Conspiracy and Contingency

Conspiracy and Contingency

How to Deal with Fake Necessities

Thorsten Botz-Bornstein

ANTHEM PRESS

Anthem Press
An imprint of Wimbledon Publishing Company
www.anthempress.com

This edition first published in UK and USA 2025
by ANTHEM PRESS
75–76 Blackfriars Road, London SE1 8HA, UK
or PO Box 9779, London SW19 7ZG, UK
and
244 Madison Ave #116, New York, NY 10016, USA

© 2025 Thorsten Botz-Bornstein

The author asserts the moral right to be identified as the author of this work.

All rights reserved. Without limiting the rights under copyright reserved above, no part of this publication may be reproduced, stored or introduced into a retrieval system, or transmitted, in any form or by any means (electronic, mechanical, photocopying, recording or otherwise), without the prior written permission of both the copyright owner and the above publisher of this book.

British Library Cataloguing-in-Publication Data
A catalogue record for this book is available from the British Library.

Library of Congress Cataloging-in-Publication Data: 2024951929
A catalog record for this book has been requested.

ISBN-13: 978-1-83999-313-8 (Hbk)
ISBN-10: 1-83999-313-8 (Hbk)

Cover Credit: By Francesco Carta fotografo/Gettyimages.com

This title is also available as an e-book.

CONTENTS

Introduction: Conspiracy as Pharmakon ... 1
1. The Conspiracy Theory as a Work of Art ... 11
2. Alternative Modernities ... 33
3. Coincidence, Accident, Virus ... 49
4. Animism and the Sense of Order ... 65
5. Ressentiment, Kitsch, and "Absolute Contingency" ... 81
6. Contingency through the Ages: Determination and Mystification ... 101
7. Evolution, Meritocracy, and Fake Science ... 121
8. The Loss of Unity ... 137
9. French Philosophy of Contingency ... 161
10. The Aesthetics of Contingency ... 171
11. Contingency in Eastern Philosophies ... 191
Conclusion ... 207

Bibliography ... 217

Index ... 229

INTRODUCTION: CONSPIRACY AS PHARMAKON

What do baseless conspiracy theories, algorithms, and meritocracy have in common? All three avoid contingency and frantically look for necessities. The COVID-19 crisis has brought about a proliferation of baseless conspiracy theories that reject, among other things, official accounts of the virus' origins and remedies, and sometimes even the existence of the virus itself. Conspiracy theories very often link events to secret plots concocted by powerful conspirators, whether it be Bill Gates or Big Pharma. The exceptionally powerful surge of unjustified conspiracy theories during the COVID-19 crisis has several already famous causes: there are increasing ways for new media to massively spread misinformation, and there has been a growing distrust for conventional scientific ideas among large parts of the population. In this book, I examine another dominant driving force: the desire to find apparently reasonable explanations for phenomena that are purely random and contingent. Many baseless conspiracy theories emerge because contingency is not accepted, and necessities are looked for at all costs. David Aaronovitch defines conspiratorial thought as a reasoning that "attributes deliberate agency to something that is more likely to be accidental or unintended" or which attributes "secret action to one party that might more reasonably be explained as the less covert and less complicated action of another" (Aaronovitch 2011: 5). Nothing happens by chance and there must be a plan or an intelligent design behind everything. A large part of this book deals with "contingency phobia." This special phobia is not only manifest in the conspiratorial mindset, but it appears in Western culture as a recurrent psychological, cognitive, and scientific pattern. It is the cause of a variety of other phenomena that have become emblematic for liberal democracies, such as the contemporary algorithm culture or the obsession with merit and ranking. Not only does the conspiratorial mindset reject a world of contingency and strive to create a universe structured by a necessary order: life coaches, algorithm engineers, and neoliberal meritocrats all do the same. This book analyzes these phenomena by using the same criteria: How do humans deal with contingency, and how do they try to establish necessities?

Conspiracy and Contingency

For the most part, conspiracy theories are political or scientific; some combine political themes with religious convictions, while a few are also cultural or racist. Often, though by far not always, theories that are called "conspiracy theories" in common language are implausible, irrational, and delusional, as well as accusatory with a strong tendency for self-victimization. Whenever there is a crisis (such as AIDS or a terrorist attack), there are conspiratorial explanations of this crisis. While most baseless conspiracy theories might be relatively harmless, some can have serious consequences and can inflict considerable damage on individuals and societies. The myth of the Protocols of the Elders of Zion, for example, helped Hitler come to power and justified his extermination program.[1] When accumulated over decades, conspiratorial thinking can create a toxic culture with deleterious effects on the politics and economy of entire countries. According to Daniel Pipes, in the Middle East, the presence of conspiracy theories "explains the regions' record of political extremism and volatility, its culture of violence, and its poor record of modernization" (1997: 2). It has been said that Russian president Vladimir Putin's actions—as well as those of preceding Russian leaders—have been strongly determined by the conviction that the world is hostile toward Russia. The rejection of contingency is central. Those leaders negate the autonomy of individuals as well as the existence of collective spontaneous movements that are often fortuitous and *not* planned by outside powers. Instead, one systematically ascribes them to manipulations organized by the enemy. Studies of the KGB archives (see Minic 2022) have shown that, in 1968, a conspiratorial vision led to violent actions in Czechoslovakia. The politburo saw the spontaneous insurrection as an imperialist conspiracy and acted accordingly. It is indeed possible to say that the recent invasion of Ukraine is based on a similar anti-contingency mindset.

In this book, I look at how various ages, cultures, and philosophies have dealt with unwarranted conspiracy theories, or how they *might* have dealt with them if they had encountered them. Why do baseless conspiracy theories appear more often in certain ages but less in others? I concentrate on the question of contingency. How would various philosophies have handled a disaster

---

[1] Though the *Protocols* had been proven a forgery, they became extremely popular in Germany and were part of Nazi propaganda (see Levin 1973: 62).

such as the coronavirus, which is ostensibly due to a coincidence? What might have prevented them from attributing it to a conspiracy? Some philosophies make groundless conspiracy theories quasi-impossible because they find original ways of combining contingency with ontological, theological, or cosmological premises. Nietzsche, instead of attributing the coronavirus to some predominant evil, would probably have faced the pandemic with tragic irony. For him, conspiracy theories were fabricated in "dark corners, secret paths and back-doors" (Nietzsche 2006: 21) by the "ressentiment man." Sartre, who believed that contingency provides a chance to break with oppressive systems and bring us existential liberty, would probably have called the coronavirus an absurdity, not because it is more absurd than other things, but simply because *everything* in this world is absurd. We must find reasonable ways to live within contingent constellations. I also show that Eastern philosophies like Daoism and Zen Buddhism have tried, more consistently than Western philosophies, to depict the world in terms of contingency or facticity. These philosophies link contingency to the phenomenon of existence, which makes the emergence of gratuitous conspiracy theories difficult or quasi-impossible. In philosophy, the existential dimension of contingency is called facticity, but unlike contingency, facticity has no opposite, which means that we cannot flee from facticity toward necessity and must instead put up with it. While contingency is constantly measured against regularity—a process that can lead to despair and resentment—facticity can contain its own intrinsic coping mechanism.

My idea is of course not new: psychologists have found that contingency avoidance plays a significant role in shaping how people interact with conspiracy theories and post-truth narratives, and research in cognitive science and social psychology (Goertzel 1994) has examined how biases and epistemic closure are involved in belief systems that avoid contingency. Ralph Keyes (2004) has shown how uncertainty avoidance, which can be understood as a sort of contingency evasion, can explain why individuals may gravitate toward ungrounded, oversimplified, and emotionally charged explanations that offer a sense of control. An increasing number of researchers have observed the amalgam of unfounded conspiratorial thinking and religious practices of all kinds.[2] One speaks of belief, apocalypticism, scriptures, and conversions. It has been found that the far-right conspiratorial movement QAnon is a new religion (Argentino 2023). Since the 1980s, conspiratorial thought has indeed become an integral part of many millenarian belief systems, and

---

[2] D. Robertson, *Religion and Conspiracy Theories* (2024), and a volume edited by Egil Asprem et al., *Religious Dimensions of Conspiracy Theories* (2022).

most American evangelicals have become millennialists (Barkun 2018: ix). While such studies typically explore certain religious traditions, the present book goes beyond such considerations and engages in a broader philosophical debate that transgresses the border between religion and philosophy.

Already for Karl Popper, the conspiracy theory came "from abandoning God and then asking: 'Who is in his place?'" (Popper 1969: 123), which means that it was a substitute religion. To a large extent, factually unfounded conspiratorial ideation seems to be linked to the loss of cosmological, epistemic, political, and theological landmarks of necessity, a loss that became flagrant in European civilizations in the late Middle Ages. In Antiquity and in the Medieval world, a solid cosmological basis could still provide a world order that was incontestably necessary. In early modernity, any vision of a centralized universe, whose micro and macro aspects are controlled by God, was forfeited. Once the closed cosmos of Scholasticism had faded, people found themselves submitted to a constant "doubt whether the world could even originally have been created for man's benefit" (Blumenberg 1985: 137). Cosmological decentralization, most often going hand in hand with the decentralization of authority, confronted humans with coincidences, randomness, and a feeling of uncertainty with which they had to cope. However, concepts like Popper's do not explain why unwarranted conspiracy theories are so dominant in the Middle East, a region where no real crisis of faith has taken place. "Unlike the West, where conspiracy theories are today the preserve of the alienated and the fringe, in the Middle East they enjoy large, mainstream audiences," writes Pipes (1996: 2). Here conspiracism seems to be due not to the "loss of God" but to the strong presence of religion. Apart from religion, the phenomenon can be traced to the "specific nature of Middle Eastern politics, especially pan-movements and its autocracy" (5), as Matthew Gray confirms when writing that "in the Arab world, the common conspiracy theory sees the state as having been co-opted or as being under the control of foreign governments" (2010: 7). Similarly, the intense conspiracy culture in the United States is due to a political tradition, which is the American myth of absolute freedom, which is so much idealized that it can never be materialized. It is certainly interesting that more than fifty years after Popper's "loss of God" theory, Donatella Di Cesare speaks of a vacuum created by democracy, a vacuum that must be filled with authoritarian regimes that conspiracy theorists often call for (2021: 29).

There is, of course, a discipline supposed to amend this loss of necessity: this discipline is science. However, science turned out to be a double-edged sword as it stands for both necessity and contingency. Science can provide necessary explanations for many things, but at the same time, it is science that has produced the world of contingency. Already the narrative of Adam and

Eve attributes the loss of a necessary unity and the fragmentation of the world to the biblical temptation to eat from the tree of knowledge. Eating from the tree meant obtaining knowledge about good and evil and thus indicated a shift away from unity toward particularities. An overarching necessity was lost. Scientific knowledge always signifies an awareness of multiplicity, that is, an awareness of the potentially contingent character of things. Science fragmented the unity of existing necessary orders. Once this was done, it would seek new necessities to replace the old ones. Therefore, in the end, science remains ambiguous: historically speaking, it is the source of both confusion and necessity.

Unfounded conspiratorial thinking can set in as a result of precisely this contradiction. It can seek to "repair" the loss of necessity in its own way by inventing alternative sciences, alternative truths, alternative religions, and alternative necessities. The problem is that these "necessities" remain entirely random. Conspiratorial thinkers of the bad kind do not really fill in the gaps that science has left open but merely reproduce the (in their eyes) "negative" view of science that is already reflected in the biblical narrative about temptation. They do not provide an organic view of the universe; nor do they point to scientific macro principles about, for example, the benefits of vaccinations. Though they often pretend to explain entire world systems, as their reasoning remains incoherent and random, they create even more fragmentation.

Chapter Presentation

In Chapter 1, I establish the term "conspiracy theory" and present my methodology. I explain that there is nothing *formally* wrong with conspiracy theories, which is why I shift the focus from an examination of the *conspiracy theory* to an examination of the *mindset* by which these theories are influenced. There is nothing formally wrong with conspiracy theories, but something is most often wrong with the mindset that produces them. Using this approach, I find a way around the particularist-generalist problem: I concentrate on the "aesthetic" aspect of conspiracy theories. Examining only particular cases is not satisfying, while generalist projects are implausible in epistemological terms. However, they are not implausible in aesthetic terms. In the end, I am not interested in the epistemological content of conspiracy theories but in the *thinking style* they deploy. A mindset determines the aesthetic appearance of theories as well as the way in which they are appreciated. Generalist statements can therefore be made in aesthetic terms: people are attracted to baseless conspiracy theories not because they find them plausible but simply because they like them.

In Chapter 2, I ask whether conspiracy theories are compatible with, or perhaps even products of, modernity and Enlightenment. Enlightenment has always produced *alternative* Enlightenment movements in its margins, and unwarranted conspiracy theories are products of this development. Pipes detects an anti-modern element in unwarranted conspiracy theories, and Keeley (2006 [1999]) and Cassam (2019) argue that conspiracy theorists reject modernity and espouse premodern views. I do not agree with this. The typically dystopian profile of the conspiratorial mindset projects neither anti-modernities nor utopias but rather "alternative modernities." The conspiratorial mindset can appear as a sort of country receiving refugees from the world of modernity by creating its own sort of modernity. I conclude the chapter by explaining how the connection between science and pseudoscience is related to the topic of contingency.

In Chapter 3, I analyze a highly contingent phenomenon that can be encountered in everyday life: the accident. The accident is contingency, and usually it is thought of as unreal until it *really* "just" happens. *When* it happens, it gives us a feeling of strange existential concreteness. I analyze the coronavirus as an accident (without saying that it really was one) and thus as an existential experience.

As the accident has the ambiguous existential status of the uncanny, in Chapter 4 I develop an ontology of uncanniness with the help of Freud's, Heidegger's, and Derrida's thoughts on contingency. The conspiratorial mindset rejects both the accident and the uncanny and attempts to create a fictional universe structured by a necessary order. Again, it creates an alternative reality. I further explain that constructing regularities in a chaotic world is a natural bias because perceiving regularities and their disruptions is part of the human survival instinct. Research has shown that "people tend to prefer explanations that make reference to a person's intentions over explanations that present the event as accidental" (Bortolotti and Inchino 2020). However, this tendency should remain moderate and contained, which is not the case for conspiratorial thinking. Like the religious fundamentalist who refuses evolution because it is too random, and who replaces it with acts of deliberate and necessary creation, so the conspiratorial mindset refuses to attribute anything to chance and looks for necessities, even when these necessities are only imaginary.

Why are some people so skeptical of contingency? Chapter 5 examines contingency skepticism. Coincidences are unlikely to happen, and a certain skepticism toward coincidences is normal. The coincidence disrupts the regular order because suddenly, the environment is no longer understood. Also, the occurrence of too many coincidences can signify danger. Both Ernst Gombrich and Karl Popper explain that our mind establishes order because we have a sense of balance. Organisms have developed a sense of order through their evolutionary struggle for existence because "perception requires a framework against which to plot deviations from regularity" (Gombrich 1979: xii). At the same time, coincidences can have positive effects, as they permit us to escape from dangerous situations. To grasp a coincidence at the right moment can be a matter of survival, too. Both the incapacity or unwillingness to see necessities *and* the categorical rejection of coincidences are pathological. The conspiratorial mindset might be suffering from a pathological sense of regularity and refuse to recognize coincidences as such. The idea of a pathological "contingency aversion" has been formulated by Georges Canguilhem.

Conspiratorial thinking is motivated by yet another source. Many unjustifiable conspiracy theories spring from feelings of "sublimated revenge": some injustice has occurred, sometimes a long time ago, and cannot be amended because the opponent is too powerful. Max Scheler, following Nietzsche, calls this diffuse feeling of vengeance "ressentiment," and ressentiment is also a core motivation for the conspiratorial mindset. Ressentiment is not an accusation, because accusations are always directed against concrete persons or institutions that have committed concrete crimes.

In Chapter 6, I review the intellectual history of Western societies and examine how contingency has been handled in different époques. In Antiquity, contingency could not cause existential problems. Unexpected events could be attributed to the goddess Fortuna (Tyche) or to divine providence, thus turning the coincidence into a necessity by tracing it to a pseudo-cause. The Christian Middle Ages saw the world and everything that was in it as God's creation and thus as necessary. Contingency could rarely spark major anger because it was possible, at any moment, to turn away from contingency toward a necessary world created by God. If a random event was evil, it could be ascribed to Satan, and the alternative, God's necessity, was always available. Like in Antiquity, conspiratorial thinking existed, but it would rarely appear in the form of the angst-ridden mania that would become typical for later époques.

Chapter 7 shows how in history, two leading cultural paradigms, contingency and necessity, alternated from background to foreground several times. Contingency represented a subject of interest between the époques of Aristotle and Descartes. After Descartes, contingency almost disappears from philosophical debates, though not because it had been scientifically solved, but, paradoxically, because science and philosophy abolished divine determinism.

The nineteenth century was overwhelmingly deterministic, but at some point, Darwin reintroduced contingency into science. Later, the modern world, with its meritocracy, science, and evaluations, reconnected with philosophies of necessity. A modern Puritan work ethic laid the foundations for a "perfect world" culture that would be largely contingency-phobic. In these most recent developments, conspiratorial thinking begins to play an important role. Both liberalism and meritocracy strive to overcome contingency by trying to replace random conditions (to which humans are submitted by birth) with the more "necessary" laws of the market. I show that, just like the conspiratorial mindset (as says Popper), liberal modernity aspires to reach God's necessities in another way. All three—the religious, the meritocratic, and the unwarranted conspiracist interpretations of the world—repress the idea of contingency. However, this is not the only possible liberalism. In "real" liberalism, so I explain, merit should not be seen as its driving force; liberalism's driving force should instead be diversity. Merit-based liberalism, with its exaggerated competition, unified merit scales, and forced comparisons, reduces diversity by neglecting contingency.

In Chapter 8, I describe more closely the handling of contingency in the modern age. The rise of statistics profoundly transformed the conception of coincidence in the nineteenth century: contingency is no longer opposed to certitude. Contingency is now feared less because sophisticated psychological and technical coping mechanisms have become available. At the same time, the world becomes more unstable, fluid, and thus also more contingency-dependent. The profusion of multinational capitalism and finance culture, the rise of social media, and the increase of risk factors produced by industrialization and its pollution have made humans more aware of contingency than ever. The conspiratorial mindset develops within this modern epistemic paradox. Everything is contingent, but at the same time, everything can be calculated. The conspiratorial mindset does not suggest a "back to necessity" movement. It does not suggest a medieval, God-centered worldview in which all actions revolve around a powerful center. Nor does it engage in real science. It accepts a "fluid" postmodern world but also invents fictional necessities to which it desperately clings.

Chapter 9 is about the "French philosophy of the coincidence," which was influential around 1900. While Engels had rationalized history to the point of letting the mystery of contingency disappear under the glaring light of determinism, these French philosophers adopted the opposite approach: they depicted the world as a manifestation of contingency but demystified it to the point of making it coterminous with reality. This is directly opposed to the conspiratorial mindset, which cancels coincidence and mystifies necessity. French philosophy of contingency bears resemblances to ancient philosophies as well as to East Asian philosophies of contingency. The main idea is that contingency is real and that necessities are only abstractions. These philosophies are the most efficient intellectual weapons to be used against baseless conspiracy theories.

In Chapter 10, I describe an "aesthetics of contingency." Both the conspiracy theories produced by the conspiratorial mindset and ressentiment are kitsch, mainly because they are narcissistic and recycle subjective feelings. Indulgence in one's misery means that one refuses to realistically face problems in order to solve them; instead, misery is transposed onto the more "aesthetic" level of indulgence. Like the narcissist, the conspiratorial mindset does not accept any insult to its vanity. Indulgence in one's misery overlaps with Scheler's ressentiment, which establishes another pertinent link between ressentiment and kitsch.

Classical Western (Aristotelian) approaches to contingency oppose the necessary to the contingent, and the real to the ideal. As a result, in the Western tradition, art is not real because it is not inscribed within the realm of the necessary (as nature is believed to be). Art contains contingency. However, given that there is a strong link between contingency and creativity, it is possible to say that in art, this contingency-dependent creativity makes the creation more "real" than the factual world of non-art. In art, the contingent is real, whereas necessities (such as the rules of art) are abstractions.

Usually, when it comes to creativity, the Western way of thinking reserves a prominent place for contingency. There is, however, in more recent times, a strong tendency to rationalize creativity and to find necessary rules also in the realm of art. The algorithm has become the main tool employed to replace contingency with necessity. An algorithm is a self-contained mathematical operation used in data processing and automated reasoning. Algorithms are used to predict musical trends and even to compose pieces that follow the necessary rules of these predicted trends. As they leave no space for contingency, algorithms follow the cognitive model of the conspiratorial mindset.

The last chapter is devoted to contingency in Eastern Philosophies. In general, Eastern philosophies avoid the obsessions with necessity that are common in Western culture. More consistently than Western philosophies, Eastern philosophies try to depict the world in terms of contingency or, rather, as a realm in which the contingency/necessity dichotomy has been overcome. For Daoism, for example, the world is in a state of constant transformations (*hua* 化) from which necessary essences are excluded.

It might appear that I do not offer a solution to a problem but engage in this book mainly in an analytic project attempting to explain why some people believe conspiracy theories that ought not to be believed. However, this is not the case. Overall, and especially in the last chapters, I show how the world and its events can be explained and given a meaning without falling into either contingency fatalism or the determinism of the conspiratorial mindset.

The alternatives I present (which are taken from both the Eastern and the Western philosophical traditions) highlight the notions of play and game as essential terms for a true philosophy of contingency. Play faces contingency "head on": it neither avoids coincidence by transforming it into necessity, nor does it fall into deterministic fatalism.

Contingency must be seen for what it is: an impossibility to predict the future. Life is an undetermined game, and even God is a gambler (as Stephen Hawking said and as will be discussed in this book). If we accept life as facticity, we will be neither surprised by contingencies nor resent them. I also suggest irony, or more precisely, Nietzsche's tragic irony. The ironical belief that much of our fate is due to coincidences avoids the poisoning of the mind through ressentiment. Fate is not determined, not even by our worst enemies. Contingency is real, and it can lead us out of painful conditions. Coincidences cannot be fought off, but they can be integrated, in an existentialist manner, into the game we are playing. I explore this line of thought through the description of the "aesthetics of gambling." Accepting loss as the outcome of a game helps one cope with contingencies. The good gambler does not plunge into desperation when losing; they do not initiate a frantic search for "necessary" alternative (conspiracist) explanations. Contingency is both a condemnation and a chance, which is why it can never be an evil. It should not instill ressentiment or a conspiratorial mindset but rather skepticism, restraint, and tolerance, which are also the three major virtues of a good gambler.

In this book, I take a philosophical perspective by concentrating on the tensions between coincidence and necessity and by contemplating a conundrum that philosophers have attempted to decode for centuries. I identify sources that other disciplines examining conspiracy theories—for example, political science, anthropology, psychology, or sociology—have rarely seen as primary. Political scientists focus on the macro level and construe conspiracy theories mostly as national or regional phenomena, whereas anthropologists, psychologists, and sociologists tend to focus on the micro level. Some philosophers have devoted their work to particular conspiracy theories, too, for methodological reasons that I referred to above. The present study is an example of practical philosophy, depicting the conspiratorial mindset as an organic and dynamic phenomenon by crystallizing cognitive and cultural "necessity-contingency patterns" that can be found in politics, culture, religion, and science.

Chapter 1

THE CONSPIRACY THEORY AS A WORK OF ART

Before proceeding to the analysis of contingency-necessity problems in conspiratorial thought, the term "conspiracy theory" needs to be clearly established. Given that the definition of the conspiracy theory has been a hotly debated topic in recent years, it is necessary to carefully present the methodology that I intend to use. I define a conspiracy theory as a framework of analysis that seeks to explain events through a conspiracy. Often, conspiracy theories lean toward a belief that a group of people who share a common ethnic, political, national, or religious origin plot to harm another group's interests. These theories can be warranted or unwarranted, though in common language the assumption that they are unwarranted is most current. It does not mean that the warranted ones are rare. Often, conspiracy theories that are labeled as unfounded have later been substantiated. Very often, attempts to point out illegal acts and atrocities authored by governments and big corporations are too easily discredited by labeling them conspiracy theories. Famous cases are the Watergate affair, the Tuskegee Syphilis experiments, the Iran-Contra affair, or, more recently, the vast surveillance program by the NSA. Multinational companies have a history of plots and counterplots to benefit themselves at the cost of the general population. Another example is Enron's conspiracy to manipulate the supply of electricity to inflate rates in California (see Orr and Husting 2018). Or a classical case is that of the tobacco industry when, in 1999, a Florida jury declared the seven largest American tobacco companies guilty of misrepresentation and conspiracy to conceal the addictiveness and dangers of cigarette smoking. It is certainly true that the U.S. government regularly lies about its programs and agenda and famously misled other governments into the Iraq War through a conspiracy. These patterns are systemic and theorizing about them means revealing them. Governments and companies lie and dub those who reveal their barbarities "conspiracy theorists" as if that alone were proof enough for the irrelevance of their concerns. "Peaceful, law-abiding people ought to be allowed to freely assemble and pursue their inquiries without infiltration," writes Hagen (2022: 140).

The meaning of "conspiracy theory" is ambiguous (warranted or unwarranted), and the question arises whether the term should be dropped from academic vocabulary altogether. The ambiguity already concerns the term "conspiracy." Conspiracy sounds bad because conspiracies tend to work against the interests of larger communities, are non-democratic, and not transparent, in which case, a theory that aims to reveal an existing conspiracy has a positive function. But then again, some conspiracies work toward good purposes and revealing them would be an ethically bad action. Pigden defines the conspiracy as

> a secret plan on the part of a group to influence events partly by covert action. Conspiracies therefore can be either good or bad, depending on the purpose, circumstances and methods used. "Conspiracy" as I use it, is not necessarily a pejorative word. However, in a democracy, where politics is supposed to be above board, there is perhaps a *presumption* (but no more) that conspiracies are morally suspect. (Pigden 2006: 26)

For these reasons, we cannot speak of conspiracy theories in general epistemological terms. A class of phenomena that can be good and bad at the same time has no formal epistemological significance. Hagen has brought the epistemological dilemma to a point. If there are some conspiracy theories that are true and warranted, how can we still offer a valid definition of what a conspiracy theory is? Are the warranted ones exceptions? But "how many exceptions are there? And which theories are the exceptions?" (Hagen 2022: 1). What Keith Harris (2018) attempts to establish as the non-falsifiability or epistemic vice of the conspiracy theory only applies to the unwarranted ones. Furthermore, not all unwarranted ones have these vices; Harris sees that some unwarranted conspiracy theories (UCTs) do not have epistemic vices such as non-falsifiability or hermetic closure. Other failures that they do have can also be failures of real scientific theories.[1]

A priori, there is thus nothing *formally* wrong with conspiracy theories. Chemtrails, Sandy Hook-as-false flag, the faked moon landing, anti-vaxxers, flat earthers... These theories are not wrong because they are conspiracy theories. They would be wrong in whatever shape they took (Coady affirms this in 2023: 759). The people who designed them were sloppy with facts, connections, deductions, and several other things, and these failures would

---

[1] Harris acknowledges the misuse of errant data and lack of self-criticism, as well as the dogmatic acceptance of certain sources of information as reliable (2018: 256).

be fatal for any kind of theory. The problem is not that conspiracies are being theorized about but *how* the way of thinking unfolds and by which mindset it is influenced. If conspiracy theories necessarily had inherent structural problems, they could not produce as many warranted results. Above this, even the theories that have been proven unwarranted can (and perhaps even typically do) adhere to many essential scientific rules. Conspiracy theorists of all kinds amass impressive details and evidence; they do not have a closed epistemology but are open-minded (as I will explain in Chapter 8). In Chapter 4, I show that the conspiratorial mindset has a very keen sense of observation and detects irregularities that others do not notice.

Conspiracy as Pharmakon

When a disease is at the same time not a disease, it becomes difficult to talk about it in medical terms. Difficult but not impossible. The conspiracy theory is something like a *pharmakon* that can be good or bad depending on its use and on the context. Raab et al. (2013) state that conspiracy theories are "a common, regulative and possibly benign phenomenon" (1). Douglas and Sutton report that "recent findings call into question this rather pathological view of conspiracy beliefs. Far from being limited to people who are paranoid and delusional, research suggests that conspiracy beliefs are common and may be characterized as the product of everyday cognitive processes" (2018: 7). When the use depends on the environment, on a mindset, or on a specific belief or attitude, that is, on something that *general* epistemological considerations cannot account for, the discourse needs to change. Just like a medical doctor can speak, when necessary, in non-medical terms. One possibility is, of course, to examine only particular cases, but I am not content with this option. General statements about phenomena are useful because they elucidate what these phenomena are essentially. The particularist-generalist debate is over whether we should define conspiracy theories neutrally (it can be either rational or irrational to believe, depending on *particular* cases) or pejoratively (holding that these theories are *generally* irrational). Particularists are not arguing that all conspiracy theories are rational but rather that it is not the case that all conspiracy theories are irrational. I agree with the particularist claim that conspiracy theories are often true, but do not consider this finding essential or even interesting. Instead, I am trying to find a way around the particularist-generalist problem.[2]

---

2 On the difference between "generalist" and "particularist" see Buenting and Taylor 2010. The generalist view attempts to assess conspiracy theories without considering

How can the unwarranted conspiracy theory (UCT)—the theory that we are interested in—be defined? A classical definition of the UCT comes from Keeley's 1999 article:

1. A UCT is an explanation that runs counter to some received, official, or "obvious" account.
2. The true intentions behind the conspiracy are invariably nefarious.
3. UCTs typically seek to tie together seemingly unrelated events.
4. The truths behind events explained by conspiracy theories are typically well-guarded secrets, even if the ultimate perpetrators are sometimes well-known public figures.
5. The chief tool of the conspiracy theorists is what I shall call "errant data."

(Quoted from Clarke 2002: 138, who synthesizes Keeley's points.)[3]

Though all characteristics apply to the unwarranted theory, a conspiracy theory that manifests all these characteristics can still be warranted (as Keeley admits). Warranted conspiracy theories can run against official accounts, the intentions behind the conspiracy can be nefarious, the seemingly unrelated events can turn out to be related against all odds, and the errant data can turn out to be important indicators. Clarke notes that it is not clear whether Keeley believes that these are necessary or sufficient conditions. They are neither nor. My point is that what Keeley describes is simply the "aesthetic" aspect of a conspiracy theory: he describes what most of these theories *look like*. Even his choice of words is telling: we have *seemingly* unrelated events.

Both warranted and UCTs can have the same "aesthetic" aspect, but most of the time, the warranted ones don't. In warranted conspiracy theories, the dots tend to look more connected, and so on. Most probably, in a warranted conspiracy theory, only a limited number of the above characteristics will apply. The problem is that as long as we do not know if the seemingly unrelated events are related or not, or if the errant data are important or not, and so on, we cannot make epistemologically valuable statements about the theory. In principle, any UCT is potentially warranted until we have checked the facts. However, this does not disable any judgment about it. We can still say what the theory "looks like." We can issue a statement about the theory's

---

particular conspiracy theories. The particularist wants to assess the rationality of a conspiracy theory on a case-by-case basis.

3 Keeley's main argument in this article is that the conspiracy theorist desires a rational rather than an absurd universe in which sometimes "shit happens," as Pete Mandik (2007) names it in his article on Keeley.

aesthetic appearance. Consequently, and this is my point, we can make generalist statements about what we believe most UCTs look like.

Shields (2022: 3) believes that the main characteristic of an UCT is that the "'views' [the theories] are distinctly flawed." The problem is that we are often unable to recognize if they are flawed or not. But despite this, we can judge the theory aesthetically and *relatively* pertinently conclude that it looks like an UCT. The conspiracy that conspiracy theorists normally talk about is different from the conspiracy of criminal groups who cover their tracks. A police inspector who tries to track a criminal conspiracy develops a theory about a conspiracy. He is not a conspiracy theorist in the common understanding. His theory can be flawed, but even in that case, we would not call it a conspiracy theory. What distinguishes an inspector's (perhaps wrong) theory from an UCT is the aesthetic appearance of the theory.

Imagine something strange has happened, and we are offered two alternative explanations. Both explanations are conspiracy theories, but one is warranted and the other one is unwarranted. We have no knowledge about the facts (it has happened in a faraway country). Can we distinguish the warranted from the unwarranted one? The only approach feasible is to judge the theories aesthetically. When too many items from Keeley's list are used, when the statements *appear* exaggerated, when the tone is too obsessive, when there is some disproportional aggressiveness or relentlessness, we will be inclined to classify the theory as *probably* unwarranted. We will also look at the contexts. If the person who designed the theory has already produced other unwarranted theories, we might conclude that she is a conspiracy theorist of the bad kind. Everything listed here comes close to evaluations that are common in the realm of aesthetics.

My suggestion to see the conspiracy theory as an aesthetic phenomenon makes sense for another reason. A theory can manifest Keeley's characteristics to certain degrees. In one theory, the dots that the theory is trying to connect are only a little unrelated. In another one, they are very unrelated. When the dots turn out to be connected, the theory has a chance to be warranted. Aesthetically speaking, a conspiracy theory can be (and can look) more or less warranted. By contrast, epistemologically speaking, while any theory can likewise be more or less warranted (as epistemology considers probabilities), the "more or less" will always be seen as a drawback. The aim of science is to exclude contingency and to establish truths with absolute certitude. Aesthetics does not have this strong ambition.

In this book, I understand the conspiracy theory as an aesthetic phenomenon. I concentrate on the aesthetics of the unwarranted ones because I find them problematic in the present civilizational context. Aesthetics is the science that looks at the outer appearance of phenomena while trying to refrain from structural, ethical, and scientific questions. To make it simple: I am not interested in the content but in the thinking style of the conspiracy theory, which shifts the problem from epistemology to aesthetics. I am not interested in the question of whether the dots are *really* connected or not. The factual content or the coherence will definitely decide whether the theory is unwarranted or not; but this is not the part that attracts my attention. Why? First of all, because most of the time I do not know the facts anyway. There are too many conspiracy theories, and judging every theory case by case through fact-checking is, in my opinion, not the task of a philosopher. I intend to make general statements about these theories; and these statements can only be obtained by limiting the inquiry to the "looks" of the theory. After all, theories are also aesthetic phenomena as we know since T. Kuhn's writings on the choice and arbitrariness of aesthetic criteria in science (see Machan 1977).

We can make generalist statements, but only in aesthetic terms, and this reasoning is not supposed to give in to the generalist position but rather attempts to circumvent the particularist-generalist distinction and the debates linked to it. In the end, my concern is with unwarranted theories, but—perhaps a little paradoxically—the question whether the theory is warranted or unwarranted is secondary.

The problem with many philosophical writings on conspiracy theories is that the authors strive to decide *with certainty* whether something is an UCT or not. In that case, the study will most likely move away from philosophical considerations and become an empirical forensic study or some anthropological research program. Hagen believes that "to really be justified in confidence regarding the truth or falsity of a particular theory of any historical event, one must carefully investigate the relevant empirical facts and evaluate the quality of the best arguments on a case-by-case basis" (Hagen 2022: 205). The problem is that philosophy cannot be purely particularist, which is why I view groundless conspiracy theories as something more akin to art. In art, there are features that make us inclined toward certain judgments, but there are no clear scientific premises leading to these judgments. This goes for the observer who tries to understand whether something is a warranted conspiracy theory, as well as for the "practitioner" who adheres to a certain theory. In the end, everything is a matter of "liking." Also, in art we need to consider the context. Even if we don't know much about art, we can reasonably suppose that a painting hanging in an elevator is not the original chef d'oeuvre of a famous artist.

Classifying a conspiracy theory, whether warranted or unwarranted, as an aesthetic phenomenon can also—though it does not have to—imply the following. The person who adheres to a conspiracy theory does so not for the purpose of revealing a conspiracy but rather because they like the theory.

They have an aesthetic appreciation for the theory. This might not always be the case, but it is important. By contrast, the person who designs a warranted conspiracy theory is more likely to do so for epistemic reasons. This person does not have a conspiratorial mindset. The person with a conspiratorial mindset can reveal a really existing conspiracy; but in aesthetic terms, their theory does remain a conspiracy theory even when it is warranted.

One can also develop an unwarranted theory for epistemic reasons. Governments that spread unfounded conspiracy theories purposefully falsify facts. Obviously, my generalist aesthetic model is more suitable for what Shields calls "Non-Dominant Institution Conspiracy Theories" (non-DITS) and less for "Dominant Institution Conspiracy Theories" (DITs) such as McCarthyism or the Bush administration's linking of Iraq and Al Qaeda. Still, aesthetically speaking, DITS and non-DITS *can* look similar, be it only because there can be overlaps. One reason for relative similarities is that people who produce them can have similar aesthetic preferences; another reason is that the target group prefers theories that have certain appearances, and the producers (both DIT and non-DIT) cater for their tastes.

The Conspiratorial Mindset

I hold that most people in the non-DIT group are attracted to baseless conspiracy theories not because they find them plausible but simply because they like them. They might say that they find them plausible, but plausibility was not the first reason they engaged with them. Very often, the reason they find them plausible is that they liked them in the first place. The concept of "conspiracy-belief," defended by some researchers, covers some of these personality patterns and will be discussed below. Another possibility is that one who finds a conspiracy theory plausible has found a warranted one. They were *probably* driven by epistemological motives but could just as well have been driven by aesthetic motives. The latter approach might also find warranted ones. What is important is that their motivations were different.

For all these reasons, I will speak in this book mostly not of conspiracy theories but of the "conspiratorial mindset." This possibility emerged in the *Le Monde* debate, an initially French debate that has received much feedback in English-speaking academic journals. It is not excluded that a person with a conspiratorial mindset believes in a warranted conspiracy theory. Motivation and driving force are a matter of mindset, which is why I believe it is better to talk about mindsets than about the conspiracy theory as such. The conspiratorial mindset engages—actively and passively—in conspiracy theories. It defends them and produces them. The conspiratorial mindset is a mindset that has a *taste* for conspiracy theories, some of which are warranted, some less warranted, and most of which are unwarranted. The unwarranted ones are often the aesthetically most attractive ones, as several authors have pointed out. Räikkä writes: "The explanations of social events provided by historians and social scientists tend to be relatively boring, as they refer to all kinds of accidents and unintentional side-effects of actions, whereas conspiratorial explanations resemble action movies" (2009: 458). Cassam recognizes the aesthetic value of these theories too, suggesting that "Conspiracy Theories are morality tales with all-knowing and all-powerful villains and naïve victims who have no idea what is really going on until the truth is revealed by the Conspiracy Theorist" (2019: 58). Conspiracy theories can be found beautiful, exciting, soothing, reassuring, pleasant [...] The person who has a conspiratorial mindset "likes" conspiracy theories in the same way a person can like hard rock or paintings by Paul Klee. They like these theories too much, to the point that they foist conspiratorial explanations on all sorts of events. In comparison, the police inspector who reveals a conspiracy of criminals by producing a "conspiracy theory" has no conspiratorial mindset. He does not like his theory but simply spells it out because he thinks it makes sense.

In principle, epistemological considerations of conspiracy theories are stillborn unless the approach becomes completely particularist; until it becomes particularist to the point that it is no longer *philosophically* interesting. Case-by-case studies should not be called conspiracy theory *philosophies* but better be scheduled as empirical studies in intellectual history. The main problem is that, generally speaking, conspiracy theories are neither true nor false in principle. They can be both, but whether they are true or false depends on what? Conclusive empirical studies of particular cases enable us to spell out the reasons. But as philosophers, we must also be able to make general statements about conspiracy theories, and these general statements can only be aesthetic. We cannot define a conspiracy theory generally in epistemological terms. First, there is no structural difference between the true and the false theory (see Stokes 2016: 35). The thought model that we call conspiracy theory is not a false theory. Designing a theory by tying together seemingly unrelated events, collecting errant data, finding a truth that is a well-guarded secret [...] all this is not a wrong approach per se. UCTs are different from superstitions, which, though the events that the superstition predicted can indeed occur, will always remain erroneous. In Chapter 6, I talk about the irrationality of superstitions and contrast them with the rationality of conspiracy theories. In Chapter 5, I show that, from a Nietzschean perspective, the conspiratorial mindset is rational in a manner similar to Socrates and dialecticians. The idea of a conspiracy theory as a general model remains valid when we consider that its potential truth or falsehood does not depend on the theory itself but on the mindset with which the theory is connected. The mindset will exaggerate connections, overestimate errant data, and so on. Again, the outcome is secondary. Everything the theory says *could* be true, and often we do not know. What matters is the mindset, and the mindset manifests itself through the aesthetic. Theoretically, a conspiratorial mindset can be enamored with a warranted theory and present it in a way that it looks like an unwarranted one. We would then say that it *looks* like an unwarranted one. The conspiracists may end up being correct, but likely for the wrong reasons, which means that the line between the reasonable conspiracy theorist and the unreasonable conspiracist is blurry, and the gray area encompassing both types may even be vast.[4] I thus agree with the particularists that the generalist project is implausible—but only as long as it is epistemological. A generalist project that says what conspiracy theories *look like*, and which leaves open whether they are warranted or unwarranted, is possible and desired for an understanding of conspiracy theories. Epistemically, particularism is a correct position, but generalism, though epistemically incorrect, is focused on those kinds of conspiracy theories that are most problematic for society (QAnon, vaccine skeptics, flat earthers [...]). The particularist wants to examine each theory on its own merit and make only particular statements. Paradoxically, the aim is to arrive at a more general understanding of the conspiracy theory that includes not only the unwarranted ones but also the warranted ones. Ideally, "conspiracy theory" should no longer have negative connotations but be neutral. My aesthetic definition of the phenomenon works toward precisely this aim but in a completely different fashion. Something which looks like a conspiracy theory can be both warranted and unwarranted; I simply leave it open whether the theory is good or bad, warranted or unwarranted. Through a phenomenological reduction, I see the theory as an aesthetic phenomenon, and like this, I avoid the definitional debate altogether: I am not attempting to define "conspiracy theory" at all, which sets me apart from both particularists and generalists. Instead, I focus on *conspiracy endorsers* and try to explain why certain conspiracy theories (warranted or unwarranted) are attractive to them. Strictly speaking, I am at odds with neither particularism nor generalism but believe that the particularist-generalist debate is not helpful in understanding the nature of conspiracism, that is, the practical, on-the-ground everyday reality of people with bad beliefs.

---

4 For example, most people would have agreed, a few years ago, that the COVID lab leak theory is an unwarranted conspiracy theory. As more evidence and more experts and official (governmental and scientific) organizations seem to confirm the existence of a lab leak, this conspiracy theory becomes a more plausible explanation.

Conspiracy Theory Philosophies

Conspiracy theory philosophies emerged in the 1990s, and since about 2006, the correct definition of the conspiracy theory has taken much space in philosophical, sociological, and psycho-sociological writings. Much research concentrates on the status of the conspiracy theory as a warranted or unwarranted theory.[5] Pigden (2006, 2007), Dentith (2014, 2019, 2024), Hagen (2022), Basham (2006, 2018), Danesi (2023), and Räikkä (2019) have multiple times pointed out that conspiracy theories can also be true (see Basham and Dentith's "Social Sciences Conspiracy Theory Panic: Now They Want to Cure Everyone" for a good summary). In general, these studies aim to provide a more conceptual view of conspiracy theories and, instead of writing them off as mere pathologies, misguided assumptions, or fruits of somehow particularly vulnerable and inadequate minds, they look into, for example, the philosophical and linguistic aspects of conspiracy theories to explain them as phenomena and their appeal to humans. This book develops a broader perspective by explicitly straddling not only multiple Western perspectives but also embracing globally diverse perspectives.

Pigden writes that "if conspiracy theories were taboo, there could be no question of impeaching the President [Nixon] for high crimes and misdemeanors'" (2007: 237), which is correct. Still, according to Cassam, Pigden has made a name for himself as a conspiracy apologist (see Cassam 2019: Chapter 4). The reason for this derogatory term is not that particularists are defending any specific conspiracy theory (or that they would perhaps theorize anything racist or antisemitic), but rather that Pigden employs relativism and concludes that since we all more or less blindly believe what history books claim, we are all conspiracy theorists (2007). This position has been called a "minimalist definition" of conspiracy theories and has been endorsed by Basham, Clarke, Keeley, and Dentith. Melina Tsapos (2023) writes that in this case the term "conspiracy theorist" no longer has any meaning, and I support this observation. In Pigden's case, one should at least specify which history books: we will then note that we can put more trust in some books than in others. There is propaganda in all history books, but we must also recognize that there can be different degrees. In the end, unless we have time to check most facts, all

---

5 While much of it is useful, some important items, though interesting and sound, do not contribute to my narrative about conspiracy and contingency and can only be mentioned in a cursive fashion. For example, the question if governments should engage in cognitive infiltration of conspiracy theory producers, as suggested by Vermeule and Sunstein, has been lengthily discussed by Coady (2017), Basham (2018), Hagen (2022), and others; it is not interesting for my project.

we can do is note an aesthetic difference between what is written in such books and some wild conspiracy theories that are generally believed to be unwarranted.

The writings of Coady, Dentith, Hagen, and Basham go in the same direction as Pidgen's. Hagen writes that "the aim of this book is to make serious consideration of conspiracy theories respectable among the sophisticated" (2022: vii). The further aim is to make conspiracy theories available for critical thinking. His book is "a defense of conspiracy theories as potentially warranted" (18). There is nothing to say against this, and Hagen's book is an impressive intellectual exercise. Conspiracy theorists can perform an important task when they investigate conspiracies. However, when Coady writes that "conspiracy theorists do not deserve their reputation for irrationality, [that] we should recognize that conspiracy theorists so understood are at one end of a spectrum, and the really worrying form of irrationality is at the other end" (Coady 2007: abstract), he seems to go further.[6] Coady admits that "*some* dismissive uses of the concept seem to be legitimate" (his italics). Like others, he seems to pay lip service to the fact that unwarranted theories exist. Fourteen years later, he sounds more radical when he likens conspiracy theory to the word "heresy" in medieval Europe and compares psychologists who analyze conspiratorial behavior to the Inquisition (Coady 2023: 757) because they persecute "heretic" conspiracy theorists. There are certainly "cases of psychologists being used by the state to persecute people for believing in real conspiracies" (759), but Coady's discourse becomes general to the point that he depicts all conspiracy theory criticism as a conspiracy in itself. Do conspiracy theory critics who analyze theories about reptilians running the world have the same ethos as the Inquisitors?

Others, such as Quassim Cassam, Keith Harris, Guilia Giulia Napolitano, and Kevin Reuter, have argued against the above approaches.[7] The vast majority of psychologists and social scientists are also—directly or indirectly—opposed to these advances. As mentioned, I do not want to join the discussion about what Tsapos calls "the conspiracy definition dilemma" (2023), though what does bother me is the relevance. While I find that Coady, Dentith, Hagen, Basham, and Pigden formulate objections that are *somehow* relevant, I wonder *how* relevant they are in a public sphere that is strongly undermined by fake

---

6 Otherwise, the article provides a good analysis of the phenomenon. Conspiracy theorists exaggerate certain claims, which does not make them irrational by definition. I agree with this, which is why I shift the discussion to the conspiracy mindset. Being prone to exaggeration is not an epistemological feature but concerns the mindset.
7 The *Le Monde* debate, which is described in Duetz and Dentith 2022, helps to understand the pro and contra positions.

news, QAnon, Putin, ISIS, Alex Jones, and dozens of similar influencers and sources that spread conspiracies about Bill Gates and 5G. Is it so important to criticize those who talk about the conspiracy theory in the form of a social disease? It is certainly essential to defend those who point out real conspiracies; but I also contend that the conspiracy theory discussion needs to be embedded into a larger social context and not be limited to epistemological questions.

Before coming back to this, I want to point out another problem. Most of the "pro-conspiracy" authors do not draw clear limits between the epistemological and the political. Pigden gives the following reason why he wants to eliminate the conspiracy theory's negative connotations: "The concept of a conspiracy theory as it is commonly employed is a chauvinist construct. It is not to be understood in terms of governments generally, but in terms of *Western* governments" (2007: 229). Like Coady, Pigden presents negative talk about conspiracy theories as a conspiracy. It is "the West" that oppresses the non-West by not allowing them to develop conspiracy theories (read: to examine existing conspiracies and theorize them).[8] The chauvinist West dismisses these attempts as conspiracy theories. One problem is that the "non-West" is doing the same when the West points out, for example, the influence of Russia on Western media. The other problem is that epistemological and political motivations get mixed together. Other researchers have put forward motivations similar to Pigden's. Orr and Husting criticize that "mainstream news frames Muslim-majority nations as populated with irrational conspiracy theorists from primitive cultures, rather than by individuals with well-founded concerns" (2018: 82). Here we have a fight against stigmatization. We should "take conspiracy theories seriously" to understand them better and to deal with them in a more adequate way. However, given that so many conspiracy theories are epistemologically unjustifiable, the proclamation to "take conspiracy theories seriously" sounds a little clumsy in rhetorical terms to say the least.

Still another problem is that by producing neutral epistemic definitions of the conspiracy theory as something that is, as such, neither good nor bad, neither warranted nor unwarranted, we are "driving a wedge [...] between the academic and the public discussion of this phenomenon," as pointed out

---

8 Hagen integrates "the West" into the definition of the conspiracy theory, too: it is "an interpretation of a historical event that runs counter to an official account and suggests that elements within a Western government have behaved in ways that seem particularly egregious" (2022: 123). Only Western? Are anti-Chinese or anti-Russian conspiracy theories impossible?

Napolitano and Reuter (2021: 2042).[9] Why would such a wedge be harmful? Again, it's a matter of rhetoric. Napolitano and Reuter highlight the "folk intuitions about the concept conspiracy theory," which they believe should be sustained. Since in common language, a conspiracy theory is "the unnecessary assumption of conspiracy where other explanations are more plausible" (Aaronovitch 2011: 5) and most often denotes a false (e.g., metaphorically "paranoid") thinking style, there might indeed be reasons to use the term in this fashion, even when it is—epistemologically speaking—incorrect (so long as we are unable to establish the facts). Just like, as I wrote above, a medical doctor can speak in non-medical terms about a pharmakon (a disease that can also be benign) when deemed necessary. Cassam suggests distinguishing between Conspiracy Theories and conspiracy theories (2019). This vocabulary, handy as it is, might again be difficult to sustain in terms of rhetoric.

My aesthetic approach solves the "folk culture" problem. In most cases, we will not say that something *is* an UCT but that it *looks* like one. However, I do not stay in the realm of neutrality. The person who has a conspiratorial mindset *looks like* a conspiracy theorist *of the bad kind*. They like conspiracy theories too much—and will *most probably* be attracted to unwarranted ones, be it only because these are the aesthetically more engaging ones.

Some epistemologists say that UCTs are problematic because believing them is irrational with respect to evidential considerations. However, some indefensible conspiracy theories are rational in the sense that they develop their own rationality. I do not share Harris's (2018) claim that conspiracy theories are irrational by definition. Instead, I deal with them as artistic expression, and in art, nothing is rational or irrational. Some conspiracy theories look irrational at first and turn out to be rational later. For me, the flat-earth theory is a work of art more than anything else, perhaps similar to Dadaism. It is imaginative, quirky, absurd, provocative […] and wrong. The fact that the proponents of this "art" advertise their work as a theory must be taken into consideration, but this "art" should still not be judged by the strict standards of scientific theories.

It is useless to talk of rationality. The only way out of these multiple dilemmas is to shift the analysis from epistemology to aesthetics; to not look at the factual content (true or false) but at the thinking *style*. We will then be in the realm of probabilities, shadings, preferences, and degrees, and not in the realm of definitions and evaluations. None of Keeley's conditions for a conspiracy theory are necessary; the parameters he enumerates merely make us

---

9 A term with less negative connotations is "plot," though it is also predominantly negative.

inclined toward certain conclusions. Already Richard Hofstadter, a pioneer in conspiracy research, found it useful to insert the word "style" into the title of his early book on conspiracy theories: *The Paranoid Style in American Politics*. A paranoid mode of thinking exists, but it is no more than a style that manifests itself to different degrees. As Dentith correctly points out, this style is not revealed by a clinical diagnosis as a case of psychological paranoia. "It denotes a paranoid mindset, but—crucially—not actual paranoia" (2018: 97). Dentith states that those who reject conspiratorial thought as paranoid often identify it with a clinical condition. He cites Richard Pipes as an example, though it is questionable that Pipes really believes all conspiracy theorists to be literally sick. Does he think that the entire Middle East suffers from a psychological disease? The belief in UCTs is rather a cultural coloring similar to a political taste. That said, it is not excluded that some cases of the conspiratorial mindset are due to real paranoia. Nor can it be excluded that an intensification of this mindset can lead to real paranoia. Hagen denies major paranoia input in conspiracy theories and makes this very generalist statement: "Many social scientists also conflate 'conspiracy theories' with 'the paranoid style' […]. But most conspiracy theories, especially the interesting ones, do not posit this" (246). I assume the "interesting" ones are here the warranted ones. Why can metaphorical paranoia not be seen as an "interesting" aesthetic manifestation?

Conspiracy Mindsets and Conspiracy Beliefs

Epistemic analyses serve the purpose of establishing what can be called an UCT and what can't. However, this is not the purpose of my study. As I will explain, in too many cases, it is almost impossible to answer that question. What I am interested in is the following: once we face a *probably* UCT (without the possibility of knowing for sure), what do we call this? Which existential and psychological forces drive people to invent or believe in a theory such as the flat-earth theory (or theories by Alex Jones, or QAnon, or ISIS)? Why do some people develop a conspiratorial mindset? I will show that such mindsets unfold by following certain aesthetic patterns, one of which is the contingency refusal. I refrain from talking about the content, that is, about the mostly ethical contents and concentrate on the aesthetics, that is, on the "how" of the baseless conspiracy theory. Whoever develops a mindset that sees too many conspiracies suffers from a thinking style that is determined by and attracted to the "aesthetics of the conspiracy theory." As mentioned, theories are not only epistemological phenomena but also aesthetic. Hagen believes that "when evaluating theories, one should focus on the most plausible versions" (181). Yes, when evaluating them in terms of plausibility, but things change when we evaluate them in terms of aesthetics. Basham writes that "epistemology determines ethical response [...] not the other way around" (2018: 42). It does so only as long as we see conspiracy theories as particular ethico-epistemic phenomena; the observation becomes redundant when we see them as general aesthetic phenomena.

In this book, I will always talk about theories that *appear* unwarranted, and strictly speaking, the word "unwarranted" should most of the time be preceded by "probably." As this would make the text too cumbersome, I left it out, but the reader should keep in mind that most of the time I talk about an UCT, I mean one that is *probably* unwarranted. By "probably unwarranted" I mean that it *looks* unwarranted. Sunstein and Vermeule tried something similar when considering only unwarranted ones. However, they focused on those that are "demonstrably false" (2009: 206). Generally, it does not work because, in too many cases, it is impossible to conclusively demonstrate the falsity. I do not deem it necessary to demonstrate the falsity because I work within the realm of aesthetic probabilities. By becoming aesthetic, I also avoid the dogmatism of Neil Levy, who holds that "there is a class of official stories that, other things being equal, we ought to accept. Responsible believers ought to accept explanations offered by *properly constituted epistemic authorities*" (2007: 187). This is a naïve belief in authorities that excludes the possibility that authorities can make mistakes or conspire.

With "mindset" comes another term that seems to be useful: conspiracy belief.[10] "Even for secular believers the theory itself begins to take on the characteristics of a sacred scripture. It is privileged knowledge, the possession of initiates who alone see the world in its true light, through the lens that conspiracism provides," writes Barkun (2018: 10). Napolitano proposes to define conspiracy theories as a certain kind of belief. I am sympathetic toward this concept though I have some reservations. First, there is something pertinent in this idea. An UCT is not a theory but "a particular way of holding a belief in the existence of a conspiracy" (2021: 86). This can explain why "individual conspiracy theorists remain committed to their favored conspiracy theories even when these exhibit clear signs of degeneration" (Clarke 2002: 143). Second, Napolitano's concept of conspiracy belief aims to abstract from the content and concentrate on the "how" of the thinking. It concentrates on conspiracy beliefs and not on the content of the explanation. Facts are *believed* in; they are presented in a believing fashion. The word is here used in the religious sense of "believe in" and not of "believe that," though the limits between both are often floating (just like in religious belief). What the facts

---

10 Goertzel (1994) was the first to suggest that conspiracy beliefs form a belief system.

are is secondary. Third, belief is linked to aesthetics: even Hofstadter likens his notion of style to belief: "Style has to do with the way in which ideas are believed and advocated rather than with the truth or falsity of their content" (2012: 5). Fourth, theories can be either refuted or not, whereas a belief cannot be refuted.[11] Nor can a mindset be refuted. We move away from epistemology toward the study of beliefs and aesthetic questions.

However, there is a problem with "conspiracy belief." First, those who produce UCTs do not necessarily believe in them themselves. The tale of demonic communist forces ready to take over the country that the U.S. administrations promoted during the Cold War was a conspiracy theory. We do not suppose that the government believed this. However, even when they do not believe in them, they can still have a conspiratorial mindset.[12] Their mindset might not necessarily be driven by paranoia or other dark psychological forces but simply by greed or the will to power. Many a YouTube influencer can be suspected of such motivations. Governments and powerful economic institutions launch conspiracy theories (DITs) because they look for political or monetary benefits. We can imagine a politician who, despite not believing in any conspiracy theories, points them out to his public whenever he sees the opportunity to do so, believing that such a tactic would afford him political gain. A similar attitude could be attributed to a clout-chasing YouTuber. But in both these cases, though the conviction with which they hold these conspiratorial beliefs may be debatable, they nonetheless are engaging in a conspiratorial mindset, given that the statements they make follow the same logic. As I mentioned, the conspiratorial mindset concerns more non-DITs and not so much DITs; but it is not entirely inappropriate to say that McCarthyism Conspiracy Theories or the Bush administration's linking of Iraq and Al Qaeda are due to a conspiratorial mindset.

Second, these "beliefs" are not expressed, formulated, and claimed as beliefs but as theories, which is why I hesitate to look at conspiracism as a belief system. The person with a conspiratorial mindset typically does not claim to merely "believe" but rather attempts to formulate their ideas in a style akin to a theory, often with copious amounts of evidence, and this is important. Nor do the producers of UCTs ask the public to "believe in" them, but they try to convince them through a pertinent theory. Also, if we base our

---

11 On the difference between a conspiracy theory and a conspiracy belief, see Duetz and Dentith 2022: 42.
12 In the end, there is no final answer to the question of whether the U.S. administration had a conspiratorial mindset. They probably would have to produce more of these theories to give the impression that they have a conspiratorial mindset.

definition on belief, we need to reestablish a structural distinction between the warranted and the UCT, which is just what we want to avoid. The warranted one is a theory and the unwarranted one isn't? In reality, both are theories, but they can be influenced by different mindsets. We reach a paradoxical formula that expresses the problem that so many philosophers and social psychologists grapple with: UCTs are theories that can be believed in. They do not become beliefs because they are believed in, but rather remain theories.[13]

Still another possibility is to talk about conspiracy narratives. Current conspiracy theory research does not focus enough on the conspiracy theory as a narrative. The fact that these narratives include theoretically formulated claims makes the phenomenon complicated, but one should stick to the aesthetic approach. These theories are aesthetic narratives that one can feel attracted to and in which one can believe.

It is important to insist on the "theory" status of the UCT for still another reason. The conspiracy theorist can claim that these are *only* theories. They have chosen to operate in the realm of theory because, in this case, hard facts might matter less than they do in empirical research. I do not agree with Di Cesare that "theory," "far from having the rigor and seriousness of the scientific model, has here has a derogatory value" (Di Cesare 2021: 22). The theoretical way of thinking is speculative by definition and removed from the world of experience. Cassam writes that "one special feature of Conspiracy Theories that makes them different from other accounts of conspiracies is that they are speculative" (11). Speculation unites the artistic and speculative effects. Through speculation, the UCT comes closer to art: artistic expressions, their values, and the analyses that attempt to grasp them, are more speculative and not empirically measurable. Given the degree of speculation (which is another word for theory), it is important to continue seeing unjustifiable conspiracy theories as theories.

In theories, facts matter less. The conspiratorial mindset can exalt this paradigm. An empirical statement affirming that the earth is flat is simply a false statement. This statement can only subsist—if at all—as a theory. In that case, this theory includes the assumption that the real facts about the earth have been concealed from us by the powers that be. The theory shifts the attention from obvious facts to some evil authorities that are purely theoretically established. Facts matter less; most important becomes the theory

---

13 Hagen warns to "conflate *belief* with various ways of *giving some degree of credence*" (Hagen: 230). He seems to address the difference between "believe in" and "believe that." I think Napolitani means "believe in" as in religious belief.

that explains why and how the facts are hidden. This theory can be found aesthetically attractive.

What does it mean to look at mindsets and at the aesthetics instead of at the content and the epistemological value of theories? One consequence is that the facts matter less. Somebody might believe in things that are perfectly true and correct and still have a conspiratorial mindset because the way they reach conclusions is determined by those thinking styles that we identify as conspiratorial. When too many points from Keeley's list apply, they *should* not have believed it, but liked the warranted theory for the wrong (aesthetic) reasons. The term "conspiratorial mindset" is thus most appropriate. A mindset is determined by beliefs as well as by theories, and it determines beliefs and theories. Especially, it determines the aesthetic appearance of theories and the way they are appreciated.

Not everybody who believes in a baseless conspiracy theory has a conspiratorial mindset. Furthermore, the phenomenon is not a scientifically established black-and-white matter. One might believe in an UCT just a bit, without being entirely committed to it. One might deem it only possible. One might be undecided about its warranted or unwarranted status. Something like "half-belief" exists in religion, as postmodern theology has established (see Vattimo 1999). Half-belief is a term that should be used in conspiracy research. Similarly, one can be "a little paranoid." I can ask myself: "Am I perhaps paranoid?" I do not mean the clinical condition but I am examining my own reasoning. We all know that we can be tempted by unwarranted conspiratorial interpretations. Social psychologists have shown that belief in conspiracy theories is relatively normal (Bost et al. 2010). The question is: To what degree? I might sometimes be prone to (half-) believe in an UCT, but I do not have a conspiratorial mindset.

Many of the recent studies on conspiracy theories split the phenomenon of conspiracy into classes, types, and subtypes with the aim of clarifying the epistemological value of these theories. I have shown that I have reservations about these approaches. Furthermore, my study is not analytic but synthetic as I open the field of conspiracy research toward a new field: contingency. It is, of course, not entirely new: Coady alludes to the "coincidence theorist," whom he opposes to the conspiracy theorist. Willman talks about "contingency theories," which I will attend to at several places in the book, especially in the conclusion. I also mentioned in the introduction the psychological and cognitive science approaches that examine contingency avoidance. For Coady, the contingency theory exists in the form of an epistemic theory and not as a mindset: the "coincidence theorist fails to connect the dots, no matter how suggestive of an underlying pattern they are" (2007: 197). However, one can have a contingency mindset to different degrees. I might be skeptical about certain connections that other people deem necessary.

I am not willing to add more to these definition debates because, in reality, I am interested in something else: the existential value of unfounded conspiracy theories by linking what Leibniz calls *Kontingenz* to existence and by contrasting it with existence as experienced by the conspiratorial mindset. I also analyze how the conspiratorial mindset has penetrated other areas of society without taking the shape of a conspiracy theory. For example, the abundant reliance on algorithms or the staunch "belief" in meritocracy is rooted in the same contingency phobia that feeds the conspiratorial mindset. In all these areas, the aesthetic approach is more viable.

By choosing this terminology, I do not narrow the field to psychology. "Mindset" and aesthetics include politics and many other things. Cassam insists that conspiracy theories should be understood first and foremost in political terms, as forms of political propaganda (2019: 5). However, republicans, neo-Nazis, or communists have different mindsets, which determine their political actions. They also have different aesthetics. Cassam is not disinclined to recognize mindsets as relevant criteria when writing that "having a 'conspiracy mentality' or being 'conspiracy-minded'" represents a "measurable individual difference" (40). He also points to material conditions: "The conspiracism of many African Americans has nothing to do with their personality or their political ideology, it's just an understandable reaction to how they have been treated" (55). Mindsets are not fantasies: they can be used in philosophical evaluations.

In everyday life, we rarely judge conspiracy theories by checking facts, simply because most often we do not have solid evidence or first-hand knowledge of a theory's *factual* falsehood. This is especially true in knowledge societies in which more and more knowledge is outsourced. Our sources are mostly simply the media, or what scientific or educational institutions have transmitted to us, often over a long time period. Our beliefs about, for example, *man-made* global warming, are rarely derived from first-hand observations. Nor can we test the large-scale effects of COVID-19 vaccinations ourselves. We do not have first-hand forensic evidence about 9/11. This means that we use outsourced knowledge, not to establish what is really true or false, but rather what *looks* likely or unlikely. Often, for conspiracy theories, the degree of likelihood matters more than the truth value. Theoretically, many unfounded conspiracy theories *could* be true, but we simply find them unlikely. Sometimes we approach them with "half-belief." The so-called truth or falsehood of the conspiracy theory does not *only* depend on the truth or falsehood of the facts, but on a variety of "aesthetic" criteria. Lee McIntyre calls such constellations "post-truth" situations because truth no longer exists as a mere fact, and the facts are "subordinate to our political point of view" (McIntyre: 11). We accept facts based on who or what we trust. The conspiratorial mindset crystallizes this post-truth phenomenon.

In addition, UCTs are often constructed in such a way that it is impossible to *prove* them false. "Conspiracy theories are unproven *by design*," writes Brotherton (2015: 62). Archaeologists cannot prove that aliens *did not* visit Earth. This "self-sealing reasoning" (Lewandowsky et al. 2013b: 8)[14] or "self-insulation" (Napolitano 2021: 87) follows the pattern not only of appeal to ignorance fallacies but also those of begging the question fallacies. For example, statements coming from an institution whose proofs we intend to use in order to refute the theory will be dismissed because the institution is said to be part of the conspiracy. The conspiratorial mindset shares this strategy with fundamentalist religions and cults: a critic of theism will be dismissed because she will be said to have been brainwashed by atheist societies. It is as though a psychoanalyst were to simply dismiss a critic of their psychoanalysis by declaring them mentally ill. Arguments will be dismissed, not on the basis of counterarguments derived from facts collected from a realm unsupported by the theory itself, but on the grounds of the same theory that the opponent is trying to disprove. One might even attribute theories that later turn out to be false to the opponent and say that he "planted" them as a strawman to divert attention.

Another reason why the modern conspiratorial mindset is difficult to refute is that the theories it invents are often relatively complex. This is part of the aesthetics of the UCT. It is often difficult to keep track of the facts or the links between facts. Complexity can be used as a rhetorical weapon meant to instill the feeling of ignorance in the listener. The same strategy is used by religious sects and fundamentalist religions: often, critics are not allowed to question basic components of the teachings unless they have obtained extensive knowledge about a mass of details that would require years of study. At the same time, and paradoxically, the conspiratorial mindset's aim is to explain difficult and complex events by reducing them to a single, often simplistic, idea. Many UCTs subsist only because the *real* complexity of a situation is passed over, either on purpose or out of lack of genuine understanding of politics, culture, science, and so on. I will provide examples in Chapter 4. It is useless to argue against conspiratorially minded people by presenting factual proofs. For Pipes, they "are virtually immune to rational argument" (1997: 1–2).

---

14 The article has been retraced for legal reasons (the legal framework of the surveys was insufficiently clear) and not for scientific reasons.

Of course, sometimes the theorizing itself can be shown to be deficient. For example, a person submitted to the conspiratorial mindset might not deduct conclusions from premises but put the conclusion first and match premises afterward. This would be a real epistemological mistake. Another pattern that can help to identify a conspiratorial mindset is that it desperately searches for powerful necessities and categorically rejects contingencies, even when contingency should be included in the theory. While this can reveal an epistemological deficiency, it also creates a certain aesthetic impression.

All these are reasons why factual correctness cannot be the main criterion for judging a conspiracy theory. The main problem is not that the facts, causes, and events are fake; sometimes they might even be true. What makes these theories suspicious is the strange way in which the theory's elements interact. This is what I call the aesthetic side of the conspiracy theory. The arrangement of facts is often too random, or a bizarre internal dynamic potentially distorts the proportions of various items. But the consumer can find the theory exciting and engaging just for these reasons. Further, in many cases, we do not think that these theories are *entirely* false (unless they manifest internal contradictions), but we still recognize them as exaggerated or reductionist. We judge them aesthetically.

Furthermore, we judge conspiracy theories by looking at the people, their location within conspiratorial environments, their precedents, and the sources they use. Often there is some amount of truth even in baseless conspiracy theories, but the exaggerations, reductions, the obsessive insistence on certain recurring patterns, as well as the feeling of resentment and emotion that speaks through their rhetoric, style, and aesthetics, make us suspicious. We find the form of discourse production problematic and conclude that this might be an unwarranted narrative. Most commonly we look at ten features that I list here, which are partly covered by Keeley 1999, and which I extend and slightly modify:

1. Random facts are connected to each other, and not entirely plausible correlations are established.
2. Too many phenomena are explained through malign plots, even when other explanations are possible. The worst intentions are too systematically imputed to individuals or to certain groups without much evidence.
3. Much importance is attributed to errant facts (neglected by, and often contradictory to, official accounts). More importance is attributed to irrelevant facts than to significant facts.
4. There is much emphasis on secrecy.
5. Uncontrolled hatred crops up.

6. A particular explanatory pet pattern is used too repetitively.
7. The selection of certain facts and the omission of other facts are biased.
8. Too many official facts are dismissed.
9. The number of skipped evidence is too high.
10. There is a dogmatic distrust in institutions such as the press, science, or universities.

Of course, a conspiracist too could use points 7, 8, 9, and 10 to support their own theory, stating that in their opponent's account "too many unofficial facts, are dismissed," that it displays "a dogmatic distrust in those institutions" that they regard as trustworthy, and so on. It is theoretically also possible that all points apply without the theory being unwarranted. But this is unlikely. The list functions similarly to an aesthetic scheme used in art to detect, for example, kitsch. When too many items match, it is likely (though still not certain) that a work is kitsch.[15]

---

15 My list necessarily differs from one that would try to enumerate epistemic, and not "mindset" data, though there are overlaps. Dentith (2019) lists as typical for the construction of a conspiracy theory: selectiveness, errant data, disinformation, the use of prior information, secret evidence.

Chapter 2

ALTERNATIVE MODERNITIES

It has been said in the introduction that the conspiratorial mindset very often creates its own alternative world. Just as superstitions were part of the medieval lifestyle, in modernity, for many, the unwarranted conspiracy theory has become a way of life. And like all lifestyles, conspiracism is often not a matter of epistemic representation but of acquaintance, repeated perception, and habit. The term "belief" is here justified to some extent. Beliefs are often created not on a scientific or factual basis (believing *that*) but on a cultural basis (believing *in*). Many overarching assumptions about how the world works are acquired, not through analysis, but through acculturation. That this is a matter of mindset and not of rational cognition is evidenced by the fact that people who believe in one baseless conspiracy theory do very often also believe in many others.[1] They can even believe in theories that mutually exclude each other. Hagen (2022: 158–60) believes to have shown that writings by Wood et al. (2012) and Goertzel (1994), which attempt to demonstrate that such contradictory beliefs exist, are scientifically flawed. The problem is that both the former and Hagen's argumentations are purely epistemological. In aesthetic terms it is rather normal that somebody is attracted by two theories that are not entirely compatible. Just like I can like two types of music that "exclude" each other. Unwarranted conspiracy theories are therefore not *only* false theories, but also cultures, subcultures, or tastes that develop a dynamic of their own. And just like the latter, they cannot be opposed by working with "true" and "false" as criteria, but, at best, with the criteria of "likely" and "unlikely."

What is the conspiratorial mindset more precisely? Before delving into problems of contingency and necessity and their relationship with conspiracism,[2]

---

1 See Brotherton: 95. Goertzel (1994) coined the term "monological belief system model," which suggests that believing in one conspiracy theory causes a person to be more likely to believe in others. Though this model has never been empirically tested, it has been influential.
2 I also use the word "conspiracism," which has most likely been coined by Frank Mintz in his *The Liberty Lobby and the American Right: Race, Conspiracy, and Culture* (1985). It was

it is useful to identify the functions and the particular places that unjustifiable conspiracy theories occupy in the lives of *modern* citizens. Are these theories against any "enlightened" way of thinking, are they compatible with it, or perhaps even *products* of modernity and Enlightenment? The preliminary argument that I formulate in this chapter is that "Western Enlightenment," as broadly understood as possible, has always produced a non-Enlightenment thinking or an alternative Enlightenment movement in its margins, and that the unwarranted conspiracy theory is a quintessential product of this development. Unwarranted conspiracy theories are not simply manifestations of an "*anti*-Enlightenment thinking"; quite to the contrary, they result *from* modernity and thus seek alternative ways of being "enlightened." My findings concern more the "non-Dominant Institution Conspiracy Theories" (non-DITs) than the dominant ones (DITs), though there are overlaps and cases where DITs are concerned, too. I already said in the last chapter that DITs cannot as frequently be traced to a conspiratorial mindset as non-DITs.

One could have expected that modernity, with the advancement of science and rationality, would have eliminated or at least *reduced* flawed conspiratorial thinking. The contrary is the case: as I will show, it has constantly increased in popularity. Science suggests truths that are plausible, but the problem is that these truths have become increasingly difficult to understand for non-specialists; and especially in terms of aesthetics, they are not attractive. As a result, pseudoscience invents implausible truths that are nonetheless appealing, and the conspiracist sphere does the same.

What are the reasons? Daniel Pipes detects an anti-modern element in unwarranted conspiracy theories because, according to him, almost all of them seem to have been directed against four population groups: Jews, Freemasons, Britons, and Americans. Why these four? Because all four "share two outstanding characteristics: modernity and idealism" (1997: 151). Jews, Freemasons, Britons, and Americans symbolize progress. Like nobody else, they have been pushing ahead in science, modern politics, and modern lifestyles; or at least that's how it appears to the conspiratorial mindset.

Pipes' observations are extremely generalizing, but they do contain some truth. One could conclude that the conspiratorial mindset is thus anti-modern, but that would be a mistake. The conspiratorial mindset does not want to leave the current world and step into a medieval universe à la Tolkien. Just as religious fundamentalists do not want to live a life entirely identical to the one presented in ancient scriptures; fundamentalism is not traditionalism

---

then taken up by Daniel Pipes in his *Conspiracy: How the Paranoid Style Flourishes and Where It Comes From* (1997: 5).

(though there can be some overlap). Keeley (2006) and Cassam (2019) argue that conspiracy theorists reject modernity and espouse premodern views. I rather believe that the conspiratorial mindset—just like fundamentalism—has what Michael Mazarr calls a love-hate relationship with modernity: "[Fundamentalists] do not really hate modernity; they hate its failed hopes—the fact that it has not offered their country, or people, or culture the benefits it promised. Radical anti-modernisms represent the humiliated anger of the jilted lover more than a true commitment to premodern life" (Mazarr 2007: 71). Similarly, the conspiratorial mindset does not reject modernity but has instead often *been rejected* by modernity, which incites the protagonists to create an alternative modernity. I will explain the rejection paradigm in this book with regard to the conspiratorial mindset but will here provide the example of religious extremism, because in Fundamentalist Islam, the pattern becomes particularly clear. Many conservative Islamic activist groups base their vision of an ideal Islamic state not on a retrospective or nostalgic model but in fact on a new model and thus suggest an alternative modernity. The most recent wave of Islamization does not signify a return to traditional Islam and its scriptures; rather, one should "see in the Islamist movement elements of a forward-looking project: it is a populist attempt to redefine modernity in Islamic terms," as writes Margot Badran (2009: 224).[3] In the past, Ayatollah Khomeini saw himself as a progressive innovator of Shia thought, and Salafis often see traditional Islam as a degenerate version of a pristine Islam that needed to be replaced with a utopian version of Islamic culture. Similarly, the Muslim Brothers see themselves as an "avant-garde that was ahead of and even above the ordinary masses" (Ahmed 2011: 53). Though their visions of Islam remain culturally conservative, all these movements launch, in the form of a modern project, a plan to revive an ideal God-made Islam from the debris of human-made traditions.[4] According to Bassam Tibi, fundamentalists do not want to modernize Islam but rather "Islamize modernity" (Tibi

---

3 Inayatullah and Boxwell confirm that in Islamic fundamentalism, "traditionalism becomes a by-product of modernity" (2003: 13).
4 I am aware of some *theological* differences. In traditional theologies, both on the Christian and the Muslim side, the future is supposed to signify a fall of the material, corrupt world (though believers can be saved). The word "utopia" was coined rather late, in the Renaissance, by Thomas More (1478–1535). Only in the humanist context of the Renaissance, when philosophy was sufficiently detached from religion, could people think of building their future on their own. In the new secular context, the *ou-topos* could emerge as a non-existent place located in the future. In the present discussion, I am addressing political and cultural implications, and not theological ones. See also Botz-Bornstein 2019b, Chapter 5 on the topic of forward-looking Islamism.

1998: 32): "Although fundamentalists do draw on traditions, they do so clearly within a modern context and with a nontraditional mindset" (29).[5] For Minoo Moallem, fundamentalism is even "a modern discursive formation" (2005: 10). These movements are not conservative in the sense of eighteenth-century European conservatism, which simply contradicted the transformative social forces of modernity. On the contrary, an optimistic notion of progress points to the future in order to establish a utopia: "The arrow of time points [...] forward even when the teacher looks over his shoulder for guidance on where to aim," writes Roger Griffin (1992: 32).

There are similarities between the conspiratorial mindset (the mindset that likes unwarranted conspiracy theories) and fundamentalist theologies, but there are also some differences. The conspiratorial mindset does not work in the service of a re-enchantment of the world: conspiracy theories are not uplifting, nor is the conspiracy theory a substitute for fairytales. While religions can have this function, the tales of the conspiratorial mindset are, most of the time, too complex and too "scientific" to be accepted by any traditional fairytale anthology. Second, unwarranted conspiracy theories are almost always not utopian but dystopian. Though conspiratorial thinking has often been integrated into religious thought, it is unlikely that the predominantly negative mindset of conspiracism will ever become a principal driving force of a religion, especially not of a radical one. Radical theologies prefer not dystopian but utopian models. They talk less about conspiracist entanglements and more about the possible liberation from current constraints, even when these constraints are due to conspiracies. Though traditionally, monotheistic religions frown upon the concept of human progress and hold that "utopia" (the ideal world) remains located in the past, they also reject outright nihilism. Paradoxically, though they believe that the future signifies the fall (see note 7), most typically, they aim at creating a feeling of optimism with regard to the future.

The nihilism that is relatively current in indefensible conspiracy theories appears as strangely "utopian-dystopian" (I will elaborate below on the fact that much unwarranted conspiratorial thinking has been related to

---

5 This is not necessarily true for American Christian fundamentalism, which should rather be defined as a "militantly antimodernist Protestant evangelicalism" (Marsden 2006: 4). American Christian fundamentalists are rather an "arrière-garde" whose strategy often limits itself to a simple opposition to cultural changes, which is more in keeping with classical conservatism. Originally, the Salafist movement launched in the 1870s by Jamal ad-Din al-Afghani and Mohammed Abduh did *not* challenge the premises of the Enlightenment. Islamic and Protestant fundamentalism construe the word "fundamental" differently.

depression). As a result of their dystopian profile, undue conspiracy theories—much more than utopian radical religions—project neither anti-modernities nor utopias but *alternative* modernities. Utopias strive to overcome a given state of affairs by becoming *more* modern, whereas conspiracism does not strive to be *more* modern but *alternatively* modern.

There is still another reason why the conspiratorial mindset cannot have a utopian profile: one of its main driving forces is a pronounced utopia aversion. Ever since the Enlightenment, the Western world has been dominated by optimistic utopian thinking, and the conspiratorial mindset resents this utopian strain. Pipes characterized the four favorite conspiracy groups (Jews, Freemasons, Britons, and Americans) not only as modern but also as idealistic. The conspiratorial mindset resents the modern world's preponderant idealism. Despite all this, in many respects, the conspiratorial mindset remains modern. For example, it criticizes conspiracies; conspiracies should indeed not occur in modern, democratic, transparent, and law-abiding societies. Or when it came to the recent coronavirus, "conspiracy scientists" would often recommend surprisingly *modern* panaceas such as the antimalarial drug hydroxychloroquine or the antiparasitic medication Ivermectin (which were not recognized by most international health authorities). Another indicator, on which this book concentrates, is that the conspiratorial mindset looks for necessities and rejects contingencies, which is a prototypical scientific approach as well (even though it will not be pushed through in a scientific fashion but only in a more "aesthetic" fashion). Pointing to hidden necessities is exciting, engaging, thrilling [...] It is paradoxical that these apparently "modern" theories can inspire social movements that can appear archaic in some other regards. The reason is that they are "alternatively" modern. Decades ago, Fredric Jameson called "a poor person's mapping" the way how the poor and uneducated orient themselves in the complex landscape of capitalism (1988: 356). They find secret conspirators rather than real oppressors.

Low-Tech Enlightenment

I said above that the modern world, still strongly driven by Enlightenment values, is utopian, and that the conspiratorial mindset, at least when concentrating on non-DITs, resents this optimistic utopianism. Why would the current world that we are living in be considered an ideal place or a utopia? To understand this, one needs to put oneself in the shoes of the conspiratorial mindset. From the perspective of those who have been excluded from modernity, the contemporary industrialized world can indeed appear to be an ideal place—but a place *too* ideal. After centuries of struggles, the late Enlightenment managed to create a universe in which everybody is liberated, and in which everything, even art and sexuality, is democratic, tolerant, well-organized, and ranked. Experts solve all kinds of problems with the help of theories. Data analysts handle the most sophisticated calculations enabling precise predictions about the future. The latest state-of-the-art model of progressive Western civilization is the post-industrial society, which has generated a world in which knowledge is the most valued resource and the most valued form of capital. The inhabitants of this world are international and cooperative, invest in creativity, and appreciate the work of professionals such as scientists and designers. Resilience, flexibility, and pioneerdom are the official virtues. This late Enlightenment world is so perfect that it has even incorporated its own self-criticism: it politely encourages democratic institutions like NGOs and humanitarian associations to criticize whatever they can; these institutions are part of the system.[6] The problem is that, precisely because of its perfection, some people cannot find their place in this system. According to Baudrillard, "the more the system is perfect, the more people are left out" (2005: 69). For some, this knowledge-based meritocracy is no ideal abode but has rather become a place ravaged by what Michael Sandel calls the "tyranny of merit." What Cassam and Shields name the "death of expertise" is due to this pervasive perfectionism.

The situation is similar to what happens in music or art: when synthetically enhanced music becomes too impeccable, or when photos are digitally enhanced to a state of perfection until their correctness becomes too pure and too formal, some musicians or photographers refuse this culturalization and aestheticization and look for alternative, low-tech methods. This is precisely what happens in the late Enlightenment world: those who are left out develop their own "low-tech Enlightenment thought" of which the baseless conspiracy theory is the prototype.

"Low-tech Enlightenment thought" becomes the favorite option of alt-modernists, a group that can comprise protagonists as diverse as Islamic terrorists, Brexiters, and flat-earthers. What these people all have in common is that they want to step out of systems that were once believed to be progressive, inclusive, and well-disposed toward "the people." At the same time, they do not reject all modern ideals. They are "alternative modernists" who try to create new forms of Enlightenment. Often, they might merely *pose* as modern without implementing any social or epistemic models that others would

---

6 Post-industrial societies are so "perfect" that they can even afford the massive creation of what David Graeber (2018) has called "bullshit jobs." Post-industrial societies are dedicated to expanding administrative tasks that are unnecessary and do not make a meaningful contribution to people's work. More on Graeber will follow below.

recognize as modern in any significant way. But even so, they cannot be classified as anti-modern.

Nassim Taleb would probably call the perfect system that I describe a "Platonically designed" system. The problem with such systems is not that they are "bad." They are good but uncanny precisely because of their perfection. In parallel, alt-modernists perceive modern people not so much as bad and dangerous, but rather as uncanny. Non-modern people are "simply" dangerous. Non-modern people come running into your country with spears, while modern people invade your country without you even noticing it. The latter are uncanny because they present a continuous *potential* danger, which gives rise to the conspiratorial mindset. The uncanniest ones are actually the "post-moderns," be it only because they are difficult to define. Of course, I am talking here of non-DITs more than of DITs.

The conspiratorial mindset is a sort of country receiving refugees from the world of modernity. As mentioned, Keeley (2006) and Cassam argue that conspiracy theorists reject modernity and espouse premodern views, and that the conspiracy theory embodies "a thoroughly outdated worldview and a perspective on the meaning of life that was more appropriate in the [nineteenth] century" (Cassam 2019: 17). I hold that the conspiratorial mindset wants to move from one modernity to another. The conspiratorial mindset perceives modernity, with its science, liberal democracy, correctness, and everything else that depends on it, as a well-oiled machine determined by evil necessities that constantly work against them. The present world is not acknowledged as a fulfillment of utopian wishes. Eventually, the conspiratorial mindset wants to flee not into a utopia but into a dystopia. This mindset does not spell out its vision in positive terms but defines its new modernity mainly negatively, that is, as a dystopian world determined by conspiracies. It does not want to join the utopian type of modernity but creates an alternative dystopian modernity that is nonetheless modern.

Hofstadter saw as the main source of conspiracy theories "a frightening view of the opposition as the superhuman incarnation of perfect evil" (Wilentz 2012: xx). Again, the main threat is not the system's evil character but its perfection. Perfection makes these systems run smoothly and imperceptibly, which is uncanny. The uncanniness becomes particularly perceptible when the perfection is aestheticized, that is, when the systems become aesthetically superior or even elegant. The conspiratorial mind is not entirely wrong when feeling a weakness in this perfection. In theoretical thought, elegance can be a weakness because it shows that the theory is too far removed from the "non elegant" practice and reality. Taleb writes: "Elegance in the theories is often indicative of Platonicity and weakness—it invites you to seek elegance for elegance's sake" (2007: 285).

Many practitioners of the conspiratorial mindset are those who have been excluded from this perfect world. Cassam (and others) confirm that "conspiracy interpretation of the world flourish in the context of marginalization, poverty, and other negative life circumstances" and people "who are conspiracy-minded are more likely to see themselves as being at the bottom of the social ladder" (2019: 56). Research has shown that "marginalized or minority groups have a propensity towards conspiracism [...] since any minority, especially one under threat or perceiving itself as so, will develop a sense of fear and seek an explanation for the situation" (Gray 2010: 30). Peter Knight confirms this too, writing that much conspiracism takes place in groups of non-privileged minorities (2000: 117–67). These authors approve the above assumption that unwarranted conspiracy theories are mainly held by individuals or communities that are excluded from official systems (though sometimes even an entire state can have a marginalized position within a global system). Similarly, Michael Sandel, in his analysis of anti-meritocracy, concentrates on the underdogs of society.

Sometimes there are factors like poor analytical thinking skills[7] or depression. Research on paranormal beliefs (which are the basis of many conspiracy theories) has highlighted a "depressed" state of mind, which is otherwise not surprising for a subculture that is basically dystopian.[8] It is, of course, wrong to conclude that those who tend to believe in varieties of unwarranted conspiracy theories are always losers. The mere existence of DITs contradicts this. Though many are underdogs, not all practitioners of the conspiratorial mindset are dropouts. Many are well integrated into late Enlightenment post-industrial, globalized societies, and play by the rules of the "perfect system." However, even ostensibly modern people can be alt-modern and strive to act within modernity in a different way. Even integrated people can have resentment against the elite. Sometimes a certain group dynamic can draw rather atypical people into conspiratorial cultures. DITs are different as they do not generally try to create an alternative modernity. They are not excluded from modernity. Shields cites Paul Wolfowitz, Bush's Deputy Secretary of Defense and one of the driving figures behind the invasion of Iraq, who was obsessed with Saddam Hussein being the cause of all evil. He was a powerful,

---

7 Lewandowsky et al. 2013b single out "unreflexive counterfactual thinking" or the "lack of a cognitive control mechanism that requires an hypothesis to be compatible with *all* the available evidence" (8).

8 Mikušková and Čavojová distributed questionnaires about paranormal beliefs and found that, in general, "depressed people and people lower in analytic thinking [...] were more credulous" (Mikušková and Čavojová: 8). What is true for the belief in paranormal phenomena would also concern the belief in unwarranted conspiracy theories.

well-educated conspiracy theorist of the DIT kind. Why was he like this? Here the will to power might partially, though not fully, explain the conspiratorial mindset.

Some suggest that the conspiratorial mindset is always produced by the political Right, which is not true either. Though skepticism toward utopianism makes the Right a typical customer of unwarranted conspiratorial thinking styles, some radical left-leaning political thought linked to wokeness and political correctness can be classified as conspiratorial too. Already in 1964, Richard Hofstadter noted that paranoid gesticulations can afflict radical movements on the Left as well as on the Right.[9] Mass phenomena like QAnon or the conspiracy culture that developed around Trump supporters like the Proud Boys show that most of the conspiratorial mindset is a product of the Right and possibly fought by the Left.[10] But on the Left, some versions of neo-feminism seem to depict a rather implausible male conspiracy against women; others depict racial conspiracies that are often warranted but also sometimes unwarranted because exaggerated.

No matter who they are, for alt-modernists, conspiracism represents a safe haven in a world of hostile excellence. The conspiratorial mindset is against the "perfectionated" brand of Enlightenment. Despite this, it continues sharing with its modern enemies some of the premises most dear to the Enlightenment. For example, it follows the idea of liberation.[11] Conspiracy theories can signify freedom from a world one resents; however, as the conspiratorial mindset constantly deconstructs the existing "perfect" modern system by detecting more and more conspiracies, in the end, it does not obtain real liberation. One reason—which will be attended to in Chapter 5—is that "conspiracist liberation" is often fed by resentment: the conspiratorial mindset easily gets entangled in resentment-inspired visions of the world. Initially, by pointing to a conspiracy, the source of humiliation is seemingly located. However, one cannot combat conspirators in the same way one combats, for example, oppressive employers. The conspirator is evasive by definition, which reinforces the feeling of victimization. In the end, there is no liberation. The only thing that remains constant is a questionable feeling of superiority and the belief that the enemy has been degraded, as notes Pipes:

---

9 According to Coady, many of the earliest conspiracy theories were due to conservatives accusing leftists of producing conspiracy theories (Coady 2006: 3).
10 Coady holds that "conspiracy thinking is indisputably an activity of the extreme Right" (n. 4).
11 Liberation was important before Enlightenment, for example, in Gnosticism, but the idea of freedom became central through Kant.

"Conspiracism deprives the accused of their humanity and makes them vulnerable to elimination as though an unwanted pest" (1997: 180).

The Paradox of Knowledge Production

The complex, unwarranted conspiracy theory as we know it today emerged in the eighteenth century. While accusations of scapegoats such as Freemasons, Jews, or any outsiders had already abounded in the Middle Ages, the most outstanding period for groundless conspiracy theories in Europe (as well as in the United States) begins around 1750, that is, precisely when the Enlightenment kicked off in earnest. It happened in connection with the French Revolution, that is, with the *preparation* of the revolution. Jovan Byford traces "the roots of the conspiracy tradition to the immediate aftermath of the French Revolution and examines the social, political, and cultural factors that contributed to its emergence" (2011). Baseless conspiracy theories already existed during the *Ancien Regime* (see Geoffrey Cubitt's book on conspiracy theories in France). As a matter of fact, they have always existed, but initially, thoughts about conspiracies were relatively trivial. With the Revolution, they morph into "all-consuming theories" (Brotherton 2015: 22) or full-fledged world-system theories. In other words, they acquired new aesthetic dimensions. In modern conspiracism, history is often believed to be "set in motion by demonic forces of almost transcendent power," as Hofstadter had analyzed (2012: 29). I examine these historical developments in Chapter 6. In this chapter, I want to demonstrate that the more recent conspiratorial mindset is an "alt-Enlightenment" phenomenon because, in some complex way, it remains linked to typically modern developments. It has already been said that science, which has been a dominant social force since the Enlightenment, has not only raised the level of knowledge in societies, but that it has also enabled the spectacular spread of unwarranted conspiratorial thinking as well as the transformation of this thinking into a sophisticated pseudoscience. The reason is that there is a logical correlation between the production of knowledge and the production of non-knowledge, into which we should look now.

It sounds counterintuitive that the Enlightenment should have helped to produce stupidity, but the idea is perfectly consistent. First, it is linked to the above-mentioned paradigm: the more a system is perfect, the more it excludes those individuals who cannot enter the system. It has already been explained that this system is not bad but rather uncanny. Bad systems provoke counterreactions in the form of revolts and revolutions. Bad systems will sooner or later be done away with and be replaced by better systems. In contrast, a perfect but uncanny system triggers the creation of alternative systems. The perfect system is not to be abolished; instead, it often remains functional and even useful. It is alongside this system that alternative truths and alternative sciences emerge. Meanwhile, the original truths might remain appreciated and continue to be used. Homeopathy does not want to *destroy* regular medicine; normally, it merely desires to exist next to it as an alternative medicine. The conspiratorial-minded person who believes in unscientific theories will, despite their anti-science skepticism, most probably head for the hospital when sick and benefit from "regular" science. This means that one does not resent the system as such but only its perfection, which is experienced as humiliating. Its perfection makes us feel our ignorance, our helplessness, as well as our hopeless disconnectedness from a world of science that has become extremely complex. As a result, the conspiratorial mindset designs scientific systems that are less perfect but more relatable, or, as Donatella Di Cesare, says, more "readable." Di Cesare summarizes the situation as such:

> Conspiracy theory is the immediate reaction to complexity. It is the shortcut, the simplest and quickest way to get to the bottom of a world that is now illegible. Those who resort to conspiracy cannot stand anxiety, open questions. They cannot tolerate living in a changing and unstable landscape, they do not accept being foreign. They show themselves incapable of recognizing themselves, along with others, exposed and vulnerable, without protection, but therefore freer and more responsible. (2021: 1, my trans.)

The Enlightenment believed that with the rise of scientific thought, superstitions and obscurantism would eventually disappear. The opposite is the case. As science develops, pseudoscience develops in parallel. First, this has to do with the above-described perfection of systems from which certain parts of the population are excluded. But this pattern also works on a more general level. Logically, with any increase in information, not only a society's total amount of knowledge swell, but also its amount of ignorance. As knowledge becomes more complex, it can no longer be mastered by non-specialized individuals and needs to be outsourced to experts. Most of us accept the experts' opinions at least to some extent, but some just don't and thus create their own knowledge base. Thus, alongside evolutionism flourishes creationism, alongside historical science flourishes fictional history, alongside archaeology flourishes treasure hunting. Alternative low-tech knowledge appears, of which the unwarranted conspiracy theory is a prime example. "Each of us typically thinks he or she (in isolation from others) possesses a far richer model and a far more detailed explanatory scheme than we do. Individualism is intuitive, but it is wrong," writes Neil Levy about conspiracy theories (2007: 183).

This parallel development of knowledge and pseudo-knowledge surfaced most clearly in the late nineteenth century. The sudden progress of biological science created, especially in Germany, Italy, and France, large amounts of pseudo-scientific madness in the form of racial inequality theories, social Darwinism, scientifically justified nationalism, and antisemitism. "Raciology" evolved in parallel with, or precisely *because of,* the nineteenth century's fulgurant scientific progress. Furthermore, the pseudo-knowledge qua knowledge pattern has also been supported by liberal democracies. According to Christopher Lasch, the classical liberal Ludwig von Mises held that "in order to break the existing pattern of dependence and put an end to the erosion of competence, citizens will have to take the solution of their problems into their own hands. They will create their own 'communities of competence'" (Lasch 1979: 235). In liberal societies, everybody has the freedom to find their own knowledge.

Unwarranted conspiracy science is the bad mirror image of good science. It is bad for various reasons: it distorts real science not only by using sloppy methodologies but also by pretending to explain everything, something that real science does not do. They "dream of a complete intelligibility of History," as writes Di Cesare (2021: 14). However, this mirror image could not exist had science not been taught in schools and become a part of modern culture. This process has become most dramatic with the internet, which allows not only more people to gain information, but also more people to provide (false) information. The internet enables us to debunk unwarranted conspiracy theories faster than ever before, but it also accelerates the production and spread of ignorance. This is how conspiracism could evolve from the fringes of political discourse to a mass-cultural level. Notable is not only the quantitative spread of conspiratorial ideation but also the push toward its "theoretical" sophistication. The conspiratorial mindset uses an ever-larger variety of facts and methods, most of which are supposed to appear scientific. The high output of today's "conspiracist science" productions was not thinkable in earlier eras. Modern conspiratorial ideation requires at least a superficial understanding of intricate facts, the ability to use some statistics software, as well as the ability to present these facts in a relatively systematic way (or at least to pretend to do so).

Furthermore, one can even say that democracy helped these theories to flourish; not only because of the introduction of free speech but also for a more intrinsic reason. Many of these theories are based on the assumption that the state is holding back information and that it is cheating its citizens by distributing fake news and fake research. Such expectations could only emerge *because* of the democratic experience. In non-democratic societies, there was no expectation that the state *should* disclose all information. Democracy fostered suspicions that conspiracies are prevalent. This can be positive or negative. In negative cases, the expectation of democracy fosters conspiratorial thinking that believes in unwarranted theories. Often the conspiratorial mindset wants democracy, as testified by the appeals to democracy among anti-vax demonstrators. It remains a contradiction that those who cannot be well integrated into the modern world and loathe the elite with its Enlightenment progressive politics also seem to loathe any "democratic" politics. But the pattern follows an intrinsic logic: democratic regimes are identified with the "best world utopia" concocted by the elite. In reality, democracy is not really declared evil, but real democracy is seen as unachievable. Democracy is only a counterfeit behind which elitist evil powers are hiding. The conspiracy theory is thus meant to fill a void that democracy itself has created and which Di Cesare describes as such: "One can understand the astonishment of citizens projected into the scenario of democratic modernity. And, together with the astonishment, also the uncertainty, the perplexity, the anxiety" (2021: 29). The void must be filled with authoritarian regimes that are believed to serve the people's interests better than the hated elites. The contradictions that the above account contains show once more that the conspiratorial mindset is not a matter of knowledge and plausibility but rather of aesthetic preference. The flat-earther does not believe in the flatness of the earth because they find it plausible in the first place. They prefer this option because they *sympathize* with a given idea. More precisely, it is not the idea that the earth is flat that they find attractive but rather the thought that here an important truth has been dissimulated to citizens by the conspiring governments. One can use the word "belief," but then again: Why would they "believe" such things or "believe in" such things? They do not believe them because they find them plausible. If they find flat-earth theories plausible, then it is only because they found them attractive in the first place. The conspiratorial mindset resents a perfect system of dissimulation and creates an alternative truth. At the same time, its proponents will continue boarding airplanes and trust that the pilot will find their way according to a conventional belief in a "round earth."

Wherever there is Enlightenment, there is alt-Enlightenment. Wherever there is a system, there is also a counter-system, and this pattern can be detected in any domain of social life. The more a society is "perfect," at least from the perspective of applied puritanism, whenever authorities attempt to eliminate all signs of deviance, debauchery will grow elsewhere, unseen and underground. Authorities have always been aware of this. Traditionally, the Catholic Church supported institutions like carnival during which an unusual amount of deviance was permitted. In certain countries, prostitution or certain drugs have been legalized with the aim of controlling "alt-movements" before they become unseen and uncontainable. The conspiratorial mindset is one of these "underground" subcultures, and to some extent, liberal governments follow the principle of carnival. On the internet, although there has been a recent push toward more control, there remains a high degree of tolerance for the conspiracy sphere because its total suppression could arguably turn it into an even more vigorous and more dangerous subculture.

Another important reason for the push toward pseudoscience is the over-scientification of the life world in the twenty-first century. Daily matters like eating, working, and exercising are increasingly supported by chemistry, psychology, statistics, algorithms, and rankings. Knowledge about daily matters is outsourced to dieticians, lifestyle workers, personal trainers, home designers, and life coaches (about the latter I will talk more in Chapter 11). "Baby Manager" apps transform the lives of newborn babies into numbers by issuing ideal sleeping times, feeding times, and crying times, and provide parents with the ideal algorithms about childcare (and also much anxiety). It is thus to be expected that conspiratorial worldviews use more and more complex "scientific" theories. When science is literally in your hand (in your phone) all day long, more pseudoscience than ever is bound to emerge. When societies were not as swamped with this kind of expert knowledge, this could not happen so easily. In addition, the Baby Manager app projects, again, a utopian, perfect world system that can easily be resented because it emphasizes necessities where contingencies obviously would play a role. Experts create a "Platonified" world of necessities, and conspiracy theorists create their own "scientific" necessities in parallel. Their alternative theories provide explanations that are supposed to be systematic, though in the end, the result is frustrating because the so-called necessities are not plausible.

But let's be fair to the alt-modern person. It is true that not all modern achievements are exciting, that not every new technology is useful, and that not all modern art deserves to be celebrated. Not all traditions deserve to be abandoned, and not all kinds of nationalism are archaic. Do we not all sometimes have doubts about the pertinence of certain data analyses? Are we not sometimes skeptical of "Platonically" designed working worlds whose impenetrable perfection is supported by algorithms? Is much of the work of HR consultants, communications coordinators, PR researchers, financial strategists, and corporate lawyers, all of whom David Graeber analyzes, not often truly "bullshit" in the sense of mindless, narcissistic, and superfluous hyper-activity? Not all neoliberal merits are worth being desired, and arguably few self-development courses have ever brought the advertised well-being. Do we not all regard some of the late Enlightenment values with a critical eye, especially those that lead to excessive evaluations and standardization? Forgas and Baumeister write that "our own epoch is based on the dominant cultural and moral values of the Enlightenment: the shared belief that humanism, individual liberty, and equality are universal, desirable, and natural values" and ask: "Is this not also a fiction?" (Forgas and Baumeister: 6). There is something alt-modern in all of us, only to different degrees. Many are dubious, but, fortunately, not everybody fully embraces a conspiratorial mindset. In this sense, Pigden is right in saying that we are all conspiracy theorists. But this idea should not lead to relativism.

I want to conclude this chapter by explaining how the connection between science and pseudoscience is related to the main topic of this book: contingency. Enlightenment has very much been built on scientific principles of necessity, with the result that the elitist correctness of the Enlightenment world can easily be perceived as dictatorial (especially) by those who are not already in its system. Then the adherents of the new alt-modern culture try to find new necessities in the realms of science, politics, and culture, and create a parallel conspiracist universe. The purpose is to reestablish a sovereignty and dignity that had been lost to knowledge networks that appear aloof and incomprehensible, and upon which the adherents feel they have no influence.

What about contingency? What about this quality that has always perturbed order, progress, science, belief, and many of humanity's firmest convictions? The problem is that both science and the conspiratorial mindset, both moderns and alt-moderns, look for necessities *only*. Both modern people and their alt-modern alienated cousins have difficulties dealing with contingency. Both are caught in ancient dichotomies that oppose progress to anti-progress, and Enlightenment to anti-Enlightenment. Both see their own productions as necessities. However, a large part of the universe that we are living in (anthropologically, scientifically, and philosophically-conceptually speaking) is made of contingencies. Humans are "beings of possibilities" (Möglichkeitswesen) by definition, as says Hans Blumenberg (1997: 212). And possibilities always imply contingencies. By choosing from possibilities, humans shape their destinies and manage to create themselves. Contingency slips in everywhere. Even the most modern way of life is not founded on necessity alone but on a slew of arbitrary decisions. Sometimes, as says Cassam, we have to accept the coincidence: "Why was Oswald himself shot by Jack Ruby while in police custody? From a modern (as distinct from premodern) perspective, all we can really say is: shit happens" (2019: 17).[12] But this is precisely not the modern perspective but a perhaps "postmodern" one that is difficult to adopt.

---

12 Cassam divides the "nothing happens by chance" reaction into three parts: the intentionality bias (there must be an intention behind it); the confirmation bias (the tendency to look only for evidence that supports what one already believes); and the proportionality bias (the scale of an event's cause must match the scale of the event itself) (XX).

This book attempts to develop not an alternative "science of necessity" (as the conspiratorial mindset does) but a worldview that is more strongly rooted in contingency. We are condemned to choose, and choices can depend on contingencies. For a long time, religion had taken this thought off people's minds by providing, when it came to choices, incontestable necessities. Today, through what Nassim Taleb calls "epistemic arrogance," specialists peddle necessity in a way that is not very different from conspiracy theorists: "We overestimate what we know, and underestimate uncertainty, by compressing the range of possible uncertain states (i.e., by reducing the space of the unknown)" (Taleb 2007: 140). Taleb does not address conspiracy theorists but mainly traders eagerly theorizing about random events. Or he addresses businessmen in dark suits who attribute their success to elaborate and scientifically established schemes, though it is often/largely merely due to chance: "A large section of businessmen with outstanding track records [are] no better than randomly thrown darts" (Taleb 2001: 22).

Be it narcissistic businessmen, algorithms, rankings, baby manager apps, or a whole working world full of useless jobs: the result is a perfect world model that can easily be resented by others. The only theory that can make the utopian "perfect world" model of late Enlightenment look more penetrable, accommodating, and humane, is one that establishes a contingency perspective. Finally, through such a perspective, much of the conspiracy sphere that is opposed to the Enlightenment culture of necessities could disappear in parallel.

Chapter 3
COINCIDENCE, ACCIDENT, VIRUS

The present book concentrates on how the conspiratorial mindset handles the phenomenon of contingency. Contingency can appear everywhere: in science, art, politics, religion, and everyday life. As mentioned, conspiracists tend to search for necessities and are reluctant to attribute certain events to chance. Everything happens for a *necessary* reason. So, what is contingency? When seen in isolation and abstractly, contingency is a logical and philosophical concept; however, even as an abstract concept, it has various shades of meaning, some of which need to be clarified first. Most basically, when what happens is neither necessary nor impossible, we speak of coincidence or of contingency. Sometimes the coincidence's causes are known, sometimes they remain unknown. The Oxford English Dictionary defines "contingent" as "of uncertain occurrence; liable to happen or not; happening by chance; fortuitous; conditional; not predetermined by necessity [...]" (Stevenson 2007). The coincidence is thus the event, and contingency is the concept trying to grasp the fortuity or the "coincidentality" of the event. In German, the coincidence is characteristically called *Zufall*, which means that an event unexpectedly "falls" into an environment and potentially determines other events. "Coincidence" expresses here the scholastic *accidere*, which means "to occur" (which is *vorfallen* in German) and which obviously gave its name to the accident. In Greek, the coincidence is *endechomenon* or *symbebekos*. Aristotle speaks in his natural scientific works (for example *Physics*, B 6: 197 b 32–35) as well as in his logical treatises (for example *Prior Analytics* 46b–47b) and *Metaphysics* (for example 1025a) of the "*kata symbebekos*" (chance event),[1] which subsequent generations of philosophers saw as an undetermined cause in the sense of the *accidens*. Scholasticism applied the *symbebekos* to language by seeing it as that which is not *necessarily* present in language, but which occurs

---

1 *Symbebekos* is especially dealt with in the fourth and fifth books of the second part of the *Physics*. Aristotle introduces conceptual precisions by talking about *symbebekos*, *tyche*, and *automaton*. The concept of contingency embraces all three plus *endechomenon*. All four can occur even when no determinate reason for the event can be recognized.

unnecessarily and is thus accidental (see Mauthner 2012: 61). Aristotle applies the word *endechomenon* in various slightly differing ways, but most often it is that which is "neither necessary nor impossible" (*On Interpretation*, 25a37–41, 29b29–32, 32a18–29, 33b17, 22–23). "Contingent" as the modern translation of *endechomenon* has thus become common.

In modern thought, contingency and coincidence are commonly used interchangeably, a convention that was most probably introduced by Kant. In *The Critique of Pure Reason* (1974: 119), Kant uses the words "*das Zufällige*" (and not *der Zufall*) for what Leibniz, in his *Theodicy*, had called *Kontingenz* (I, §39). Leibniz's terminology was still in keeping with a medieval theological tradition of *contingentia* as God's absolute freedom (meaning that God is not bound by necessities), which will be further examined in Chapter 6. By calling coincidence *das Zufällige* (which is linguistically close to *der Zufall*), the difference between coincidence and contingency almost disappears. Kant thus secularizes contingency and creates a non-theological understanding of contingency that would become current in modern thought.

Both Leibniz's "Kontingenz" and Kant's *das Zufällige* are the antithesis of the necessary. They represent an actuality (Wirklichkeit) that could also not be, but which remains different from the merely possible. Despite these generally accepted overlaps, some subtle distinctions between contingency and coincidence remain pertinent. Contingency is still a *mere* potentiality, whereas coincidence can be seen as the actualization of this potentiality. Contingency is what enables coincidence. Contingency can be seen as the "space" in which coincidence happens, which means that single events or micro-events called coincidences unfold within a macro sphere of contingency. The micro-event and the macro structure can have separate (though most probably interdependent) existences. This becomes clear when one considers that the micro-event can be turned into a necessity without canceling the general contingent context. For example, through genetic engineering, one can "neutralize" the coincidences that cause a human being's genetic particularities. By doing so, one establishes a finality: the child will not be born with features that are generated coincidentally but rather in a way that fulfills the parents' wishes. Here the single coincidence becomes a necessity, but the macro structure, that is, the contingency of birth or the fact that one is born even though one *could* as well not even have been conceived, maintains its open-ended character. Being born cannot be subjected to a finality and remains inscribed in a sphere of contingency. While coincidence is the absence of finality, a certain "macro contingency" will subsist. Such shifts between micro and macro considerations with regard to coincidence will be further discussed in Chapter 8.

As mentioned, the coincidence is also the medieval *accidens*, and coincidence and accident have always been linked. In today's understanding, an accident is an unfortunate coincidence, and its causes are usually—though not always—known. An accident can have a low probability (for example, when a brick falls off a roof onto somebody's head) or a higher probability (when this happens during a storm). What matters is that there was no intention and no plan behind the act. The only thing that distinguishes an intentionally staged event from an accident is contingency, and this contingency arises from either a (possibly temporary) inability to control or from negligence. A tempest, though fortuitous,[2] is not an accident, but it can cause an accident. There are thus two events: the brick getting loose and the brick falling on a passerby's head. The latter is the accident, and the former is what caused the accident. A brick getting loose might be an unlikely event and can be seen as a coincidence under certain circumstances. But it becomes an accident when it falls—through a second coincidence—on somebody. If a driver drives through a storm ignoring all meteorological warnings, we might say that the event is the result of human behavior that should have been better controlled; but it still led to an accident, and not to an intentionally staged event. Speeding a car is an intentional action and can result in accidents, but the driver's intention has not been to produce an accident. The higher the probability, the more we are inclined to see it as "less" of an accident. Balancing on a balcony railing and falling to one's death is a coincidence because it did not have to happen. But the probability of the coincidence happening was high, and we might have some reservations about calling it a mere accident. Why did the individual in question balance on the railing in the first place? Suspicions of suicidal *intentions* will naturally emerge. Still, while some acts are intentional and others are unintentional, often there are gray zones between them. We see that the surrounding circumstances (such as depression or the temporary loss of control of a situation) could have led to the same result (falling from a balcony railing), even without clear intentions. In that case, we might call it "almost an accident." The conclusion is that not all accidents are alike and that we inscribe them on a scale of probabilities and classify them as "real" accidents or, on the lowest level, as "almost accidents."

Whatever happens by chance could also not have happened. It is therefore intuitive to believe that coincidences are "less real" than those events that happen necessarily. However, from another perspective, it can appear that the coincidence is the perfect unity of actuality and possibility, and that it therefore expresses something more "real" than anything else. This chapter and the following two will explore this line of thought. The accident is a

---

2 Fortuitous has two meanings: "happening by chance rather than intention" and "happening by a lucky chance; fortunate." I use it in the more technical, first sense.

case of a "real coincidence": in the moment it "really" happens, it gives us the uncanny feeling of a concreteness that suddenly and unexpectedly flares up within our existence. What was only seconds ago an abstract probability, and real only for others, suddenly has dramatic and disproportionate consequences on our own, real lives. Often, we say in such climactic situations: "Now I understand that these unfortunate things can not only happen to others but also to me."

These thoughts are important for the relationships between the conspiratorial mindset and contingency. Something negative clings to the coincidence, and it has to do with uncanniness. The accident is uncanny, and the degree of uncanniness is inversely proportional to its probability: the less probable it is, the uncannier it appears. When the most unlikely of events causes considerable damage, it gives us this strange experience in which something that feels rooted in the unreal has now become real, and its experience of realness has thereby become exalted. The outcry "I can't believe it" expresses this epistemic contradiction. "Can one know something and not believe it?" asks Pascal Massie. "Not only did it not have to happen, but in a sense, it should not have happened" (Massie 2011: 14). The peculiar skepticism expressed by the "I can't believe it" statement is triggered by uncanniness.

The experience of such a coincidence is not simply an experience of what is not necessary. The latter could simply leave us indifferent: we would not *experience* it but merely notice it. "Experiencing a coincidence" means to be confronted with an event that *could* have reasons but apparently happened without any necessary reason. We are surprised because we miss the logic, probability, or utility of the event and might thus suspect other reasons behind it. The coincidence can shatter beliefs in facts, persons, symbols, and theories that were thought to be infallible. Wars, disasters, hyperinflation, financial crashes, but also private events such as unexpected deaths, can create feelings of incredulity toward a reality that suddenly appears uncanny.

The impression that "it *should* not have happened" is much reinforced in situations where "nothing" has happened for a very long time. Nassim Taleb experienced his first "Black Swan" (the most unlikely thing to happen) in the form of the Lebanese war: "After close to thirteen centuries of remarkable ethnic coexistence, a Black Swan, coming out of nowhere, transformed the place from heaven to hell. A fierce civil war began between Christians and Moslems" (Taleb 2007: 7). The second Black Swan arrived for him in 1987 as a stock exchange trader when the largest market drop in history took place, but which "all these intelligent-talking Platonified economists with their phony bell curve-based equations [had been unable] to prevent, or at least forecast," not even the day before (Taleb 2007: 18).

Consequently, Paul Virilio sees the accident as a product of a real contingency. The accident was the most unlikely thing to happen, but *when* it happens, it looks more real than anything that could have been measured and calculated *in* reality. Because of this reality effect, the accident will always remain extraordinary, no matter how much we try to explain it retrospectively, using all sorts of measurements and calculations. We find that "the colossal dimension of the accident surpasses us" (Virilio 2005: 34). In other words, while we try to rationalize the accident's "what," we realize that we cannot rationalize the "that." The excessive speed of the driver explains the accident, but only in the sense that it explains "what" happened, but not "that" it happened. It did not have to happen; many speeding cars do not have accidents. The accident surpasses us even more when the "what" of the cause is minimal (for example, a minimal surplus speed) and the result is disproportionate (leading to the passengers' deaths). While the "what" can be linked to certain causes, the "that" is bound to remain strange and mysterious; if not, it would no longer be an accident.

The young Heidegger tried to grasp such and similar experiences by looking at "it-sentences" (es-Sätze) such as "it rains" or "it storms." In his doctoral dissertation from 1914, he picked German sentences like "es blitzt," "es regnet," "es kracht," which were for him "Being-events" (Seinsereignisse), that is, events that "just happen" (1972: 126). In some languages, such it-sentences tend to be used for meteorological phenomena, which, given the potential danger associated with some weather events, come close to accidents. Instead of saying "there is rain" or "there is thunder," languages have found formulas that highlight not the "what" but the "that" (daß) of the event. In the "it" of "it rains" or "it thunders," the event takes place without any specification of the "what," which can therefore be understood as a pure presence or, in Heidegger's later formulation, as Being or "Being itself" (das Sein selbst). Being is here detached from space and time. While the "what" must always take place in a concrete space-and-time world, the "that" just happens. The "that" is not inserted in a narrative but apparently stands on its own. Should a "what" be introduced into such a sentence, it would blur the instantaneous manifestation of the "being that." "It rains water" does not have the same effect as "it rains." "Being that" is pure facticity and contingency without causes traceable to space and time. It "just" rains. The contingency happens for Heidegger in a momentariness (Augenblicklichkeit) that is not determined by any time-spatial measurements.

An accident is always such a "being that." In the existential experience of the accident, which is an experience of the contingency of being, or of facticity, we concentrate on its strangeness and unpredictability as though the event were linked to a mystical power that existed beyond reason, common sense, and even beyond all math and logic. Math and logic might be able to calculate the "what" of the coincidence in the form of probabilities and even see this as an interesting challenge. But when we are struck by the "that" in the form of a fortunate or an unfortunate accident, the unpredictability transcends common sense, math, and logic. "The coincidence is the undesirable host of common sense," writes the French promoter of the Vienna Circle philosophy, Marcel Boll (1966: 3). Just like math and logic, common sense is led by the inextinguishable belief that everything which happens has a reason. It is the same common sense that also concludes that living organisms are simply too complicated to be due to coincidences and that they therefore depend on intelligent design. Common sense cannot imagine that coincidences construct their own macro sense without the interference of an outside intelligence (for example, the reason of a creator). Though in popular language, the coincidence is used in the sense of an event that cannot be explained, common sense—just like math and logic—desperately looks for necessities.

Often the reason for this behavior is that contingency is more difficult to establish than necessity. For example, if a natural disaster happens, it is relatively easy to attribute it to the negligence of politicians or to the industry that destroyed the environment; it is more difficult to argue (politically and in front of a public) that coincidences played a predominant role and that the event is *not* due to any necessity. Even when a coincidence is accepted as such, thinking about it tends to be "paralogistic." Very often, one presupposes the existence of logical patterns, which is, once again, due to nothing other than common sense. The coincidence evades reason, and common sense quickly produces paralogical biases, for example, when suggesting that the coincidence is always "fair," meaning that chances must be equally spread, and also that a coincidence must not happen too often. When random numbers are drawn, they are expected to be heterogeneous and not to display too much regularity. These assumptions are false because they work with ideas of hidden necessities. Chance is here explained through necessity while, in reality, there is, within any restricted space, no equitable dispersion of coincidences. Other mistakes are also common. The size of the sample is often not evaluated within the totality, or the particular event and the general context will be confused. Too quickly, one assumes that what is true for the general must also be true for the particular.

In everyday life, we tend to draw comfort and reassurance from this fallacious way of thinking. We are often satisfied when our false ideas are confirmed by experience simply because nobody has bothered to search for counter-samples. In statistics, this attitude is called confirmation bias, and it plays an important role in unwarranted conspiracy theories (together with the proportionality bias and the cognitive bias). Too easily, common sense accepts what confirms our beliefs. That this is oftentimes a matter of belief becomes clearest in religions. Religions often search for confirmations of some truth (the existence of God, the supernatural state of a guru, etc.) by interpreting signs that they find only because they were looking for them. Counter-samples are not considered. The cognitive bias that makes people see regular and necessary patterns in randomly generated data is also linked to the human "sense of order" that has been confirmed by evolution and that will be examined in the next chapter, and which is also related to the proportionality bias. However, the sense of order can also be perverted by confirmation biases. Nassim Taleb has forcefully attacked the paralogical attitude that looks for necessities, even when chance is the only explanation. According to him, this is typical of people who owe their success to chance but do not want to admit it. The conspiratorial mindset has the same attitude and displays it in a very systematic fashion and often without any scruples. However, the conspiratorial mindset inverts Taleb's scheme and tries to appear as one whose *failures* are not due to chance but due to hidden necessities.

The Coronavirus

It is certainly important that the coincidence is similar to a disease or a virus. It represents a risk for individuals and societies not only because of its potential danger but also because it is obscure, always in motion, constantly destroying and re-creating itself, and never satisfied. Any contact with the coincidence should be avoided. In this context, the COVID-19 pandemic had a particularly strong existential impact. According to Turkish writer Orhan Pamuk, it "provided an opportunity to think more deeply about who we are, what really matters and what we want, both as individuals and as a society." He speaks of "the sense of the uncanny experienced by the stricken populace [that] will also determine the depth of their anger and political discontent" (Pamuk 2020). It appears that in the contemporary world, uncanny experiences can be made more frequently than in bygone eras. On the one hand, civilization has developed devices such as disaster prevention methods, vaccinations, and insurances, which can decrease the damages caused by unfortunate events. On the other hand, the disproportionality between the coincidence and the consequences it entails has dramatically increased because of the inflation of economic interdependence between entities. Linkages between events now extend into a global sphere, and this also concerns the consequences of accidents. According to economists Schwab and Malleret, earthquakes and storms cause more damage today than in the past because of likely chain reactions of economic consequences. Especially, chain reactions happen faster, which is why coincidences can also cause more dramatic existential experiences.

Did COVID-19 teach us a lesson about contingency? Obviously, the coronavirus epidemic came out of the blue and is a typical contingency experience. When untamed contingency threatens our comfortable civilization, our Cartesian fantasies of control feel dangerously weakened. In the case of the coronavirus crisis, technology, management, logistics, and much statistics, quickly forced contingency back into apparently necessary structures of regularity, productivity, and progress. However, some kind of "Black Swan" shock remained in people's minds.

If we consider the coronavirus to have formed itself in nature, we might call this an accident, though only in a metaphorical fashion; the more appropriate term would be coincidence. The DNA of a cell assembled viral proteins and nucleic acid in a way it could produce new virus particles, which then escaped from the cell. If the coronavirus had been unintentionally released from the Wuhan laboratory in China into the outside world, then this is an accident. However, the evaluation of human responsibility can be complex and lead to controversies. A stock market crash can be construed as a coincidence because an overly complex web of factors led to unexpected results. But just like in the case of a car accident due to speeding or multiple malfunctions of the car, we esteem that human intervention could have avoided this coincidence, whose probability had been rising in parallel with irresponsible behavior. Lack of control links the coincidence not to human intention, but still to human responsibility. It would have been possible to better appreciate the probabilities; still, the failure to do so will usually not be attributed to intention.

As mentioned above, *too much* negligence can lead us to say that this was not an accident: this "accident" was predictable, and not seeing it coming was almost like producing it. In stock market crashes, it has been noted that often, right before the crash, investors seemed to not recognize the disastrous character of the situation because they did not *want* to recognize it. They were blinded by their enthusiasm, by theories that amounted to ideologies, or by group dynamics. "Intention" here becomes a complex matter because it is multilayered, not purely rational, and emotionally determined. Traders did not intend to produce the stock exchange crash, but they ignored the signs that announced it and thus did not prevent it. Also, they indirectly helped create the bubble in the first place.

The origin of the coronavirus has not yet been entirely elucidated, but there are basically two options: either it was produced by nature, that is, through a "zoonotic overflow" (as leading scientific journals like *Nature, The Lancet,* and *Science* had maintained for months after the first appearances), or by scientists when experimenting with viruses, most probably in the Wuhan

Institute of Virology. Even if the virus was human-made, it does not necessarily follow that its creation or its release into the environment was planned and deliberate. Its creation and release can still be—and most probably were—due to contingency.

The appearance of the COVID-19 virus has had unusual global repercussions. In the past, many pandemics have played important roles in shaping human history, but this latest one has had more dramatic economic consequences than all recorded ones because, as mentioned above, interdependence between economic entities, as well as the size of these entities, has increased. Though the coronavirus killed fewer people than recent other pandemics, its economic consequences have been multiple times more dramatic. Schwab and Malleret compare the virus not with sanitary phenomena but with specific economic events. The coronavirus

> has been more severe and has occurred much faster than anything else in recorded economic history. Even in the Great Depression in the early 1930s and the Global Financial Crisis in 2008, it took several years for GDP to contract by 10% or more and for unemployment to soar above 10%. With the pandemic, disaster-like macroeconomic outcomes—in particular exploding unemployment levels and plunging GDP growth—happened in March 2020 over the course of just three weeks. (Schwab and Malleret 2020: 25)

For most people in the world, the disease was not threatening to them because of its lethal power or because of the possibility of getting infected, but because of the economic and social consequences it engendered, which quasi-inverts the pattern of previous pandemics. Though 32 million people have died of HIV since the early 1980s, in general, people are not aware of a significant social or economic impact, except, perhaps, in Africa. Also, in the popular mind, the AIDS pandemic could conveniently be linked to a limited population group. Additionally, comparisons of the COVID-19 epidemic with earlier epidemics in economic terms are awkward because most of the time, we simply do not have much information about the *economic* consequences. While public memory of past pandemics tends to remember the victims of infections, notions of their economic or social impact tend to take a backseat. The reason is either that these repercussions were managed relatively well or that the contemporary mind has relegated them to an apparently irrelevant past whose conditions are incomparable to those of our present world. Cholera, the Black Death, and the Spanish flu clearly belong to ages past. The Spanish flu (1918–1920), the most severe pandemic in recent history, infected an estimated 500 million people (one-third of the world population) and killed 675,000 people in the United States alone and around 50 million worldwide. However, this pandemic seems to have unfolded not only in a distant past but also under special circumstances: a World War had imposed poor living conditions and bad nutrition on millions of people. As a result, the context appears incomparable to what we find today, at least in the Global North. Because the world was at war, the degradation of the economy due to this pandemic cannot be realistically measured. After World War II, several influenza pandemics arose in settings comparable to those of the year 2019, but they had relatively little impact on the economies of the developed world. The influenza pandemic of 1957–1958 emerged in East Asia and later reached coastal cities in the United States. The estimated death toll was 1.1 million worldwide and 116,000 in the United States. The 1968 flu pandemic was first noted in the United States and led to an estimated number of deaths of 1 million worldwide and about 100,000 in the United States.

The new pandemic subjected many of those living in well-organized environments—often in "first world" countries where the future tends to be relatively predictable—to an encounter with an entirely unexpected destiny. First, the events could not be intuitively linked to existing historical patterns simply because, in the public consciousness, large-scale pandemics had been relegated to a distant past. Second, if we consider the virus to most probably be due to a coincidence, we recognize the highly unusual character of this existential experience. All over the world, individuals with safe jobs lost their livelihoods because somewhere in China, a virus happened to make its way into the human population (whether this was due to an accident in a lab or from nature). How can a coincidence like this have such widespread repercussions? The conspiratorial mindset suspects an evil plan behind it. As a typical Black Swan phenomenon, COVID-19 is unlikely and unpredictable but has a massive impact. As with any Black Swan, once it has happened, we concoct explanations that make it appear less random and more predictable than it was. The coronavirus is uncanny because it *should* not be, but it is. Non-modern epidemics are dangerous because they "simply" kill. However, this modern epidemic is "one of the least deadly pandemics the world has experience over the last 2000 years" (Schwab and Malleret 2020: 2). At the same time, it is more uncanny than other epidemics because it manipulates the economy with an invisible hand, which makes it an ideal target for the conspiratorial mindset.

Conspiracies in Risk Societies

The German sociologist Ulrich Beck (1944–2015), who worked in the area of risk studies, would have been interested in the social management of the coronavirus of 2020. Beck's main hypothesis is that as capitalism evolves, risk-taking evolves in parallel: "In advanced modernity the social production of *wealth* is systematically accompanied by the social production of *risks*" (Beck 1992: 19/German 1986: 25). Consequently, advanced societies spend much time and energy on debating, preventing, and managing the risks they have themselves produced. But Beck goes further. The risks that are viable in industrial societies would not be viable in just any capitalist system: risk societies produce sensibilities, moralities, reasonings, and responsibilities that transcend the typical risks of capitalism since they can no longer "be understood by means of the interlocking interests of the market, as was still possible in the bourgeois and industrial societies" (74/98).

In his own studies, Beck mainly considers the risks of pollution. As industrialized societies release more and more poison into the air and food, there is the constant risk of an accident, which these societies attempt to attenuate using various methods, especially statistics. In 1986, Beck writes, in a special "pre-preface" to the German edition of his *The Risk Society*, about the Chernobyl catastrophe, which had happened in the same year. He is struck by the fact that the risk now travels across borders like a meteorological phenomenon in the form of a "nuclear cloud" that cannot be contained by walls, fences, or the military. "Far away in the West of the Soviet Union occurs [...] an accident" (Beck 1986: 8). The accident just happens, it comes like the weather and cannot even be seen. "It simply rains" nuclear particles. There was a risk, but the risk was *only* a risk, which means that the danger was not real but only potential. Suddenly, an invisible cloud empoisons people, which adds to the uncanniness.

The coronavirus and global warming (both of which are a privileged subject of unwarranted conspiracy theories) are newer editions of Beck's uncanny scenario. The Munich sociologist pertinently observes that whatever is invisible is given to theorizing and speculation. He mentions Hume, who held that knowledge about risks is always theoretical knowledge. A risk, which is invisible, is not necessarily scientific, but we require it to be "scientized" (*verwissenschaftlicht*):

> As we have known at least since Hume [...] presumptions of causality escape our perception. They must always be imagined, implied to be true, believed. They are theory. In this sense too, risks are invisible. The implied causality always remains more or less uncertain and tentative. Thus we are dealing with a *theoretical* and hence a *scientized* consciousness, even in the everyday consciousness of risks. (28/36, translation altered as one sentence is missing in the English translation)

When addressing a *scientized* consciousness that creates theories based on what is "imagined, implied to be true, or believed," it appears that Beck indirectly refers to baseless conspiracy theories without naming them. Thirty-five years after the Chernobyl disaster, the handling of the coronavirus by national governments shows that we have moved more closely toward the risk society as Beck understands it. In November 2019, risk suddenly took a central place.

But let's first follow Beck's line of thought. Beck contrasts the risk society with the class society: "The dream of class society is that everyone wants and ought to have a share of the pie. The utopia of the risk society is that everyone should be spared from poisoning" (1992: 49/65). This means that in risk societies, desire has been replaced with fear. Furthermore, the desire to have a better life is not replaced with the fear of becoming poor—as the risk of becoming poor is smaller, calculable, and more "visible"—but rather with the fear of being poisoned:

> The driving force in the class society can be summarized in the phrase: *I am hungry!* The movement set in motion by the risk society, on the other hand, is expressed in the statement: *I am afraid!* The *commonality of anxiety* [Gemeinsamkeit der Angst] takes the place of the *commonality of need* [Gemeinsamkeit der Not]. The type of the risk society marks in this sense a social epoch in which *solidarity from anxiety* arises and becomes a political force. (49/66)

Beck never explicitly addresses conspiracy theories. However, are both the warranted and unwarranted types of these theories not examples of what he names "solidarity from anxiety"? Certainly the unwarranted type more than the warranted one because anxiety reduces the rational thinking capacity. In a section only three paragraphs long called "The Scapegoat Society," Beck confirms that the risk society contains "precisely, as the dangers increase along with political inaction, […] an inherent tendency to become a *scapegoat society*" (75/101). Despite this apparent missed opportunity to elaborate more on such a closely related topic, Beck's system can partly explain the recent increase in indefensible conspiracy theories. It will be shown below that the conspiratorial mindset develops out of anxiety and ressentiment, and a desire to look for scapegoats. Furthermore, it is less often a reaction to "real" threats, such as reactions to hunger or poverty. The cause of hunger or poverty can be given the name of a person, a political system, or an institution that can be *accused*. Concrete measures can be taken and theories will not proliferate. Hunger makes us angry, but it does not create anxiety. Hunger is not uncanny but a reality experience. Historically, hunger has often led to targeted actions in the form of protests, riots, and revolutions, whereas anxiety about poisonous air does not tend to lead to action—at least initially—but rather to speculations (theories) about its origin or even its existence.

There is another difference. Anxiety does not unite social groups in the way hunger or poverty can unite. Anxiety and speculations about conspirators do not bind people together; they do not make them move forward by creating social movements. In general, people with a conspiratorial mindset feel less solidarity with each other than members of organized political movements that have clearly defined goals. Conspiracist networks are more diffuse; they are not held together by a clear political idea but rather by vague speculations. Any emergence of group coherence is also weakened by the international character of the networks through which the conspiratorial mindset is spread today. At best, anxiety produces an *uncanny* brand of solidarity, which Michael Sandel calls, without reference to Beck, the "solidarity of fear," representing a very loose form of solidarity.

For Beck, anxiety is part of a modernization program. In modernity, we are constantly anxious, not about what we know, but rather about what we do *not* know, or what we do not know well enough. And in modern societies, there are more and more things about which we are ignorant. It has been explained in Chapter 2 that an increase in civilization increases not only a society's total amount of knowledge but also its total amount of ignorance. Today, more than ever, knowledge needs to be outsourced. Even scientists become increasingly "ignorant." Evolutionary biologist Stephen Jay Gould mentions that modern models of causal flow in physics have become so complex "that we have had to reach out to colleagues explicitly trained in rigorous thinking about such issues," whereas older models "have served us well for centuries" (Gould 2002: 28). Such a resignation to outsourcing did not occur in past societies because one could then still hope that newly acquired knowledge would be taught in schools and penetrate society in some way. One could expect that the individual would be able to keep up at least with the knowledge they need in their everyday life or in their profession because professions were not as "scientized" as they are today. Believing that society will somehow catch up with the knowledge it produces is a mindset symptomatic/typical of industrial societies.[3] In knowledge societies (or post-industrial societies), the individual (and this concerns *all* individuals) is increasingly dependent "on external knowledge" (*fremdwissensabhängig* for Beck, 53/70).

---

3 Beck is obviously aware of the coming of the post-industrial society but concentrates here mainly on the difference between industrial and pre-industrial. "Post-industrial" means for him especially the reduction of pollution.

According to Beck, all this is part of an inevitable modernization process. Whether this process should really be scheduled as modern can be questioned. One can also interpret it as a weakening of the Enlightenment ideal "to see with your own eyes" or to think for yourself. The outsourcing of knowledge also adds to the anxiety (which Beck sees as an integral part of modernization, too), which the Enlightenment program never intended for. In any case, the conspiratorial mindset desires to reestablish its knowledge sovereignty, which it believes has been lost to a world of experts who constantly discuss matters which it does not understand but which increasingly invade its life space. In the end, the conspiratorial mindset launches a conspiratorial altmod knowledge project.

Did the COVID-19 crisis transform societies? Despite the above-described parallels between today's post-class society and Beck's risk society, there remain important differences, and the COVID-19 crisis has made this very clear. According to Beck, in modern nations, authorities tend to downplay the risks of air pollution because they are interested in progress. Governments usually deny risks, and "those who point out risks are defamed as 'alarmists' or even risk producers. Their presentation of the hazards is considered 'unproven'" (45/60). All this was true for earlier risk societies but could not be observed during the recent crisis in which, in general, governments did *not* downplay the danger. On the contrary, understating the problem now became the role of the conspiratorial mindset, which depicted the government as alarmist. In parallel with what happened in the realm of global warming, the conspiratorial mindset became "reassurist" (even though it could still remain alarmist in other areas).

A pandemic like this one essentially differs from Beck's air pollution or nuclear accidents. Beck's cases of poisoning are due to industrial overproduction, that is, to human greed that denies all risks, whereas viruses can appear by coincidence. In this sense, they are a post-industrial phenomenon. While the lab accident theory resembles the Chernobyl accident, the zoologic overflow theory stands out as something different. One cannot compare a virus with industrial air pollution. More than the Chernobyl disaster, the coronavirus depended on contingency (or could be understood as such), which is why it sparked the most frantic of searches for necessities in conspiracist circles. At the same time, there was *some* human interference (the lab accident theory), which made the case ambiguous and raised even more skepticism.

Interestingly, the coronavirus resuscitated not only the risk society's dream of "the avoidance of poisoning" that is dominant in Beck's model; it also resuscitated the old dream of a just class society in which everybody is supposed to have a share of the pie. This time, the pie was the vaccinations. Vaccinations were not a privilege, and everybody was supposed to get vaccinated. More precisely, the risk society's utopia of a "non-poisoning society" depended here on the equal distribution of capital. At the opposite end, the conspiratorial mindset fought against the distribution of vaccines and suggested that they would only lead to more poisoning. The situation is no longer comparable to Beck's classic examples of poisoning through air pollution. Here the virus was in the air and could only be fought by using another "poison." Consequently, roles were inverted: the authorities insisted on contingency, that is, on the contingency of the virus that could be efficiently fought by sticking to the necessary insights of science. Vice versa, the conspiracy sphere insisted on the willful (necessary) production of the virus that one could best escape by not being vaccinated and by leaving one's destiny to chance.

Chapter 4

ANIMISM AND THE SENSE OF ORDER

Contingency Skepticism

Usually, contingencies are perceived with surprise, especially when they have tragic consequences, such as those following major natural catastrophes or accidents. And tragic coincidences can happen in history, such as when the accidental death or sickness of a ruler significantly alters the affairs of state. As mentioned above, whenever the repercussions of coincidence appear disproportionate to the actual event that sparked them, a certain skepticism toward contingency is likely to emerge and to question whether the event *really* happened by chance. Like all events, coincidences are due to causes, but in the case of coincidence, it is either impossible or too difficult (the difference between the ontological and the epistemic coincidence will be explained below) to state *why* the event was caused by a *particular* cause and not another one. Coincidences are no miracles. Coincidences have no finality, but they have a cause, whereas wonders have no cause (and are often *retrospectively* equipped with finality). Strangely, coincidences can incite the same kind of skepticism that occurs when we are faced with wonders. This is paradoxical because normally, an explanation involving coincidence is meant to suspend hypotheses about the wondrous and the mysterious. But coincidence can become wondrous and mysterious in its own right. Should an insignificant event like a cat crossing the street lead to a car accident killing an important politician, the accidental character of the event is likely to be challenged. Why would a cat cross the street right at this time and in this place? Behind Princess Diana's mortal accident, the conspiratorial mindset sees an organized assassination because of Diana's symbolic importance. In their view, this importance cannot have been compromised by a simple accident. Coincidence-skepticism is bound to arise more often when the consequences are negative and produce considerable damage; less skepticism will emerge when the coincidence brings fortune, though this *can* happen, too. For example, when a corrupt politician says they did not embezzle any money and simply inherited it, the general framework of the event incites us to trace the event to causes other than mere coincidence.

A cat crossing the street is an *ontological* coincidence because it was impossible to predict what decision the cat would make. One type of coincidence skepticism will try to interpret the ontological coincidence as an *epistemic* coincidence. In epistemic coincidences, the causes are not undetermined, as they are in the ontological coincidence, but only unknown, or too small or too complex to reckon with. In an epistemic coincidence, to which games like roulette are submitted, the causes could, at least in theory, be evaluated and their consequences calculated; but such calculations are too difficult. In an ontological coincidence, it is simply impossible to predict the results. For many games of hazard, probabilities *could* be statistically calculated if the players were given the time to do so.[1] Then the coincidence would become *relatively* predictable. The event could still not be linked to intentionality, but it could be understood *as if* there were an intentionality behind it.

When we cannot advance any explanations for an event, we will attribute it to ontological indeterminism. This conclusion will sometimes be only preliminary because the reasons, motivations, and causes *could* perhaps be found in the future. The conspiratorial mindset suspects that the cat's behavior is not due to mere indeterminism or arbitrariness but to—so far—unknown causes. It develops a theory apparently revealing the causes and thus transforms the ontological coincidence into an epistemic one. Conspiracism tries either to match the event with an intention—which eliminates all contingency—or to point to hidden causes. The twist of the epistemic coincidence is that it does *not* affirm that the causes are scientifically impossible to determine because they are due to contingency. There is a cause, even a well-determined one, but it is unknowable, either because it is hidden or because it is too complex.

The ignorance about the cause stimulates the conspiratorial mindset. Unwarranted conspiracy theories are not always mere false cause fallacies or appeals to ignorance ("there is no evidence, thus it must be a conspiracy"). In many cases, the conspiratorial mindset turns the ontological coincidence into an epistemic one, and subsequently construes the epistemic coincidence as a decidedly obscure "determinism." The necessities or motivations remain vague and mystical and are not spelled out clearly. There is, for example, a conspiracy theory about the philanthropist George Soros who is believed to help immigrants "invade" the United States or Europe. Soros's supposed

---

1 Taleb points to the difference between the French words *"hasard"* or *"aléatoire"* (aleatoric) and *"fortuit"* [fortuitous]. The former two imply tractable randomness, whereas *fortuit* is "the purely accidental and unforeseen," exactly like a Black Swan: "*Fortuit* seems to correspond to my epistemic opacity, *l'imprévu et non quantifiable; hasard* to the more ludic type of uncertainty" (Taleb 2007: 272–73). The distinction overlaps with the above distinction between the epistemic and the ontological coincidence.

motivations for this program remain extremely unclear, and no suggestion about why he could have such intentions would stand an objective analysis. The same can be said about Bill Gates' alleged plan to release trackable microchips in vaccines in order to control humans, or that Gates had planned the pandemic altogether. Flat-earthers believe that secret powers keep us believing in "the globe." Others think that secret powers have made us believe in vaccines, evolution, the moon landing, the harmfulness of GMO food, dinosaurs, or that these powers want to submit the world to a transsexual push. What interest these powers could have in doing so is never, or only very sporadically, elucidated. The "that" and the "who" are more important than the "why." Much of this reasoning is due to what Swami et al. (2014) as well as Mikušková and Čavojová (2020) associate with lower analytic thinking capacities, which can lead to faulty intuitive thinking.[2] The researchers detected lower analytic thinking capacities in both conspiracy theorists and believers in paranormal phenomena. The classical juridical question of "who benefits" ("cui bono") *could* lead to real conspirators, but this question is most often not asked. In the vocabulary of criminology, the perpetrator's act is explained in terms of opportunity and ability, and the third important parameter is the motive. In productions of the conspiratorial mindset, the motive is often missing. George Soros manipulates governments the world all over without anyone being able to say why he is doing it. The conspiratorial mindset believes it has penetrated a deep existential sphere, but it can believe this only so long as it disregards the "what" and only concentrates on the "that." Just like in fantastic literature (see below), chance is not really dealt with, but the contingent event is turned into an unsolvable puzzle. Sometimes plausible motives do become established though: as long as the National Lottery has existed, there have been rumors that the organizers manipulate it. When the gains are so high, there *must be* a strong enough motivation to cheat. Here, *possible* motivations lead to the invention of new facts. But these motives are only established because they *could* be plausible, and the conspiratorial mindset merely builds upon this plausibility: the motive is here the foundation of suspicion, rather than an *explanation* for one.

Some unwarranted conspiracy theories are based on necessity skepticism. For example, when it comes to climate change, to links between smoking and lung cancer, or to links between HIV and AIDS, the necessary connections, though recognized by science, are often denied. The conspiratorial mindset

---

2 Swami and Mikušková's definition of "conspiracy theorist" is a pejorative generalist definition, which I do not fully share. However, as I state, it remains appropriate for many cases of conspiracism.

attributes these phenomena to contingencies, saying that those who believe in these necessities are possibly victims of a conspiracy. Popular books that are critical of climate science routinely refer to global warming as a "conspiracy" or "hoax." In this case, in contrast to how it tends to deal with the coronavirus, the conspiratorial mindset *does* recognize global warming as a matter of a natural overflow, that is, as due to contingency. The dominant idea of *these* conspiracy theories is that the scientifically accepted necessities that lead to climate change (greenhouse gases) are conspiracies in their own right that have been invented by evil powers. These evil powers present contingency as necessity.

Animism

What the conspiracy theory (warranted and unwarranted) shares with other theories is that it attempts to explain both the personal and the more extended environment in a meaningful way. Most obviously, the unwarranted conspiracy theory is sometimes a matter of giving meaning to one's life, in which case it is not merely a theory, but also a philosophy of life. Like most pseudo-philosophies, it strongly fights for a cause, which brings it close to ideologies and religious commandments. Because the motivations of groundless conspiracy theories are often obscure, the conspiracy theory can sometimes be seen as a commitment leading to salvation; salvation perhaps not in this life (since these theories tend to be very dystopian) but perhaps in an afterlife.

In this book, I concentrate on the fact that the conspiratorial mindset very often searches for powerful necessities and rejects contingencies. In this sense, many unjustifiable conspiracy theories are reminiscent of animistic worldviews because animism, too, excludes chance and contingency. Animism attributes psychological qualities to physical objects and believes that everything in the world is directed by concealed invisible forces. It endows things with consciousness, feelings, and intentionality. For animism, the wind, rain, clouds, and the sun are conscious beings following personal plans. They do not "just happen." Nor do they follow the contingent principles of meteorology or physics. Instead, they are directed by hidden powers. Similarly, the conspiratorial mindset does not believe that institutions, systems, or political situations have emerged over history—partly randomly and partly following pragmatic reasons—but sees them as the results of hidden intentions that make these institutions pursue their own evil plans. In conspiracy animism, Heidegger's "it rains,"—which the Black Forest philosopher intended to be understood as a pure presence or a "that" event without a "what"—is objectified in the form of a concrete being. It becomes an entity that we can encounter in space and time, even in the form of a person. The "what" is fleshed out with detailed intentions, feelings, and a soul. As a result, facticity is transformed into a purposeful being, which is the complete opposite of what Heidegger intended. *Why* these institutions, systems, or political situations would be subjected to such hidden forces is just as rarely accounted for in conspiracy animism as it is in regular animism. As with the wind, the rain, and the clouds, the "final why" is beside the point. All we know about these phenomena is that their actions are not due to coincidences but carefully planned by sinister, superior forces. It is rarely entirely clear why they are planning it.

In gambling, this animistic element becomes most obvious: gamblers can believe that the past, in which the gambler has lost, will influence the present and will now let them win. "I have lost so often, therefore it is sure that I will win next time." This thinking succumbs to the illusion that the past is animated like an interactive person when, in reality, it is dead. It is instructive to stay with the gambling metaphor as it is also frequently used in the philosophy of science. Jacques Monod, in his *Chance and Necessity*, detects an "animism" in the persistent belief that genetic evolution cannot involve coincidences. According to Monod, rejecting coincidence in evolution (or rejecting evolution as a whole, one might add) represents an "animist conception of man that has dominated virtually all Western world views from those of primitive cultures to those of the dialectical materialists" (from the blurb of his *Chance and Necessity*). Against this, modern biology shows that humans are the product of chance genetic mutation and that "nature's roulette" (Monod's expression from page 138/French: 122) always offers a myriad of opportunities. Especially since Darwin, biology began to explain the adaptation and evolution of species without creating external finalities. For Monod, the initial elementary events which open the way to evolution in the "intensely conservative systems called living beings, are microscopic, fortuitous, and utterly without relation to whatever may be their effects upon teleonomic functioning" (118/134). In these systems, specialized cells "possess the unique property of 'playing roulette' with a well-defined part of the genetic segments that determine the structure of antibodies" (125/144).

The conspiratorial mindset also often evokes such an animistic power. Of course, it only *evokes* this power and rarely spells it out. The procedure is comparable to what various religions do when they see random events as "signs" supposed to indicate that their guru is always right or that God wanted to speak to them. The adept is surprised because he had never noticed such signs before and ends up being thankful for these new "explanations." This reasoning rests on the presupposition that the life world is not a "dead" accumulation of random signs but is in reality animated.

Fuzzy Necessities

All animisms are driven by a resolute "anti-contingency thinking." Books from the shelves of New Age, pseudoscience, and self-help sections, bearing titles similar to "Nothing Happens by Chance," are listed on Amazon by the hundreds. Behind every "coincidence" we find hidden forces, which denotes an animism principle. However, while the coincidence is "revealed" as a necessity, at the same time, explanations remain vague and practically never point to real necessities. Similarly, the conspiratorial mindset, instead of providing evidence and clear motivations, strings together a chain of random facts to make events look "somehow" determined. We have a curious pattern of revealing-obscuring. The conspiratorial mind replaces the coincidence with a blurred and fuzzy finality, which becomes very obvious in conspiracy documentaries in which, most typically, an excessive number of accumulated events and witness statements, flashbacks, and reconstructions blur the picture instead of clarifying it. Contradictions are shown but not explored. Agreements between individuals and groups are evoked, but they are presented as immaterial and thus ungraspable. One refers to meetings of secret societies by giving their dates but leaves the identity of attending individuals obscure. Like the unwarranted conspiracy theory itself, the conspiracy documentary appears as "a massive, loose-ended whole replete with clashing personalities and contradictory ideologies" (Pipes 1997: 44). The conspiracy itself remains immaterial, which is why it *cannot* be traced to concrete necessities but only to a vague "there must be something." This ends up making it even more threatening.

The official purpose of conspiracy theories is to make sense of complex realities, but instead of simplifying reality, the unwarranted ones often complexify it even further. The search for complex epistemic determinations that is supposed to discard the ontological coincidence opens the door to the most baroque of explanatory fantasies. At the same time, there *is* simplification. In the case of a pact between several evil partners, inherent complexity is often reduced to a single cabal's master plan. Nuances are effaced, and evil is typically attributed to a single conspirator. As mentioned in the last chapter, the ambition to simplify contradicts the strategy of blurring sources and motivations through complexification and a profusion of details. The cognitive profile of the conspiratorial mindset is thus paradoxical: while it sees regularity in complexity, it also rejects official explanations because they are "too simple." In other words, "evil" as it occurs in the conspiratorial mindset is always organic. The protagonists of evil are spread over the whole planet and can appear practically everywhere; but at the same time, their organization is held together by a strong uniting force. The conspiratorial mindset functions like negative theology: like most populist "anti-system" politicians, it disbelieves in existing theories without being willing to provide a proper alternative theory. Most important to the conspiratorial mindset is that the official view be contradicted. That an alternative theory is either lacking or implausible matters very little. Gratuitous conspiracy theories are intentionally superficial and incoherent because they never intend to trace events back to sources by using critical thinking and deduction. Instead, they tend to transform the world into a big, confused surface beneath which are hidden evil subjects. Again, this is mostly due to the shift from the ontological coincidence to the epistemic one. The conspiratorial mind finds comfort in the conviction that nothing is undetermined and that there is always a hidden necessity; but as long as this necessity is only vaguely evoked, the event can be considered an epistemic coincidence, which means that there *is* a cause, but that we do not know it precisely. Mostly, the ambition to contradict official views is fed by the will to oppose a vaguely defined elite, that is, the political, economic, cultural, media, and scientific establishment (which does not prevent some elites from producing unwarranted conspiracy theories of their own).

The unfounded conspiracy theory is in competition with official versions of events that have been produced by an elite, and it is also one of the main driving forces of populist politics, which is the reason for the strong link between populism and unwarranted conspiracy theories. Populism presents "the people" as morally good and "the elite" as evil, corrupt, and decadent. The term "populism" came into use in the late nineteenth century, apace with the advancement of democracy. In the twenty-first century, populism became increasingly visible in Western countries when a newly formed range of left-wing and right-wing parties or groups began challenging established political formations. Populist politics or populism is not driven by "real" political theories such as socialism, liberalism, or fascism, but by a vague ressentiment against "the elite," which almost automatically invites worldviews approaching conspiracism. Today, the elite is generally no longer aristocratic but is instead inscribed in a system of meritocracy, that is, built around "perfect world" values such as efficiency, technology, and also democracy. As a result, populists resent all these values.

The Sense of Order

The will to discern regularities and irregularities is part of the human survival instinct. By definition, coincidences are events that are unlikely to happen, and a certain skepticism toward coincidences is normal. Recognizing and trying to reduce contingency is a civilizational process, just as the invention of tools and artifacts has helped humans "overcome their biological deficiency," as writes Blumenberg (1987: 438). However, we understand the position of contingency in society only fully when we also consider that coincidences are not only greeted with skepticism and incredulity but often with fear and hatred. When the coincidence disrupts the regular order, the environment is suddenly no longer understood. The will to reattribute the event to a regularity arises almost automatically.

Coincidences often signify danger, which is illustrated by the linguistic contact between the French word *hasard* (coincidence) and the English "hazardous." There was an ancient game called "hasard" from which the French *hasarder* is apparently derived (see Boll 1966: 116). *Hasard* probably comes from Arabic *az-zahr*, meaning "dice" and by relation, chance, and it is interesting that this word could enter the English language as an equivalent of "dangerous." In older French, *hasarder* used to mean "to risk," and the word is still used accordingly today in some literary expressions such as "hasarder sa réputation." The coincidence is seen as risky and intrinsically dangerous.

There is a tendency called psychological determinism, which implies that humans have a predilection for classic causality (see Nisbett and Ross 1980). Since chance and indeterminism create discomfort, intuitive expectations about the dynamics of the social world pushes individuals to attribute events to more or less deliberately acting agents. Once again, this can be considered animistic. Humans prefer "broad predictabilities of life's pattern through time, transcending the contingent particularities of any individual lineage," writes Stephen Jay Gould (Gould 2002: 1182). Gould reports that

> if, as a teacher, I suggest to students that they might wish to construe probability and contingency as ontological properties of nature, they [...] almost invariably respond with some version of the old Laplacean claim.[3] In short, they insist that our use of probabilistic inference can only, and in principle, be an epistemological consequence of our mental limitations, and simply cannot represent an irreducible property of nature, which must, if science works at all, be truly deterministic. (2002: 1333)

Ernst Gombrich has shown in his *The Sense of Order* that all humans (and even all organisms) have a natural inclination toward *seeing* order in chaos. Earlier, Karl Popper (1972: 341) had explained that our mind establishes order because we have a sense of balance. By establishing order, we attribute meaning to our environment. For Gombrich, this "perception of meaning can never be switched off" (Gombrich 1979: 2) because the recognition of

---

3 See Chapter 8 on Laplace.

departures from the norm is "somehow encoded in the nervous system" (4). Gestalt theory also stresses the tendency of perception toward simple shapes. Though both Popper and Gombrich's reflections clash with other details of Gestalt theory, there remain important overlaps with the latter. We first see simple configurations like straight lines and circles and perceive things in terms of symmetry; and only this vision of regularity permits us to quickly detect asymmetry.[4] Popper and Gombrich believe that organisms have developed a sense of order through their evolutionary struggle for existence because "perception requires a framework against which to plot deviations from regularity" (Gombrich 1979: xii). The word "plot" is interesting in this context because "to plot" means to conspire.[5] In conspiratorial thinking, this plot is believed to become visible as the "theorist" plots the perceived deviations against an imagined framework.

Detecting coincidences and questioning them is one of the most intrinsic human activities; however, not all coincidences are dangerous. In order to survive, a certain tolerance toward irregularities is required in parallel. The conspiratorial mindset has an exaggerated sense of order because it reacts negatively to *any* coincidental irregularities in its environment. One can say that this contingency management leads to a necessity pathology. Freud states in his *Psychopathology of Everyday Life* that normal people accept coincidental events and that their categorical refusal should be considered paranoid (Freud 1904: 81). Theoretically, an exaggerated sense of order can work *against* survival because coincidences can also have positive effects, as they permit us to escape from dangerous situations. Grasping a coincidence at the right moment can be a matter of survival, too. This means that both the incapacity or unwillingness to see necessities *and* the categorical rejection of coincidences are pathological.

The idea of a pathological "contingency aversion" has been formulated by the French epistemologist Georges Canguilhem, who has extensively disserted on the difference between the normal and the pathological. Relying on the research of the neurologist Kurt Goldstein, who established in his book on organisms and normativity (1934) that "normal" individuals accept the fact that "life means to face risks and to accept the eventuality of catastrophic consequences," Canguilhem asks whether "the embarrassment of an individual when facing life [with its contingencies] does not [...] denote a pathological state" (Canguilhem 1947: 327).

---

4 I have explained this in Botz-Bornstein 2021.
5 In much political discourse, "plot" is used in preference to "conspiracy" because "plot" has less negative connotations.

We could go further and say that, in existential-ontological terms, coincidence has a predominantly positive function, which is counterintuitive but makes sense. We want things to "coincide" in our lives. Ambition and fulfillment, prediction and result, thinking and action, emotion and intellect should not be forces that are fleeing in different directions but rather forces that work together harmoniously. When "everything coincides," we can more easily believe that we are now enjoying the fullness of life, as François Jullien has aptly expressed in his book on coincidence: "One could rather believe that to live, as such, is to coincide, that it is even the definition of life. Because being alive means to be in uninterrupted coincidence (*être en coïncidence ininterrompu*) both with the world and with oneself" (Jullien 2017: 33). It is, of course, important that such moments remain rare and that they appear spontaneously and are not sought. Otherwise, the process would resemble a willful transformation of contingency into necessity, which is precisely the strategy of the conspiratorial mindset. The "coinciding" must contain a hint of chance. Transforming coincidences into necessities does not provide satisfaction and fulfillment, which becomes clear when we think about aesthetics. In art, such willful transformations lead to the production of kitsch because, in kitsch, the expression *coincides* exactly with the required feeling: the painted reality *coincides* exactly with the reality painted. Kitsch will be examined along these lines in the next chapter as well as in Chapter 10.

Distinguishing regularities helps us make sense of the world, but the chain of regularities must be sufficiently long to be recognized as such. According to historian Reinhart Koselleck, in human history, the coincidence "severs the continuity between the experienced and the horizon of the expected, that is, between what is and what will be" (Koselleck 1983: 145), which means that the detection of a coincidence depends very much on our expectations. If we expect unrealistically long regularities, we will be struck by coincidences even though regularity existed in shorter intervals. Vice versa, regularity can be perceived by taking an overly distanced long-term view, which erases all irregularities.

The coincidence is thus in the eye of the beholder, but regularity and necessity are subjective too. The conspiratorial mindset establishes regularities on a subjective basis and attributes coincidental events to regular patterns, and this most often happens on a dogmatic basis. Humans have a natural inclination toward seeing order in chaos, but a certain tolerance of chaos is required too. The conspiratorial mindset invents a necessary order where no such order exists and where, in reality, contingency is the only source of a given event. Vice versa, a vision that detects coincidences everywhere even when events follow a relatively well-ordered regularity can likewise be seen as pathological. Such a vision can be traced to an exaggerated sense of *irregularity*, which the conspiratorial mindset also applies, for example, when attributing necessary links between facts (pollution-climate change, smoking-lung cancer, HIV-AIDS) to coincidences.

Humans need to recognize irregularities, but not every irregularity signifies a coincidence leading to an emergency such as upcoming accidents or natural disasters. According to both Popper and Gombrich, a healthy order is an order that is motivated by a sense of balance. Only a well-proportioned appreciation of both coincidence and necessity can guarantee an adequate perception of reality. In contrast, the conspiracist's strategy to replace every coincidence with necessity distorts reality. True, the conspiratorial mindset has developed a very keen sense of observation and might detect irregularities that others do not notice. But the compulsion to find an explanation for everything leads to both simplifications and complications, to the negligence of heterogeneity, and, finally, to the refusal of contingency. All this brings them close to the paranoid individual who is similarly overly alert.

It is interesting to note that Bergson makes quasi-identical statements, though in a completely different context. In *L'Evolution créatrice,* Bergson declares that the intellect is a product of evolution that developed as an analytical tool which enabled us to interact effectively with our environment. Through the intellect, we recognize the significance of events that repeat themselves (Bergson 1991: 37–39). Just like Popper and Gombrich, Bergson sees the human capacity to recognize repetitive patterns as the result of evolution. However, for him, this recognition is due to the intellect, which is "merely" an analytical tool. In Bergson's view, analysis is inadequate for apprehending the nature of continuous developments: for these events, we rather need instinct, intuition, or the ability to "sympathize" with our environment. Or we need to grasp this regularity like a rhythm that we can feel. Seen from this angle, the conspiratorial mindset can appear similar to Bergsonism because it does not reach its conclusions through analysis but through intuition. Bergson's anti-intellectualism, otherwise well directed against scientification, mechanism, and the undue mathematization of the life world, opens the door to anti-rationalist conspiracy thinking. Of course, Bergson had no intention of providing support for such theories.

Since coincidence is multifaceted, ambiguous, blind, or has no meaning at all, coincidence-phobia is deeply anchored especially in the Western psyche, which can explain the peculiar position of coincidences in Western science, theology, and philosophy. A further characteristic begins to matter in modern civilization: contingency contradicts the expectancy of progress. Often, order is conceptualized as a progressive order (or can at least be), which means that contingency finds itself against progression by definition: "We tend to begin with a preference for explanation by predictability and subsumption under spatiotemporally invariant laws of nature, and to move towards contingency only when we fail," says Stephen Jay Gould (2002: 1338). The Darwinian idea of replacing progress with models of shifting local adaptations meets with the same kind of resistance that Western philosophy and theology had already built up much earlier and for several centuries (Darwin's input into contingency thinking will be presented in Chapter 7). In the case of the conspiratorial mindset, this psychologically rooted determinism has taken on abnormal dimensions.

The Conspiracy and the Uncanny

The disruption of regularity can lead to insecurity and defensive behavior. However, too much regularity can have the same effect. When events that should be coincidental happen on an overly regular basis, we get suspicious. Both skepticisms, regularity skepticism and irregularity skepticism, are due to human survival instincts whose dynamic is twofold. First, humans must recognize regular patterns in their environments because such patterns can signify danger. Second, any irregularities can also signify danger, but they can only be distinguished against a background of regularities. "Coincidences" that disrupt the regular flow need to be discerned because they are dangerous for the very reason that they might *not* be coincidences. Recognizing the regular patterns in which these coincidences are inscribed, and thus recognizing that these events are *not* coincidences, has always been an important task.

The uncanniness of the coincidence is also due to the fact that contingency is ontologically obscure by definition. We grant existence to possibilities, which means that we blur the border between what is and what is not by installing a "could be." With the coincidence, this border becomes precarious, porous, and darkened, which leads to what can be called an "ontological insecurity."

First of all, the coincidence is not frightening because it would represent a real danger, but because it is unexplained and, furthermore, because it displays reality in a confusing fashion as what "is" and—simultaneously—as what "should not be." Freud has called the human experience produced by this constellation the "encounter with the uncanny" and established its structure in an essay (1945). It has already been mentioned above that the accident, in the moment it "really" happens, gives us an uncanny feeling of a concreteness that suddenly and unexpectedly flares up within our existence. Accidents are uncanny existential experiences because of their exuberance; and so too can be the experience of a coincidence. According to Freud, if during a trip, our boat cabin, train seat, and hotel room are all the number "62," we may be tempted to believe that it cannot be a coincidence. The person involved in this experience would find this uncanny and might be inclined to attribute a hidden meaning—a conspiracy, perhaps—to these coincidences. Is it an allusion to his future age of death? (Freud 1945: 238). The uncanny frightens, but it is not *simply* frightening. The uncanny is a subcategory of the frightening, that is, a sort of diffused fear that does not know toward what it should direct itself. And it is precisely this "not knowing" which is most frightening. When objects in our home suddenly seem to start moving, this creates such a diffuse atmosphere of the uncanny. For a moment, the doll looks as though it were alive, though we know perfectly well that it is only a doll. There is no directed action behind this phenomenon, and even if there was, instinctively we would hesitate to explore it.

We notice a strong parallel with the conspiratorial mindset. Like the conspiracy, the source of uncanny phenomena *is bound* to remain obscure. Though we are curious, we avoid any direct contact. We "discover" a conspiracy and understand that our lives are governed by hidden powers: even our most common actions are not free but controlled. This is uncanny, especially because this "understanding" remains vague and is overlaid with another understanding that tells us that all this is very unlikely. We are in disbelief, just as when the doll looked, for a moment, as though it were alive. As a result, we do not dare to explore the situation further. We might add some theoretical fantasies as explanations, but we do not dare to approach the uncanny subject to dissect and analyze it.

The uncanny follows a structure of disautomatization because it installs unexplainable alterations—which could be coincidences—in phenomena that are otherwise familiar and automatized. The source of the disautomatization remains unknown. Such events are uncanny because they also could *not* be coincidences. A further problem is that the strangeness arises "by itself": it is produced neither by an underlying intellect nor by a desire. The disautomatization of the uncanny is a "self-disautomatization": it is never constructed but simply appears; and this makes us uneasy. Attributing the event to a clear, scientific, and fully transparent source would eliminate the uncanniness. The conspiratorial mindset "re-automatizes" the action, that is, it puts the uncanny into what it believes to be a confirmed structure (an evil system, a conspiracy); at the same time, it does not dare to spell this structure out completely. Paradoxically, the mystification of the strange event is presented as a de-mystification. The coincidence is demystified by hinting at a cause, but the cause always remains partially concealed. The coincidence is not traced to a natural or logical cause, but rather to a heterodox order known only to skeptical specialists or the initiated, and, ultimately, not even to them. In everyday life, the conspiratorial mindset does not *simply* replace the coincidence with necessity because the event is supposed to remain fascinating.

It is interesting that this strategy of maintaining ambivalence replicates that of fantastic literature. Here too, the aim is not to cope with the coincidence by canceling it, but rather to transform the contingent event into an unsolvable enigma. The unexplainable coincidence is not explained but dispersed over diffuse patterns of necessity. In this sense, it becomes "aesthetic" as opposed to epistemic, which corresponds with Freud's analysis of the uncanny. The disautomatized world that we grapple with when we are confronted with an uncanny coincidence is basically an aesthetic phenomenon. Right at the beginning of "The Uncanny," Freud makes clear that he is venturing—unusual for him—into the area of aesthetics. Years after Freud, the uncanny would indeed be very much used in the study of aesthetics. The uncanny can be understood as an "aestheticized fear," which brings it close to ressentiment. As we will see in the next chapter, ressentiment can also be "enjoyed" like an aesthetic phenomenon. It will not be traced to clear sources but remains obscure. All these phenomena play into the psychology of the conspiratorial mindset.

There are a few more parallels between the uncanny and aesthetic experiences. Both the uncanny and art produce an adequate effect only if they are not too perfect (e.g., too realistic). Too much perfection destroys aesthetic enjoyment. Derrida speaks of the "art of the coincidence," which is precisely the art of the uncanny: it *must* always remain imperfect. Derrida suggests juggling as an example because, in juggling, any overly strong control of the coincidence would *remove* any impression of the uncanny. The art of juggling can only exist as an uncanny art. In order to remain uncanny, it must maintain the strange and imperfect nature of the world of chance.[6] Juggling perfectly executed by a machine is not fascinating; just as an ordinary "realistic" photo is less fascinating than a painting that perhaps aims to be realistic without completely achieving it. Perfection destroys the aesthetic. In parallel, the presentation of a conspiracy is uncannier when it is not presented as a perfectly functioning system (such as an exploitative or oppressive system that can be interpreted in communist terms) but as a strange and mysterious plot.

For Heidegger, an event like "it rains" is uncanny, and in Chapter 3 it has been likened to the uncanniness of the accident. Heidegger comes back to the topic of uncanny "that-sentences" in *Being and Time*. Already in his dissertation from 1914 (1972: 126) such sentences were considered "Being-events" (Seinsereignisse). Now, in 1927, Heidegger clearly evokes "Dasein in

---

6 "Juggling by itself would imply too much mastery in the art of coincidence, which must remain *unheimlich*, uncanny" (2007: 358). French: "La jonglerie toute seule, ce serait trop de maîtrise pour l'art de la coïncidence qui doit rester *unheimlich*, uncanny" (366).

its uncanniness: primordial, thrown Being-in-the-world as the not-at-home—the bare 'that it is' [das nackte 'Daß'] in the 'nothing' of the world."[7] The resulting existential anxiety is always "uncanny" in the sense of "not being at home" (unheimlich), which is, to him, an experience of nothingness: "In anxiety one feels 'uncanny.' Here the peculiar indefiniteness of that which Dasein finds itself alongside in anxiety, comes proximally to expression: the 'nothing and nowhere.' But 'uncanniness' also means 'not-being-at home.'"[8] Heidegger recognizes that the uncanniness usually goes unnoticed because in the everyday interpretations of our existences it is not a matter of interest—which is precisely the danger. In the section on "Idle Talk" (Gerede) in *Being and Time*, Heidegger lays down that the uncanny can, because of human negligence, become more and more "groundless" and, as I would like to add, also break forth in the form of an unwarranted conspiracy theory, which is just another type of "idle talk":

> Yet the obviousness and self-assurance of the average ways in which things have been interpreted, as such that while the particular Dasein drifts along towards an ever-increasing groundlessness as it floats, the uncanniness of this floating remains unhidden from under their protecting shelter.[9]

With Rorty, we can say that only a "Dasein that knows it is Dasein, [that knows] that it is only contingently there where it is," is an authentic Dasein (Rorty 1989: 109). Only a Dasein that is aware of its own contingency is safe from degenerating into idle talk and baseless conspiracy theories.

This chapter has pointed to a paradox contained in the logical flow of conspiracist ideation. At first, it appeared as though the conspiratorial mindset does not want to accept chance or the accident as an existential event and tries to construe it as a necessity. However, it soon became clear that the conspiratorial mindset strives to obtain an existential experience: it even wallows

---

7 "[…] das Dasein in seiner Unheimlichkeit, das ursprüngliche geworfene In-der-Welt-sein als Un-zuhause, das nackte 'Daß' im Nichts der Welt" (Heidegger 1980: 277/ German: 367).
8 "In der Angst ist einem 'unheimlich.' Darin kommt zunächst die eigentümliche Unbestimmtheit dessen, wobei sich das Dasein in der Angst befindet, zum Ausdruck: das Nichts und Nirgends. Unheimlichkeit meint aber dabei zugleich das Nicht-zuhause-sein" (233/German: 250).
9 "In der Selbstverständlichkeit und Selbstsicherheit der durch-schnittlichen Ausgelegtheit jedoch liegt es, daß unter ihrem Schutz dem jeweiligen Dasein selbst die Unheimlichkeit der Schwebe, in der es einer wachsenden Bodenlosigkeit zutreiben kann, verborgen bleibt" (214/German: 226).

in the uncanny as though this represented what Heidegger calls "Being itself." The problem is that this mindset grasps neither contingency/facticity nor necessity but merely produces an ontology determined by a strange and incoherent mixture of contingency and necessity. Nothing is accidental, but there are no clear necessities either.

Chapter 5

RESSENTIMENT, KITSCH, AND "ABSOLUTE CONTINGENCY"

Conspiracy and Ressentiment

Most of the time, the conspiratorial mindset is motivated not by the will to objectively judge the life world but rather by other elements, one of which is resentment. Many unwarranted conspiracy theories spring from feelings of "sublimated revenge": some injustice has occurred, sometimes a long time ago, and cannot be amended because the opponent is too powerful. Scapegoating (blame-shifting) and conspiracism are closely linked. However, the injustice and the enemy who caused the misfortune are rarely clearly identified, and the source of the evil remains diffuse. Max Scheler, following Nietzsche, calls this diffuse feeling of vengeance "ressentiment," and ressentiment is also a core reason for the existence of the conspiratorial mindset. Ressentiment—derived from the French word for resentment—is deeper seated and more durable than mere resentment and can be defined as an individual's frustration over his or her own powerlessness. Both resentment and ressentiment differ from anger because they include bitterness. Apart from being more intense, ressentiment is typically directed against sources that are more abstract than those that spark a simple resentment. In his 1915 study of resentment and the role it plays in moral behavior, Scheler gives the following definition:

> Ressentiment is a self-poisoning of the mind which has quite definite causes and consequences. It is a lasting mental attitude, caused by the systematic repression of certain emotions and affects which, as such, are normal components of human nature. Their repression leads to the constant tendency to indulge in certain kinds of value delusions and corresponding value judgments. The emotions and affects primarily concerned are revenge, hatred, malice, envy, the impulse to detract, and spite. (Scheler 2007: 29)

Ressentiment is charged with a diffuse kind of anger combined with fear that does not really know toward what it should direct itself. Most of the time, ressentiment is caused by hierarchies that arouse feelings of envy, humiliation, and helplessness. The ressentiment person feels dispossessed because they believe they are threatened and dominated by an ungraspable alien power. Again, this evil power is not *simply* frightening, but also uncanny because it is not clearly identifiable.

Ressentiment distorts our perception of reality, which also concerns our perception of irregularities and contingencies. Often the source of the evil cannot be identified beyond vague affirmations that "this is not a coincidence." Seneca, the first-century Roman Stoic, calls this mental disposition the "suspicion and inference" that leads to misleading conclusions: "'This man greeted me with too little curtesy; that one did not linger in my embrace; that one cut me off when I had just started talking; that one seemed to turn his face from me more than usual.' There will be no lack of rationale to back up this suspicion" (Seneca 2014: XXIV). Seneca suggests we "trust only that which we can see, plainly, with our own eyes" and disregard the rest: "It is the part of a great mind to despise wrongs done to it" and "many have taken small injuries much more seriously that they need by revenging them" (XXXII).

The attribution of fortuitous events to necessities that will never be clearly spelled out leads to the formulation of ressentiment directed against ill-defined groups (Jews, Freemasons, etc.), or sometimes against entire states that are believed to be behind an "institutional conspiracy" (vice versa, states can issue unwarranted conspiracy theories, in which case ressentiment can become an ideology). When the ressentiment is directed against concrete persons such as Soros or Gates, the necessities and motivations that could have led to these people's supposed evil behaviors tend to be presented in a vague fashion. The only thing that is safely assumed is that the conspiracy is the work of a minority or that the conspirators are financed by foreign powers.

The spread of many unjustifiable conspiracy theories is only possible because of existing ressentiment. For example, a conspiracy theory stating that the pandemic is merely a ploy staged by governments to rob citizens of their freedoms will most probably be adopted by those who *already* feel that their freedom is oppressed in some way. As mentioned in Chapter 2, the interest that many flat-earthers take in the curious belief that the earth is flat is not the fact as such, but rather the idea that the truth has been dissimulated from them by conspiring governments. This truth about the conspiring governments they find "aesthetically" attractive. Similarly, one might insist on the existence of UFO landings not because one is necessarily strongly interested in UFOs but because one looks for confirmations of the fact that the state has dissimulated important events from its citizens. Though the motivating forces of conspiratorial thinking are multiple and have been debated at length in academic circles, there is no doubt that they thrive best in climates of oppression, regardless of whether the oppression is real or imagined.

Ressentiment is not an accusation because accusations single out concrete acts of misconduct and attribute them to concrete persons or institutions that have committed concrete crimes. Accusations need to be backed up by evidence. In addition, accusations leave space for contingency, whereas unwarranted conspiracy theories are normally obsessed with necessities. I might accuse country X of exploiting my country because it has certain economic interests. Whatever the exploitative plan might be, it is submitted to contingencies, especially when the periods considered are lengthy; exploitative projects are fluid and can change over time. However, when I attribute the plan to a conspiracy, I purge the project of contingencies. As a result, the exploiter can become absolutely evil. Before, I could have admitted that my own country or even I myself might have been ready to engage in similar exploitative practices, were I put in similar circumstances. Once the plan is backed by a conspiracy theory, a notion of unadulterated evil emerges and foists uncompromising notions, not only of evil but also of otherness, upon my opponent.

Despite the ambition to establish absolute and necessary truths, both the injustice that has been suffered (which is often an insult or an injured honor) and the resulting negative feelings tend to remain diffuse. The motivations of ressentiment are not based on objective analyses from which a will to defend oneself or a will to improve society by eliminating the evil could result (both of which can likewise be accompanied by anger and indignation). Instead, they remain inspired by obscure negative feelings. The accusation is intentionally kept vague because the conspiratorial mind likes to play with probabilities so that the anger lingers in the form of ressentiment.

In May 2020, Lijian Zhao, deputy director of the Chinese Ministry of Foreign Affairs Information Department, tweeted:

> CDC [Center of Disease Control] was caught on the spot. When did patient zero begin in US? How many people are infected? What are the names of the hospitals? It might be the US army who brought the epidemic to Wuhan. Be transparent! Make public your data! US owe us an explanation!

The statement is not meant to create anger that can be directed against a particular institution. It does not directly link the Center for Disease Control to an allegedly U.S.-born coronavirus; the CDC is merely placed at the beginning of a "statement" that contains only rhetorical questions without making assertions, except the one that the United States should be transparent. In this tweet, there are no *accusations* about the U.S. involvement in the virus, but only questions about what "might be"; the way in which the statement is formulated incites ressentiment rather than anger and protest. What Canguilhem called "pathological" is here Scheler's poisoning of the mind, which creates an irrationally sustained, vague feeling of vengeance.

Conspiracy and Slave Morality

Among vague and obscure feelings, we most often find fear and anxiety, which institutions like states or religions can use for their own purposes. Similarly, the conspiratorial mindset can take advantage of existing anxieties and direct them toward aims that need to remain vague so the anxiety can continue to be sustained. One *submits* oneself to ressentiment and thus to the conspiracy, which denotes a kind of slave mentality. The 2020 coronavirus lockdown produced much social anxiety, and fake news about conspiracies was more quickly absorbed than they would have been in more relaxed situations. But the fear and anxiety were rarely consistently traced to concrete sources. In general, they might be traced to a name, a person, an ethnic group, or a country, but there is usually no plausible proof of a causal link between the subject and the event. The reason is that once evidence is provided, "real" anger, action, and revolution could emerge, and not just anxiety and ressentiment. In cases of real threats, concrete action is required, and the problem might even be solved. In unwarranted conspiracy theories, the enemy's geographical location often remains vague; or the origin of malevolent processes is often found in a past so distant that it has acquired the status of a myth rather than that of an objective historical fact. When all action is blocked, ressentiment builds up. Accordingly, Scheler writes:

> These psychical forces become repressive especially when the steady and constant pressure of authority deprives them, as it were, of an object—i.e., when the person himself does not know "of what" he is afraid or incapable. Thus fear, which always has specific objects, here plays a secondary role. Much more important is that deep blockage of vital energy called "anxiety." (Scheler 2007: 46)

Scheler traces ressentiment to bourgeois morality, which has, since the thirteenth century, gradually replaced the preexisting Christian morality which he believes—contrary to what Nietzsche held—to be free of ressentiment. But this rambling sentiment can also be found in many social movements that do not seem to have a strong link with what Scheler saw as bourgeois morality. Populist extremist movements ranging from far left to far right produce unwarranted conspiracy theories based on a feeling of ressentiment. Often, an unwarranted conspiracy represents a cause-effect relationship that cannot be elucidated through rational explanations. Both the conspirator's motivations and their desired results very often remain secret and undefinable. As has been shown, most typically, two unrelated events are perceived to be linked, such as the rapid rollout of 5G networks and the spread of the coronavirus. The correlation is non-existent, but a further problem is that no truly plausible motivation can be found for the "perpetrators" engaging in such a project. If China is seen as the driving force behind 5G, the perpetrator is faraway and almost "mythical," and evidence does not *need* to be established. The "deep state" can be seen in a similarly "mythical" light. In this sense, we are not confronted with a simple false cause fallacy but with something more complex. When the general feeling of injustice cannot be directed against a concrete source, it will be directed against a more general evil pattern. Ressentiment tends to turn against large-scale arrangements. Contingent events are single events, but the conspiratorial mindset's ressentiment is directed against coherent structures. Scheler affirms that ressentiment turns more frequently against lasting situations. Because the structure is very coherent, spite and anger cannot be relieved through vengeance, work, violence, robbery, or revolution: the enemy is simply too systematic as they act through a consistent network.

The ressentiment can also be directed against the idea of contingency as such. Coincidences might have brought misfortune in the past or prevented the ressentiment man from obtaining the merits he thinks he deserves. As a result, he establishes regular patterns that he believes to be responsible for the misfortune.

Conspiratorial mindsets are most likely to emerge when, in Scheler's terms, the "injury is experienced as a destiny" (38). When destiny is the source of resentment, the resentment is directed against a past that cannot be changed, which creates, as Nietzsche says in a section of the *Zarathustra* entitled "On Redemption," a "counter will" (Widerwille) toward the past. This is because destiny is an individual's (or group's) future, and the future is logically determined by the past. Consequently, the "counter will" is directed against an "Es war," that is, against time as a whole (Nietzsche 1969: 161–62). Destiny or fate is predetermined and is thus a necessary structure *par excellence*. In the end, it is assumed that the enemy simply dislikes one's existence and that the conspiracy is a matter of destiny. General patterns such as racism or the oppression of certain population groups are declared to be inveterate and irreversible. "No coincidence can lead us out of this predetermined condition." The result is, again, sustained ressentiment, following a vicious circle: because of the ressentiment, the conspiratorial mindset invents diffuse patterns of evilness that cannot be clearly discerned but are still supposed to be necessary and coherent; and because these patterns are diffuse and cannot be directly combated, the ressentiment becomes even stronger. The evil has become a matter of destiny, which explains why ungrounded conspiracy theories linger. The evil is incurable not only because it is so powerful but also because the evil is the main pretext for the conspiracy theory. It *must* remain present in order to justify one's terms of existence. It is part of one's destiny. Here Nietzsche's slave morality concept becomes most plausible. In *On the Genealogy of Morality*, Nietzsche states that the man of *ressentiment* "loves dark corners, secret paths and back-doors, everything secretive appeals to him as being *his* world, *his* security, *his* comfort" (2006: 21). Paradoxically, the unwarranted conspiracy theory that is based on threats can provide security as it adopts the character of slave morality. The evil (together with the ressentiment it produces) is accepted and provides comfort.

The ressentiment becomes strongest when the discrepancy between pride felt and injury suffered is the largest. Again, this is an exaltation of necessity on both sides: both pride and the injuring conspiracy are seen as necessities. Personal pride or national pride is often explained in terms of absolute necessities, especially when this pride is linked to religion. Scheler cites Nietzsche's example of Jews who believe themselves to be God's chosen people. As a result, single events that challenge this absolute necessity cannot be accepted as mere single events. Any evil that challenges an absolute truth cannot be a mere coincidence and must be systematic.

Scheler advances many more points about ressentiment that can be applied to unwarranted conspiracy theories. There is the envy and depreciation of the enemy because one was not allowed to have what he has. The old ressentiment story of the fox and the grape reflects the dynamic that leads to the creation of undue conspiracy theories, and the reason is always the tension created by the discrepancy between desire and impotence.

Contingency and Science

Many conspiracy theories are motivated by a strong distrust in science. Some are warranted and some are unwarranted. As for the unwarranted ones, the conspiratorial mindset usually does not openly engage in anti-scientific activities such as mysticism or spiritualism but rather invents an "alternative" science, as has been explained in Chapter 2. It follows the model of some— prominently monotheistic—religions that look for "scientific" (pseudoscientific) explanations in their respective holy scriptures. As "theories," unwarranted conspiracy theories claim to be scientific because they look for necessities. They are not scientific, at least they are not "good science," but the strategy is at least consistent insofar as science normally never puts up with contingency.

The aim of science and of most philosophy is to find necessary reasons underlying apparently random phenomena and to show that things only *can* happen the way they do.[1] The German philosopher Fritz Mauthner established in the *Dictionary of Philosophy* of 1910 that contingency and philosophy are incompatible because the former contradicts the ideal of clarity: "Since millennia, all clear thinkers have affirmed that the coincidence does not exist in reality, and that it is a relative, human notion, coined only to veil our ignorance" (Mauthner 1910: 634). Aristotle affirms that "nature does nothing by coincidence" (*Of Heaven*, 11, 291b, 13), and Hegel, who can at times sound rather determinist, declares in his *Philosophy of World History* that philosophy "has no other purpose than to eliminate the contingent [das Zufällige]" (Hegel 1955: 29).

Contingency, and even probability, maintains an element of ignorance, and it is indeed absurd to imagine a science founded on ignorance. When science works with probabilities, it extracts from probabilities only those things that are known. Contingency is *pure* ignorance and, normally, it cannot be used for the building of science (see Boll 1966: 17). Science can *recognize* contingency, but it cannot draw conclusions from contingency-based premises. Strictly speaking, any science of coincidences, that is, any science that builds on coincidences and draws conclusions from coincidences, is an impossibility. Science handles randomness by measuring it, which means that it separates the known from the unknown. Before the advent of quantum physics and the branch of mathematical physics called chaos theory, the natural sciences ascertained only regularities that could be taken for granted. *When* science encounters contingency (which arguably happens more often in the cultural world than in the natural one), it will not apprehend the "that" of the contingency but only its "how." Then, through a restrained perspective focused on the "how," science can reformulate contingencies as quasi-necessities. The coincidence becomes a relative necessity. Strictly speaking, probability theory is not a science but only a tool that science uses. It is a practical device, like a computing tool.

Science cannot accept contingency. Medical doctors adhere to this principle when establishing symptoms. A large part of Freud's *Psychopathology of*

---

1 More recent developments like quantum physics and chaos theory integrate coincidence into their theories. They are exceptions and will be dealt with in Chapters 5 and 6.

Everyday Life consists of attributing apparently random (zufällige) events to general rules and of explaining contingent actions (Zufallshandlungen) as "symptomatic actions" (Symptomhandlungen). Freud works within the spectrum of science that fights coincidence and finds necessities. What appears to be random is found to be determined by the invisible rules of our subconscious. In Greek, *symptoma* also means coincidence (related to *symbebekos*), which makes the symptom a sign that has no meaning as such, but that can be interpreted and explained as meaningful, as Derrida explains in his book on chance (*Mes Chances*):

> One may remark in the system the incidence of a coincidence, the very thing that falls, well or badly, with something else, at the same time or in the same place as something else. This is also the sense that the Greek gives to *symptoma*, a word that means, first of all, a sinking or depression, collapse, secondly, coincidence, fortuitous event, encounter, next, unfortunate event, and finally, the symptom as sign, for example a clinical sign. (Derrida 2007: 350)

When a fact turns out to be significant, that is, not to be a mere coincidence, it becomes what we today call a symptom. In modern language, a symptom is a necessity.

Science can *detect* coincidences, and this is true of all sciences. When sociology explains how society evolved in a contingent fashion during a certain period, it does not attribute contingency to necessity but merely describes the contingency. This description has its limits. If *everything* is attributed to contingency, the scientific account becomes unsatisfactory. Most probably, it will result in the kind of "contingency theory" that Skip Willman forcefully criticizes and which I will attend to in the conclusion. A historical narrative that attributes all events to chance lacks depth. Historical explanations must make history intelligible as a complex combination of necessity and contingency. The former cannot simply be replaced with the latter, but contingent events must be elucidated in broader contexts that provide some amount of necessity. Coincidences will then not be simply denied but, on the contrary, the coincidence will become more visible when it is put into a necessary context.

However, all this remains purely descriptive. Developing these coincidences and using their fortuity as if they were the result of scientific calculations would lead to the writing of alternative histories (counterfactual history). These histories imagine alternative outcomes of coincidences in order to show that the allegedly necessary order of history owes a lot to chance and could also have evolved otherwise. Alternative histories are converse to unwarranted conspiracy theories: the latter tend to deny coincidences and find imaginary necessities (the conspiratorial mindset believes that history is not coincidental and that it is set in motion by demonic forces and transcendent powers). Counterfactual history exalts the coincidence and denies necessities. It is based on what Coady and Wilman call a "coincidence theory."

Science looks for regularities in a world that can easily appear anarchic, and this paradigm has not been weakened in recent history. Despite the existence of chaos theory, which merely acts within a scientific niche, in the modern world, coincidence is not more but less well accepted than in preceding centuries. At the same time, we no longer observe the determinist enthusiasm that was present in the nineteenth century. It rather seems that science is embarrassed by coincidence. As a matter of fact, it should be. After centuries of necessity-searching science, should coincidence not have simply disappeared? Instead, contingency subsists, remaining beyond science's reach, as if coincidence could escape the powerful dichotomy of chance and necessity and thus mock all science. However, compared to the nineteenth century, something important has changed: coincidence is no longer an element that *needs* to be overcome through necessity (we will see in the next chapter how much the nineteenth century was determinist). As the Laplacian necessity-oriented optimism faded in the twentieth century, contingency is no longer perceived as an *enemy* of science: instead it has become its strange and freaky other. According to Baudrillard, coincidence (*le hasard*) is today conceived as an indecent and obscene pariah: "The *hasard* corresponds not to science's provisional state of incapacity to explain everything—in that case it would still have a graspable, conceptual existence—but to a passage from a state of causal determinism to another order that is also different from non-*hasard*. The *hasard* has thus no existence at all" (Baudrillard 1983: 209). The *hasard* exists but it has no existence for science, which means that contingency is no longer simply *anti*-scientific, but that it exists in a strange *non*-scientific universe. And here it can more easily be recuperated by pseudosciences that fight coincidence in their own way and establish their own necessities. In the determinist nineteenth century, coincidence was what science tried to overcome and believed it was capable of overcoming. As will be shown in Chapter 7, today coincidence pops up everywhere: in astrophysics, biology, and the humanities. Once the determinist conviction has faded, the conspiratorial mindset can take up the task of transforming embarrassing contingencies into necessities.

Hegel's "Absolute Contingency"

Can the rejection of coincidence be unethical? Hegel delves into this question. First of all, the "why did this happen to me?" attitude is self-centered and refuses to look at the "big picture" of human cohabitation. The ressentiment man believes that he was predestined for a better fate and that a coincidence (which he does not accept as such) prevented him from assuming this legitimate destiny. According to Dieter Henrich, Hegel finds that the ressentiment man "meditates and remains closed to the moral necessity, which would be 'to let the coincidence be simply a coincidence'" (Henrich 1971: 174).[2] He locks his self-consciousness into reflections on its own specificity and ruminates on his adverse fate. The ressentiment man is narcissistic, as already Seneca pointed out: "[Resentment] is caused by our excessive self-love: we think we ought to remain uninjured even by our enemies: every man bears within his breast the mind of a despot and is willing to commit excesses" (Seneca 2014: XXXI). According to Seneca, there's no other reason "why we are irritated at the smallest trifles in our own domestic affairs, and why we call our friends' carelessness deliberate injury."

Hegel does not speak of ressentiment, but often his analysis focuses on the selfsame phenomenon. The ressentiment man complains of an unfortunate coincidence that he believes to be incompatible with his individuality. In the *Lectures on the History of Philosophy*, Hegel suggests that "a will that insists only on its freedom will be pushed into vanity" (VGP II: 466), from which it follows that protest against contingency is unethical, be it only because anti-contingency vanity is based on subjectivity. In more modern terms, we would call this attitude narcissistic. Alternatively, Hegel suggests a dialectic of necessity and contingency, a dialectic that he believes to be the driving force of any evolution—natural or historical. In his *Science of Logic*, Hegel develops an elaborate theory of contingency, especially in the chapter on the modalities of reality, possibility, and necessity.

Thinking about contingency and determinism became important to Hegel as well as to Engels (see Engels' *Dialektik der Natur*) because around 1800 rationalism and a strictly deductive philosophy of science had become rather mainstream in Germany through Fichte. In the *Logic*, Hegel writes that the "unity of possibility and actuality is *contingency*. The contingent is an actual that at the same time is determined as merely possible, whose other

---

2 In Hegel, *Zufall* is the coincidence whereas *Zufälligkeit* (literally "coincidality") is "contingency," though Hegel, at some point in the *Logic*, shifts to the Latinate "*Accidentalität*" (accidentality), most likely in order to connect the term to the "accident" that can be contrasted with "substance." See Di Giovanni's note 15 on page 479 on that matter. In his translation, Di Giovanni uses the term "accidentality" extensively whereas Miller sticks to "contingency."

or opposite equally is. This actuality is therefore mere being or Existence."³ Roughly, Hegel suggests that absolute contingency must exist because, without it, there would be no necessity. It can be concluded that for Hegel, contingency and necessity are "analytically linked" (Henrich: 164) and that he believes the world to be governed by a paradoxical "absolute contingency."⁴ The totality of Being is necessary, but individualities cannot be derived from this necessity. According to Henrich, Hegel's is the only philosophical theory that recognizes the notion of absolute contingency (Henrich 1971: 171).

Hegel's concept of "absolute contingency" goes in the direction of Emile Boutroux's later "contingency of natural laws," which will be discussed in Chapter 9. It might even echo the principles of quantum physics, which integrates uncertainty and contingency into necessary natural laws. Apart from that, it takes up an old question about science: the laws of science are absolute, but why are they the way they are? Could they also be otherwise? Science can establish absolute laws, but how will this scientific activity be matched with the contingency of the world, that is, how will it be matched with the facticity that the world *could* also be different? The fact that it is such and not otherwise cannot be apprehended but must simply be accepted.

---

3 Hegel 2010: 480. German: "Diese Einheit der Möglichkeit und Wirklichkeit ist die *Zufälligkeit*. Das Zufällige ist ein Wirkliches, das zugleich nur als möglich bestimmt, dessen Anderes oder Gegenteil ebensosehr ist. Diese Wirklichkeit ist daher bloßes Sein oder Existenz [...]" (1986b: 205).

4 The term "absolute contingency" (absolute Zufälligkeit) appears only once in the *Science of Logic* and is unfortunately not reproduced in the Cambridge University Press translation by George Di Giovanni. In German, the text (ed. Meiner) reads: "[...] das Übergehen in *Anderes* ist Reflexion in sich selbst; die *Negation*, welche Grund der Ursache ist, ist ihr *positives Zusammengehen* mit sich selbst. Notwendigkeit und Kausalität sind also darin verschwunden; sie enthalten beides, die unmittelbare Identität als Zusammenhang und Beziehung und die absolute Substantialität der Unterschiedenen, somit die absolute Zufälligkeit derselben,— die ursprüngliche Einheit substantieller Verschiedenheit, also den absoluten Widerspruch" (1057). In the Cambridge translation, the formulation "absolute contingency" has disappeared: "[...] the transition into *otherness* is reflection-into-itself; *negation*, which is the ground of the cause, is its positive *rejoining* with itself. In the reciprocity of action, therefore, necessity and causality have disappeared; they contain both the *immediate identity* as *combination* and *reference* and the *absolute substantiality of the differences*, consequently their *contingency*, the original *unity* of substantial *difference* and therefore the absolute contradiction" (504). The older translation by A. V Miller (1969, Humanities Press) translates more literally: "[...] the transition into an other is a reflection into itself; the negation, which is ground of the cause, is its positive union with itself. In reciprocity, therefore, necessity and causality have vanished; they contain both, immediate identity as connection and relation, and the absolute substantiality of the different sides, hence the absolute contingency of them; the original unity of substantial difference, and therefore absolute contradiction" (571).

As philosophy and science became increasingly systematic, they recognized coincidence as a theoretical complication that they would find fundamental but also disquieting. Engels, in his unfinished manuscript *The Dialectics of Nature* written between 1896 and 1898 and posthumously published in 1925, reflects upon a dilemma. In this piece, Engels is more critical of determinism than in other works (see below) and criticizes French materialism (which, according to him, is responsible for this determinism) because it tries to entirely do away with chance in the natural sciences. However, in the end, Engels does not accept contingency and finds it "degrading." About the evolution of nature, Engels famously writes: "If the fact that a particular pea-pod contains six peas, and not five or seven, is of the same order as the law of motion of the solar system, or the law of the transformation of energy, then as a matter of fact, chance is not elevated into necessity, but rather necessity degraded into chance [die Notwendigkeit degradiert zur Zufälligkeit]" (Engels 2010: 500/German 1952: 233). In an earlier text, in his historical materialist treatise *The Origin of the Family, Private Property and the State* (1884), Engels explains how such a "degradation" can be overcome. Nature *appears* to be ruled by contingency, but science always finds necessities within this world of coincidences: "In nature, where chance also seems to reign, we have long ago demonstrated in each particular field the inherent necessity and regularity that asserts itself in this chance" (2004: 161).[5] In other words, there is necessity in chance, and science can make it visible. Engels extrapolates this to society: "What is true of nature holds good also for society. The more a social activity, a series of social processes, becomes too powerful for conscious human control, grows beyond human reach, the more it seems to have been left to pure chance" (161). Contingency is a threat, and society must be controlled by leaving nothing to the unknown, that is, to chance.

We see that Hegel's concept of "absolute contingency" is fundamentally different. For Hegel, science, even as it establishes absolute laws, does not feel "degraded" by the inner contingency of the world. For ethics, for example, this means, in Hegel's view, that humans should submit themselves to what he calls an "unconditional moral necessity" (unbedingte sittliche Notwendigkeit) (Henrich 1971: 174). But it implies an acceptance of contingency. One must be free of vanity and see contingent events as unimportant, no matter if they bring luck, illness, or death. Henrich speaks of the "letting be" of contingent being (Seiendes), which follows from the necessity of Being (Sein). Moral

---

5 "In der Natur, wo auch der Zufall zu herrschen scheint, haben wir längst auf jedem einzelnen Gebiet die innere Notwendigkeit und Gesetzmäßigkeit nachgewiesen, die in diesem Zufall sich durchsetzt" (1961: 159).

consciousness must coordinate necessity and contingency so that it accepts contingency within the necessity of Being.[6] Humans are not just submitted to the necessary natural laws of Being but can also pose their own laws. Humans are not passive receivers but progress on the path of civilization by mediating between contingency and necessity.

Kitsch and Conspiracy

It has been said that for "the worldview of kitsch everything is wonderful" (Steinvorth 2016: 211). Against this, the conspiratorial mindset holds that everything in this world is awful, which is no less kitsch. This analysis seems to collide with the classical view of kitsch as clean and, in Milan Kundera's famous formulation, as "the absolute denial of shit" (Kundera 1984: 251). Theologian John Cilliers believes that "kitsch cannot endure life's struggles. It avoids theodicy like the plague. It cannot exist in the tension of the quest for meaning […] it bypasses the reality of suffering, poverty and being truly human" (Cilliers 2010). The ressentiment-ridden conspiratorial mindset seems to do the opposite as it indulges in its own suffering. However, this is equally kitsch. Kitsch is not only self-congratulation but also the bittersweet warmth of self-pity and self-indulgence, which precisely fits the profile of the ressentiment man. Steinvorth's formulation must thus be complemented with another observation by Kundera, for whom kitsch is either shitless or *indulging* in shit in a fit of pity. Both kitsch and the conspiratorial mindset "cannot endure life's struggles" (Cilliers), and in order to make life more bearable, both bypass reality.

The conspiratorial mindset is kitsch because it often produces theories that are repetitive, formulaic, and very predictable (at least when one is acquainted with the conspiracist style) and tends to work with clichés. Though some are creative, many unwarranted conspiracy theories follow schemes similar to the one proposed by Keeley, which makes them formulaic. Furthermore, both the conspiratorial mindset and ressentiment attitudes are kitsch because they are often narcissistic: they recycle subjective feelings. Empirical research by Cichocka et al. (2016) found that gratuitous conspiracy theories are particularly appealing to narcissists because they inflate their feelings of self-worth.

---

6 See Henrich's comment: "Unter die unbedingte sittliche Notwendigkeit sich stellen heißt Aufgabe des Besonderen, Freisein von Eitelkeit, Freigabe des nur Zufälligen als des Unwichtigen, auch im eigenen natürlichen Sein, sei es eigenes Glück, sei es Krankheit und Tod. Das Seinlassen des kontingenten Seienden geschieht hier aus der Notwendigkeit des Seins. Für das sittliche Bewußtsein sind die Begriffe der Notwendigkeit und des Zufälligen so vermittelt" (185).

Again, all these features are highly compatible with indulgence. The style of thinking practiced in unwarranted conspiracy theories, the style that has been depicted in Chapter 4, is a kitsch style of thinking. Indulgence in one's misery means that one does not realistically face problems in order to solve them. Instead, misery is transposed onto a more "aesthetic" level. Like the narcissist, the holder of the conspiratorial mindset does not accept any insult to her vanity and often, loss makes her dive into a pool of ressentiment from which she rarely reemerges.

Both the conspiratorial mindset and ressentiment attitudes are defense mechanisms that try to deal with life's negative components. The rejection of these conspiracy-ressentiment strategies does not mean one needs to maintain that everything is positive: this would just be another expression of kitsch. A realistic, non-kitsch, and non-ressentiment attitude toward life must consist of finding an appropriate way of dealing with the ups and downs of life. Yes, life is tragic, but this does not signify that the whole world is against us. The conspiratorial mindset and ressentiment people choose the latter option, which is kitsch. They are nihilistic, but they adhere to a *dramatic* version of nihilism, which is distinct from Nietzsche's *tragic* nihilism. Tragic nihilism manages to bear the tragedies of life without succumbing to kitsch. Did Oedipus ever ask: "Why must this happen to me?" The dramatic nihilism of unwarranted conspiracy theories and ressentiment knows neither irony nor humor but indulges in the drama of a hopeless situation. This drama tends to be pompous and full of pathos, and usually, it is backed by a well-calculated grand narrative about the power of the "bad ones." Ressentiment people are caught in their own drama, which they perceive as (vaguely) necessary and predetermined. Of all options, they will always choose the most dramatic one. For example, during the COVID-19 crisis, they would choose a coronavirus lab leak narrative over a zoonotic overflow one because the former is more dramatic.

It has been said above that, unlike an accusation, ressentiment is always diffuse. This also overlaps with Harry Frankfurt's philosophical idea of "bullshit," which he considers to be different from lying because it *disperses* the truth. Bullshit deludes by creating confusing contexts and ambiguous definitions that work in its favor. Its "focus is panoramic rather than particular" (Frankfurt 2005: 52), which reflects the production of ressentiment. Accusations are precise, and false accusations will be considered lies, whereas ressentiment is a sort of "bullshit accusation" that is "merely" fake and phony. Ressentiment twists reality without straightforwardly lying about it, which means that it is *indifferent* toward reality, which is, for Frankfurt, the quintessence of bullshit. Given the obvious links between kitsch and bullshit (see Botz-Bornstein 2015, 2016, and 2019), one can confirm once more that the conspiratorial mindset, which operates on bullshit and not with lies, must be called a kitsch mindset.

There is only one element that *could* lead the conspiratorial mindset out of its dramatic self-enclosure in kitsch: the coincidence. Coincidences import irony into the tragedy of life, but to both the conspiratorial mindset and kitsch people, irony is alien. The deterministic ressentiment attitude does not permit a more distanced vision of a world submitted to contingency. Irony or humor are only possible when not everything is perceived as necessary. Through irony, even the most tragic chain of events can be viewed from a distanced position. In contrast, when necessity is depicted as overwhelming, we will most probably have a kitsch scenario. For the ironist, the tragedies of life or of history do not unfold alongside necessary laws but always include coincidences. "Shit happens" expresses an ironic attitude that can see even the necessary (i.e., the events that could not have been averted) as if they were coincidences. In contrast, the conspiratorial mindset is unable to depict life as a tragicomedy in which the flow of events *could* have happened otherwise. Life is a drama because it is determined by evil powers that are necessarily working against it. Of course, all this is possible only because the conspiratorial mindset puts itself or its own group at the center of the narrative, which reveals the narcissistic impulse inherent in these theories.

As mentioned in the last chapter, the kitsch person wants everything to coincide: art with reality, and expression with feeling, or her whole life with destiny. She thus transforms the coincidence into a necessity that is so perfect that it becomes "too much," which is precisely a defining characteristic of kitsch. "Being alive means to be in uninterrupted coincidence both with the world and with oneself," writes Jullien (33), but such coincidences need to be understood *as coincidences* and not as necessities. If not, one falls victim to determinism and fatalism, that is, to a kitsch version of destiny.

According to Rorty, who has probably given the best account of existing links between contingency and irony, the anti-ironist cannot accept that in the real world, sometimes patchworks do not match. He requires a perfect overlap (a "coincidence" in the sense of necessity) of the essential and the accidental, the inner and the outer self, the soul and the state, as well as cognitive truth and moral belief (see Rorty 1989: 90). Usually, the anti-ironist is a traditionalist who sees the world as basically unidimensional, serious, and necessary. *If* a contradiction occurs, she might trace it to a conspiracy. Both the ressentiment-ridden conspiratorial mindset and the anti-ironist are kitsch persons, but they are also, in Stoic terms, people who care too much about things that "just happen." They do not manage to be indifferent toward those things that they should rather be indifferent about.

Linked to kitsch and anti-irony is narcissism. It has been said above that empirical research has revealed links between receptiveness toward unwarranted conspiracy theories and narcissism. Gilles Lipovetsky writes that "contemporary narcissism unfolds in the astonishing absence of tragic nihilism" (1983: 74). The narcissist most probably prefers to be imbued with the *dramatic* nihilism of the conspiratorial mindset. Against this, *tragic* nihilism recognizes loss but refrains from attributing it to some indeterminate evil power. It attempts to see life as playful. Life is a game with losers and winners, and the stakes can change at any moment. Tragic nihilism—as opposed to dramatic nihilism—does not recycle the feeling of loss but sees life with the lighthearted spirit of the player. Good players do not reprocess negative feelings because they have no ressentiment. Of course, this view on life can be taken only if one admits the existence of coincidences, which is precisely what the tragically nihilist player does. Tragic nihilism does not submit the tragedy of the world to necessities because everything *could* also be otherwise. The evil could merely be a coincidence, and good things can happen by chance too. The dramatically nihilist conspiratorial mindset is fixated upon the oppression of its ego and, consequently, only sees the drama revolving around its own person. A more detached view would enable this mindset to see the tragedy of life as a spectacle unfolding in the distance. Tragic irony might inspire us to write satire, which is decidedly not on the agenda of the conspiratorial mindset or the ressentiment man. Instead of being ironic, the conspiratorial mindset is dogmatic. Quentin Meillassoux draws a link between necessity-dogmatism and theological dogmatism by mentioning "the kind of dogmatism which claims that this God, this world, this history, and ultimately this actually existing political regime necessarily exists" (2008: 58). Against this, the ironic mentality holds that nothing is what it appears to be and that nothing should be taken for granted. Absolute necessities do not exist, and there is always some gap between the signified and the signifier. Ironism can, of course, also develop toward the other extreme, which is equally kitsch. It can lead into the kind of relativism for which nothing matters (Coady's "contingency theorist," for example) or Alan Bloom's idea of the "Nietzscheanized left," which denies *all* truth (see Bloom 1987: 217). This is as problematic as the "absolutism" of deterministic baseless conspiracy theories. For the relativist, everything is contingent, and no judgments are possible. We can also call this position "anti-dramatic" because once everything and everybody is equal, no drama can occur. Tragedies have become impossible too, which creates the exact mirror image of the ressentiment-driven conspiratorial mindset imbued with dramatic anti-ironism.

The relativism of Bloom's "Nietzscheanized left" distorts Nietzsche's original idea of tragic irony. To admit the existence of contingency does not imply a negation of all values. The latter approach should rather be called cynicism, and, paradoxically, it is also an attitude that characterizes the conspiratorial mindset. In contrast, ironic relativism evolves out of the tragic insight that absolute, necessary truths are lost, which, once again, does not simply suggest the negation of all truths. Relativism based on Nietzsche's tragic nihilism is no straightforward pessimism. It is rather a nihilism with ironic connotations that culminates in the conclusion that all worldly matters are "tragically relative." Tragic irony prevents both fanatic absolutism and fanatic relativism. The latter is the kitsch version of Enlightenment culture, just as scientism is the kitsch version of science; and the unwarranted conspiracy theory is the kitsch version of skepticism. It is not at all erroneous to speak here of kitsch; remember that my approach toward theories is aesthetic.

In contrast, tragic irony always perceives nuances and does not paint the world in black and white, or innocent and guilty. The world is a complex game in which all elements remain interlinked, which makes the crystallization of absolute necessities very difficult. Usually, new constellations are not easily predictable.

Large parts of human history can be perceived through the model of tragic irony. Tragedies like colonialism were not built on a grand narrative directed by a quasi-absolute truth but evolved organically, always integrating both coincidence and necessity. Only the tragic irony perspective can reduce ressentiment. Nietzsche's formulation of the tragic anti-ressentiment position, which he expresses in the *Twilight of the Idols*, therefore reads like this: "Saying Yes to life even in its strangest and hardest problems, the will to life rejoicing over its own inexhaustibility even in the very sacrifice of its highest types—that is what I called Dionysian, that is what I guessed to be the bridge to the psychology of the tragic poet" (Nietzsche 1997: 80).[7] Seeing life as tragic sparks dynamic gaiety over stagnant ideas about the absolute evil of conspiracies.

The pompous dramatic ressentiment narrative that is full of pathos is a metaphysical kitsch narrative. It is both metaphysical and theological (see Rorty 1989: xv). The holder of the conspiratorial mindset is a philosopher who applies science to life, but the problem is that she accepts neither irony nor contingency. Narcissistically, she puts her own beliefs and desires at the center of the narrative and refrains from seeing single events within larger historical, geographical, or ideological contexts. According to Rorty, metaphysicians and theologians commit precisely this mistake. Contingency, wherever it exists, can come into view only within contexts that include not only one,

---

7 For more on Nietzsche's tragic irony, see Botz-Bornstein 2019, Chapter 7.

but various points of view. Irony can only develop through a perspective that is not fixated on one's own misfortune but which understands that, due to a significant number of agents and a multitude of possibilities, everything could also have happened otherwise. Irony is essential to prevent ressentiment and unwarranted conspiracy thinking. Whereas the ressentiment man says "why did this happen to me," the anti-ressentiment man says "this could have happened to anybody." To a large extent, the difference between the two depends on the applied irony.

In Rorty's terms, conspiratorial mindset people would be "metaphysicians." They see their own liberty threatened by, for example, the necessity to wear face masks to prevent the spread of the coronavirus, but do not see the bigger picture within which many other elements are interconnected. Simultaneously, as "theorists," the conspiratorial mindset tends to create overarching theories based on large-scale, vague, and unproven truths that are supposed to hold selected single events together. In this double-bind system, there is no place for chance. For example, the probability that one catches the virus exists, but it will be ignored. In parallel, a "them against us" theme functions like an absolute, metaphysical reality that exists beyond the (contingent) reality of time and space. The ressentiment person is a true metaphysician. Basically, ressentiment signifies an incapacity to recognize that social relations and institutions are to some extent contingent and an inability to deny that they have emerged over time; that social truths are always made and not found, and that contingency could have slipped in everywhere.

The conspiratorial mindset seeks reason and finds unreason. The main problem is not that she finds unreason but rather that she wants to find reason in the form of a static language. The language of science, institutions, and so on, is for her not a language made in history (as it is for Heidegger or Wittgenstein) but an abstract rule to which it opposes its own absolute counter-rule. Such metaphysical ways of seeing the world are due to ressentiment as well as to guilt. They can extend into everyday life, such as in the form of Political Correctness (PC). PC believes in a linguistic truth supposed to be "out there" as a permanent and ahistorical language. It is a language that cannot and should not be subjected to play, irony, and contingency. As a result, PC creates a reformed language that is intended to be ever closer to this supposed absolute.

Nietzsche's relativism is representative of a mindset that has interiorized the tragic sense of the world and refuses to make statements about absolute truths. The result is neither relativism nor a simplistic drama of conspiracies but rather an ironic kind of tragedy. The conspiratorial mindset does the opposite. Instead of attempting to gain a Dionysian insight into life's tragic reality and to live their lives accordingly, it prefers to escape from reality altogether by using some "scientific" theory. Like kitsch, unjustified conspiracy theories do not falsify reality but alter it. As mentioned, they do not produce lies but rather what Frankfurt calls "bullshit." Therefore, the conspiratorial mindset is not simply delusional: adherents to movements such as QAnon are most likely not the products of psychosis or serious mental illness (apart from depression or narcissism, occasionally). It is not that these people join alternative realities because they find them convincing; it is rather the fear that one could have been the victim of delusions, or that one has once again been cheated in life, that pushes them to take the leap into the conspiracy world. We can say that these worlds are "aesthetically" attractive to them. Ressentiment makes them accept a reality that is not plausible at all, but which they prefer to believe in.

Still, as I mentioned in Chapter 1, we should take the word "theory" seriously. From a Nietzschean perspective, the conspiratorial mindset is rational in a manner similar to Socrates and dialecticians. Socrates did not acknowledge the tragic sense of the world either. Socratic thought is very much against contingency, ambiguity, variety, and irony, and in this, it comes close to positivism. The conspiratorial mindset represents a fake positivism because it declares a holy war against everything that is nuanced, contingent, and tragic (though it is not as concerned with facts as real positivists are). For these reasons, the conspiratorial mindset can be likened to kitsch. Steinvorth sees kitsch as "an alternative to the tragic worldview [that] can connect to a metaphysics held by both the Enlightenment and Christianity. [...] In the end, this world is the best of all possible ones" (Steinvorth 2016: 208). For the conspiratorial mindset, the world it lives in is the worst of all possible worlds, which, in this context, does not make a difference. Sometimes it might hold an ideal image of what the best of all worlds should look like, but even then, there is, for this mindset, no mediating power between the best and the worst world. One such mediating power could be coincidence. Another one could be irony. For the conspiratorial mindset, there is only the eternal drama of them (the good ones) losing out against the bad ones. Its adherents explain this drama with the help of a theory but never recognize the situation as tragic. The dramatic state of the world is a plot invented by the Jews, the Americans, George Soros, or the Freemasons. Tragic nihilism would counter that whatever happened is not a conspiracy but just the way life is; and in this life, we must all assume our responsibility. Even Oedipus was responsible for what he did, which is highly ironic. The purpose of unwarranted conspiracy theories is always to shift the responsibility onto others. Nietzsche called this attitude "slave morality," which is to limit responsibility as much as possible and to reject all sense of guilt for the acts of others. If one thinks that other people have evil designs, one will naturally refuse responsibility not only for one's own acts but also for theirs.

All this confirms that the conspiratorial mindset is inscribed in the logic of Western metaphysics that had very early turned against contingency. Nietzsche attempted to relativize this way of thinking through tragic ironism. On the other side of the spectrum, dramatic relativism (or what Bloom called the "Nietzscheanized left") deconstructs an entire metaphysical heritage and attempts to minimize suffering through a simple escape from reality. This can easily end up as victimism, which is another path chosen by those who are submitted to slave morality. Both dramatic attitudes, the relativist and the conspiratorial mindset, are very much due to this kind of ressentiment, and both can lead to kitsch.

Chapter 6

CONTINGENCY THROUGH THE AGES: DETERMINATION AND MYSTIFICATION

Both science and conspiracy theories look for necessities in a world where a necessary order that had once been guaranteed by religion has largely disappeared, and where life and the entire world can easily appear as contingent. Warranted conspiracy theories find such necessities; unwarranted ones don't, but they *believe* that they have found them. When viewed through the optics of these "contingency versus necessity" relationships, the conspiratorial mindset turns out to be inscribed not only in a Western metaphysical tradition but in an even broader civilizational development.

Contingency has been on the minds of thinkers throughout the ages, but within various phases of Western civilization, its position has changed multiple times. In Antiquity, historians would attribute unexpected events to the goddess Fortuna (Tyche) or to divine Providence and thus turn the coincidence into a necessity by tracing it to a pseudo-cause (see the Greek historian Polybius [in Polybius: 29]).[1] When no pertinent cause could be found for events such as floods or droughts, such fortuities could be connected to Tyche or divine providence, which became very important in late antiquity. This technique could even be used for events in politics. Dylan Burns shows in his *Did God Care? Providence, Dualism, and Will in Later Greek and Early Christian Philosophy* how in the first centuries CE, Hellenic and Christian philosophers elaborated notions about providence, divine care, and fate that would shape the European mindset. Today such devices are less available, and as a result, conspiracy theorists invent new pseudo-causes. This chapter will provide a rough historical sketch of how contingency has been dealt with by thinkers throughout history.

---

1 Nassim Taleb suggests that "before the spread of what can be best called Mediterranean monotheism, the ancients did not believe enough in their prayers to influence the course of destiny" (Taleb 2001: 227).

Antiquity

In Antiquity, almost everything was perceived to be necessary, and, compared with today, contingency could not cause existential problems for the Greek or Roman individual.[2] It is true that the ancient world *did* have unwarranted conspiracy theories, for example, about "bad" emperors such as Nero, malevolent Christians, immigrants, or slaves. The existence of secret societies in Athens already spurred some conspiratorial thinking. Greek plays tell us much about conspiracies "that involve almost every facet of Athenian life." According to Daniel Pipes, a conspiracy mentality can "be traced back to the dualist religions of Iran or the mystery religions that swept the Roman Empire" (1997: 53). Secret societies were often built around mystery cults such as the cult of Demeter and Persephone at Eleusis (the Eleusinian Cult), the cult of the Great Gods at Samothrace, and the cult of Isis. They were part of the religious traditions of the Greek and Roman world. Victoria Emma Pagán (2004) wrote an entire book on conspiracy narratives in ancient Rome. "There are plots against people's lives, property, careers, or reputations, as well as against the public interest, the regime, and in foreign affairs" (Brotherton 2015: 24). Some of these plots were real, some were exaggerated and can be considered undue conspiracy theories, others warranted. Political intrigues, such as Roman senator Catalina's plan to take over Rome in the year 63, were real. However, all these conspiratorial explanations remained relatively local and personal and, when unwarranted, rarely involved superhuman or global powers; second, plots rarely adopted cosmological, theological, or existential dimensions. The explanations of events remained relatively simple tales or speeches told by orators and were rarely shaped into metaphysical or complex pseudo-scientific theories. In this sense, they were different from our contemporary conspiracy theories, especially the unwarranted ones. Much later, in the middle of the eighteenth century, a dramatic shift happened "from theories about local and petty conspiracies of self-interest, to altogether grander theories. Then the proposed plots became more mysterious, subversive, and universal" (Brotherton 2015: 22).

The Greeks had little ambition to explain single and contingent events with the help of homemade all-embracing theories. One reason is that the Greeks still had a sense of an overarching necessity in cosmological terms, and, at least as far as some Pre-Socratics and later Stoics are concerned, also

---

[2] It is also the working hypothesis of the German research group "Poetics and Hermeneutics," which published a monumental volume on contingency in 1998 (see Marquard et al. 1998, xi–xvi). It has been criticized by Ingolf Dalferth and Philipp Stoelliger (2000, Introduction).

in ethical terms. The Greeks also had complex ways of handling the coincidence-necessity problem in general. As mentioned in Chapter 3, Aristotle talks of the *endechomenon* as that which is "neither necessary nor impossible" (*On Interpretation,* 25a37–41, 29b29–32, 32a18–29, 33b17, 22–23), which thus corresponds to the idea of the contingent as opposed to the necessary as "that which cannot possibly be otherwise" (*Metaphysics,* V5 1015a33–6). For Aristotle it is clear that not everything is or comes into being out of necessity, and that some things are contingent (*On Int.* 19a17), and he is therefore opposed to any deterministic denial of contingency, such as the kind that he could encounter in Democritus's philosophy of nature. While the coincidence does not happen necessarily, it is not simply due to a hypothetical possibility either. It is rather due to chance or luck and thus, for Aristotle, "it is manifest that chance or luck is something" (*Physics* B 196 b15). In Book 5 of the *Metaphysics,* Aristotle insists that *tyche* and *automaton* are "something." Being "something" means that the coincidence is a feature of our life world that can determine our actions and even our thinking and our concepts. Still, the coincidence cannot be a reasonable basis for our actions. In the *Physics,* Aristotle maintains that effects caused by coincidences are neither good nor bad because there is no intention behind them (198b21–23).

Since contingency exists, Aristotle decides to integrate it into his ontology. Within the Aristotelian ontological framework, all beings are composed of essence and existence, which means that contingency can be an expression of the "contingency of being." "Being" is never completely "what it is" (essence, quiddity, identity), as "being" also stands for the diversity of things, that is, for existence. *Kata symbebekos* is related to the accidental properties of a being or a thing that are distinct from its essence. Aristotle's ontology is thus an ontology of contingency: the aggregative totality called "the world" is composed of both necessary essences and contingent beings, that is, of beings with contingent properties or manifestations. Again, this supports the claim that contingency is real. Contingency is ethically and anthropologically irrelevant but ontologically relevant.

While the world's diverse elements can be contingent, the existence of the universe is not linked to contingency. There is no cosmological contingency in Plato or Aristotle. Plato's cosmology is clearly finalistic and suggests a world order shaped in an ideal fashion. Platonic myths speak of the world as imbued with principles of wisdom, which is why its contemplation can lead to wisdom too, and why, finally, physics is seen as a part of philosophy. The world can overlap with philosophical aspirations, but only as long as our cosmology is finalistic. In an open-ended world, philosophy would logically and continuously lag behind the world's newest developments.

In *The Laws* (Book X), Plato clarifies the distinction between his own philosophy and that of Pre-Socratics, hylozoists, or natural philosophers, and explains that for the latter, the amalgamation of natural elements (fire, water, earth, air) is due to coincidences or luck (*tyche*) without any intervention from intelligence (*nous*) or God (889c, 5–6). For Plato, it is always the soul that guides, through the intervention of a "divine intellect" (*nous theios*), eventually leading all things to the best possible outcome (897b, 2–3). The divine demiurge in the *Timaeus* supports this idea.

Except for the natural philosophers, in Greek eyes, the order of the universe was not something that had emerged, because if it had, this would mean that contingency could have been involved. The universe must have always existed as an eternal and unchangeable being.[3] The view comes close to the Chinese idea of heaven (*tian*) as *natura naturans* or "nature naturing" (see Moeller 2006: 44). Ten thousand processes and events (*wan wu*) are not the creations of a *tian* but are simply constitutive of it. However, there is a difference with the Chinese system because *tian* is still an emergent order that is constantly negotiated, whereas for the Greeks, the stars move about regularly on fixed tracks in a spherical universe, and natural processes on earth are regular and fixed accordingly. The state of the universe is eternal and not linked to the contingency of time. The harmonious whole of nature contains an inner reason; this reason leaves—sometimes—place for chance, but it cannot be canceled by chance. Even atomistic philosophers like Democritus, Epicurus, or Lucretius, who denied holistic perspectives of the universe or any association of the world with non-material divinity, did not see the universe as entirely contingent. Even an anti-determinist philosopher like Epicurus perceived contingency to remain within the bounds of a necessary universe. As a matter of fact, even though atomistic philosophers did not accept a holistic perspective, just like Aristotle, they applied a complex positioning to contingency. For Democritus, the cosmos is moved by chance (*to automaton*) (see Aristotle *Phys.* II, 4, 196a, 24–26), but this primarily only means that it is not guided by a god. "Being moved by chance" did not mean that necessity was excluded. Democritus denied any divine determination but still believed in deterministic laws that governed the behavior of atoms. Democritus is a determinist for whom all events in the world are connected through an eternal deterministic causal chain. Nature always acts necessarily; however, paradoxically, this just means that it acts blindly. Precisely *because* nature is a necessity in and of itself, it contains no divine reason. In this

---

3 The Timaeus suggests a more complex constellation: While Being is unchanged and eternal, the cosmos is a by-product in time and becoming.

sense, for materialists, the world results from random (*mátin*) and "blind" collusions of atoms; but the collusions do still follow *necessary* laws of physics. For Democritus's teacher Leucippus, "Nothing occurs at random, but everything for a reason and by necessity" (Fragment 2).

Two centuries after Democritus, Epicurus adds a supplementary element of chance to this materialist philosophy and moves human control and responsibility to the center of materialist philosophy. However, this step can also be seen as an *overcoming* of contingency because it abandons any idea of submission to an arbitrary fate determined by the gods or the laws of nature. Until then, from a materialist perspective, nature could submit us to loops of eternal returns upon which we had no influence. The Stoics had a theory of eternal recurrence. These laws upon which we have no influence are as "arbitrary" as divine laws. Epicurus's philosophy is thus erected in opposition to any metaphysics of providence. Epicurus wants to be rational, and if coincidence exists, then this must be accepted as the most rational explanation for the existence of the world, even though better explanations might be found later. Accordingly, he argues that atoms "swerve" from their otherwise determined paths, thus initiating new causal chains whenever such a swerve takes place. Epicurus wants to break the causal chain of determinism and deny all claims that the future must follow logical necessities. This is a theory of indeterministic freedom. For Democritus, nature was still determined, and coincidence did not really exist except as a matter of subjective perception. In contrast, Epicurus sees coincidence as an objective fact and integrates it into nature. Karl Marx wrote his doctoral thesis about "The Difference between Epicurus' and Democritus' Philosophy of Nature" (1841) and endorsed Epicurus's view.

Lucretius, who lived ca. 250 years after Epicurus, gave the name clinamen to the unpredictable swerving of atoms through which the contingent character of the future comes into being. From a materialist point of view, the future is thus produced by coincidence, and nature cannot create anything without the clinamen (Lucretius II: 224). Atoms can deviate at any moment, and nothing predetermines their deviation. New constellations of atoms are not eternal and will cede their place to even newer constellations. There is an infinity of orders that arise one after another. The creativity of nature is due to this unpredictability which avoids repetition. The clinamen introduces coincidence into nature but does not create chaos. The coincidence transcends preconceived orders and provides freedom and creativity, but it does not create despair and anxiety. It rather signifies a capacity to create new constellations within a larger world order that remains basically unchanged. The idea of unity is never entirely abandoned: there is no divine plan, but there still is unity. In other words, *in its contingency*, the world remains necessary, eternal, and unified.

According to François Jullien, the clinamen "de-coincides" an order where otherwise everything would "coincide" according to legitimate norms (see Jullien 2017: 47). It creates a hiatus, that is, a break in continuity or a break in a sequence of acts, but this paradoxically means that the coincidence is the moment in which things do *not* coincide. Science, philosophy, or human thought in general, have always had difficulties grasping this "de-coincidencing" faculty of nature. An obsession with necessity wants things to coincide, that is, paradoxically, to admit no coincidence. Of course, this obsession increases once the overarching order is canceled.

The Stoics, though entirely opposed to the Epicurean randomness of nature, held that "all that is not up to us" (e.g., coincidence) should be neglected, at least in ethical terms. One best controls one's life not by fighting contingency but by *accepting* it. Accepting randomness means victory over randomness. For the Stoics, as for Aristotle, contingent events are irrelevant to human happiness. The difference between the Stoics and Aristotle is that Aristotelian morality invites us to develop our excellence within this world, which is determined by contingency and necessity, whereas the Stoics invite us to escape everything that is idle and to look for an eternity beyond time in which contingency does not matter. They live according to a natural order. In all of Greek thought, the strategy of neglecting coincidence instead of frantically trying to replace it with necessities was only possible because there was a strong belief in an overarching necessity, which assured the Greek individual that, in the end, nothing is really random.

It has been shown that the Greek world created a complex interlinking of coincidences and necessities. The resulting mindset seemed to be little inclined to search for new necessities in the form of scientifically or metaphysically backed conspiracies. The encounter with the contingent was an encounter with what "just happens." It could not be influenced, but it could also be relatively conveniently neglected as it did not perturb the order of the universe.

The Middle Ages

We do not find a real equivalent for the modern baseless conspiracy theory in the Christian Middle Ages either. Like in Antiquity, conspiratorial thinking existed, but it would rarely appear in the form of the angst-ridden mania typical of later époques. There were many heretic movements, sometimes contagious like epidemics, and talks about them could function like conspiracy theories, often unwarranted, but they had relatively short lifespans (see

Borst 1965: 173). One reason for the short lifespan is that populist theories about conspiracies would rarely be linked to absolute evil. They couldn't, as only the church could issue theories about evil. Official theories issued by the church could have some conspiratorial dimensions, but in general, they would look more like policies or ideologies.

Philosophically, the Middle Ages widely accepted the Aristotelian framework. God's creations were necessary. Contingency could spark little anger on the ethical-anthropological level because it was possible, at any moment, to turn away from the contingent world and to affirm the necessity of a world created by God. This scheme can be understood as representing the inverse formula of our contemporary conspiratorial mindset. The latter sees the coincidence as a product of hidden powers too, but, unlike the medieval Satan, these powers often remain quasi-impossible to identify. They might be named, but, as has been shown, identifications tend to be evasive. For medieval people, Satan was intangible but still conceivable as a distinct entity. And just like Descartes's evil demon, he was, at least theologically speaking, so powerful that he did not need conspirators and could simply *do* evil. In contrast, the modern conspiratorial mindset typically presents conspirators as diffuse groups or as individuals who need to team up with others in order to gain power. Concluding a pact with the devil has sometimes been an option, but it has become atypical in modern times.

During the Middle Ages, following the increasingly clearer oppositions between God and Satan, the realms of the necessary and the contingent became very clearly separated. Already in the fourth century, Saint Augustine had drawn up a two-kingdom plan in which *Civitas Dei* and *Civitas Diaboli* were not only believed to exist but in which they were laid out as decidedly distinct. To the salvation plan of God was opposed the destruction plan of the Devil who lived in the underworld. As a result, once negative events had been ascribed to Satan, their contingent character would no longer matter as these events simply became necessities. Beyond that, religious authorities could always be counted on to extinguish evil necessities by punishing the supposed perpetrators, as it happened with the persecution of witches, heretics, Jews, and other outsiders. The church was supposed to be stronger and capable of replacing satanic necessities with divine necessities; but it did not combat contingencies.

Sometimes the coincidence could be attributed to God's will to punish, and when no obvious reason for this punishment was available, one could still affirm that God's ways are unknown. In any case, whenever a coincidence produced disasters, religion could provide consolation. Modern science, at the peak of determinism, would later adopt a similar scheme by suggesting that nature does things in its own way, and that whatever from a human perspective appears to be a coincidence is, in fact, determined by laws of nature that we cannot understand.

It is true that in the Middle Ages, the church could officially replace intangible demons with concrete persons or populations. However, even this created, in this particular given theological context, a politics of accusation rather than popular indefensible conspiracy theories. Also, the resentment should not be overestimated. The Christians' resentment about the Jews' killing of Jesus did not lead to an intense resentment culture because, according to Pipes, the official resentment against Jews was not permanent: "As the Church gained in confidence, attacks on Jews faded" (1997: 53). While stories woven around evil elements could sometimes indeed have conspiratorial tones, they would rarely spark popular *theories* about conspiracies. Around 1100, secret societies had been founded in the context of the Crusades, the most famous of which was the enigmatic Catholic military order of the Templars headquartered in Jerusalem. This inspired, like all secret orders, a decent amount of conspiratorial thinking, warranted and unwarranted. However, one has to wait until modern times for secret societies to proliferate and more complex myths to be spun around them.

Beliefs in witches should not be seen as conspiracy theories either. The original belief in witches was a superstition, and religions normally had remedies against such evils, such as prayers and offerings. As will be shown below, superstitions are different from unwarranted conspiracy theories because they have historical roots and are not artificially produced, that is, merely invented. Governments are usually suspicious of superstitions, but they can produce their own unwarranted conspiracy theories. At some point, the church and the state took advantage of existing superstitions and organized persecutions that were in their own political interest. Those who organized the persecutions were not psychotic. There was both a popular and high cultural belief in the real existence of evil, and the resulting collective delusions that this belief enabled followed relatively simple metaphysical patterns based on certitude. However, normally (though exceptions existed, as will be shown below), such beliefs would not excessively proliferate but remain contained within well-structured religious ideologies. The beliefs were used by authorities who had a rationally determined political agenda.

The pioneer of modern centralized state theories, the philosopher Jean Bodin (1530–1596), concentrated in his work entitled *De la Démonomanie des sorciers*, on the fact that witches can be dangerous for sovereign powers. On the popular level, there were superstitions, but the real *resentment* was on the side of the state and the church. The same can be said about medieval accusations against Jews and lepers. When France was hit by the Black Death in 1348, Jews and lepers were singled out as causes of events because they could not be explained otherwise. Here too, politics played a role as lepers were envied for the support they received from Christian almonries. Jews were equally envied. Philipp le Bel, plagued by financial troubles, persecuted the lepers in southern France, holding that they were planning a world conspiracy helped by Arab Princes and Jews. They supposedly wanted to nominate a king from their circle. Philipp's interests were clearly monetary (see Brachfeld 1965: 113). From the eleventh century onward, theories about conspiracies organized by heretics emerged. Some of these theories were Catholic fantasies about the machinations of the devil, but many had some ground in reality. In general, heretics were not atheists but former clerics. Like regular clerics, heretics worked for the establishment of a utopia, which was the materialization of the gospel. There was thus a competitive aspect with the church, which is, again, rationally motivated (see Borst 1965: 175).

If there was a collective delusion, it was very much bureaucratized, as Wanda von Baeyer-Katte points out in her article on the historical witch trials. Popular excitement was rarely spontaneous; there were "no awkward outbursts of superstitions, no eruptive reactions against outsiders or psychologically suspect persons under the pretext of witchcraft" (Baeyer-Katte 1965: 220). Especially in a new political context, in a world in which the modern state was supposed to be consolidated, it became the task of the state to eradicate witchcraft.[4] Again, the anti-witch movement was a political project.

Miracle workers and charlatans could offer fancy explanations for random events, but the church and the state always had enough authority to contradict such beliefs. The existing superstitions rarely gained the dimensions of what would later be identified as mass psychosis. Doctrines about the existence of witches and their extermination were pronounced by authorities and were closer to rationally dictated policies that aimed to consolidate power. Witches were folk culture, and the church would use this folk culture for its own purposes by reinforcing existing phantasmata and by inducing social effects such as fear and aggression. These theories about conspiracies were ideologies rather than conspiracy theories. Witches were evil, but there was little *popular* ressentiment—in the modern sense—against witches. It would be wrong to talk about a "witch conspiracy" as witch hunts are due to a mixture of superstitions and official policies, and our modern unwarranted conspiracy theories are normally neither. Also important for many gratuitous conspiracy theories is the infiltration pattern. The fact that witches were women disabled all suspicions that they could infiltrate governments and institutions. In

---

4 Feudal lords would take over the entire jurisdiction, a task by which they turned out to be overwhelmed in many respects, as Baeyer-Katte shows.

the case of witches, the would-be "conspirators" were simply too visible and clearly identifiable as individuals; they were not diffuse groups. The witch hunt of the Middle Ages and the Early Modern period is too descriptive to be classified as a body of unwarranted conspiracy theories. Public perception of witches was more akin to that of criminals or perhaps terrorists that need to be eradicated by enforcing efficient policies.

It is worth noting that things went out of hand when the church once attempted to attribute a great evil to God. This sparked a genuine conspiracy theory. In the fourteenth century, Pope Clement VI declared the Pestilence an act of God. As this was not accepted by the people at large, counter-ideologies developed, and the people declared Jews to be the source of the pestilence.

At a cosmological level, contingency had weakened the concept of the universe as a necessary production. As a result, cosmological considerations needed to be linked to theological ones. On the one hand, it was reassuring that the church could tackle this problem. On the other hand, much of what the church decided would have no dramatic consequences for individuals anyway because, in medieval Europe, cosmo-theological debates had become very abstract. For example, theologians declared that the universe could also "not be" because God must have had the power *not* to create the world. Otherwise, God himself would be submitted to necessity, which was not acceptable. God is free to act contingently, but his will, once it is enacted, will create necessity for humans. The universe was no longer seen as self-sufficient, uncreated, and eternal and was instead due to a contingency; however, since this contingency was divine, mortal humans would simply experience it as necessity. *Contingentia* expresses the ontological constitution of the world that is created out of nothing, though it still remains firmly sustained by divine will. If God wills, the universe would be contingent to vanishing at any moment. The Greeks had coped with coincidence by elevating Fortuna to the status of a goddess and by creating cults around her, hoping to diminish arbitrariness. Christian authorities found other solutions. Augustine questioned the Greek reasoning that first conceives of Fortuna as the embodiment of arbitrariness and then subsequently tries to influence her through cultish worship (see Doren 1924: 81). From Augustine's point of view, Fortuna was irrational and, above that, contradicted the Christian idea of divine providence. For Christians, Fortuna could not serve as a basis for life or the world because she was unstable and random. Still, eventually, the church fathers' approach was not much different from that of the Greeks: they transferred contingency from an irrational Fortuna to a "rational" monotheistic God, which means that God was not *submitted to* contingency but *was* contingency. Whatever God wants, humans have to accept as necessity. Contingent events are due to providence, which is a sign of God's omnipotence. God had become Fortuna.

Fortuna reemerged most literally in religious terms in Boethius's *Consolatione Philosophiae* (AD 524), which attempted to fuse the arbitrariness of fortune with divine providence. Here, Fortuna was clearly said to work in the service of God. At the same time, contingency was no longer merely chance because once chance is God, chance is no longer blind. Contingency had become a function of God's action, his mercy, and his justice, which was again incompatible with the "blind" Greek concept of contingency. Central was now no longer the single coincidence but rather contingency as an all-encompassing concept (that could be seen as a necessity).

Augustine's theology was based on this concept of God's inconceivability, concluding that God *can* only be conceived as contingency (see Augustine *De Civitate Dei*, V. 9). Later, Islamic philosophy distinguished between the necessary and the contingent, asking whether the contingent required a cause. If yes, this cause would have to be a necessary one and not a contingent one. In other words, contingent things must have a cause that is not contingent. Ibn Sina (Avicenna, 980–1037) argues in this sense that there must be a "necessary existent," that is, an entity that cannot not exist (see Adamson 2013: 170).[5] In Latin translations, beginning in the twelfth century, Avicenna's philosophy influenced Christian Medieval and Renaissance philosophers. At about the same time, William of Ockham (1285–1347) attempted to reconcile divine omniscience with the contingency of future propositions. Though the idea of the contingent being due to a necessary source remains a logical contradiction, the argument would become very influential as an explanation of God's existence. Centuries later, Leibniz's idea of "future contingents," expressed in his *Theodicy*, would still tackle the same problem. Agamben summarizes Leibniz's problem of "future contingents" thus: "Let us suppose that someone says that tomorrow there will or will not be a battle at sea. If the battle occurs tomorrow, then it was already true the day before it would take place, which means that it could not not take place" (Agamben 1999: 263/Ital 1993: 77–78). Once again, contingency is replaced with necessity.

However sophisticated these very abstract concepts of contingency were, they would not much affect people's everyday lives, probably just because of their abstract complexity. The modern conspiratorial mindset would later adopt a very similar model, no longer focusing on single conspiracies but attempting to define large conspiratorial systems. God is here replaced with

---

5 Later, Al-Ghazali (1056–1111) declared that to assume that "some things *originate* from others is unqualified ignorance, and [that] the same holds for expressions like 'generate' or others like them, for all of them must be aligned with the intention expressed by the divine decree" (Ghazali 2011: 37).

evil, but the reasoning remains similar. Hofstadter observed that "the distinguishing thing about the paranoid style is not that its exponents see conspiracies or plots here and there in history, but that they regard a 'vast' or 'gigantic' conspiracy as *the motive force* in historical events. History *is* a conspiracy, set in motion by demonic forces of almost transcendent power" (2012: 29). History *is* a conspiracy, just like for medieval theologians' history was *contingentia* that had become a necessity.

In medieval philosophy, contingency and facticity were always understood as theological notions. The origin of the world was believed to be "contingent," which meant that it was due to divine power; and *because* it was contingent, it could not be grasped and remained mystical. Both the conspiratorial mindset and pseudosciences rationalize this mystical capacity of contingency by reducing it to mere coincidence and randomness. Next, they replace it with imaginary necessities that are mystical and cannot be grasped. In contrast, contingency, as it was understood in medieval Europe, did not suggest that the world was random but one rather attempted to design an organic view of the universe *through* contingency: while single events could be seen as random, the totality of events was held together by a divine necessity. While, in principle, this does not deviate from the general Greek worldview, in our modern understanding of contingency, the term's spiritual content is lost. In earlier époques, the idea of divine contingency indirectly always suggested necessity, and it is this paradoxical overlapping of contingency and necessity that could give a "soul" to the world. By "soul" one did not necessarily mean a divine order: a world that has a soul would rather be what we would today call a "life world" valued in terms of psychology and habitability, or which simply is a meaningful place to live in. As a necessary-contingent place, the world has a soul, whereas a world in which everything is purely necessary is just as soulless and meaningless as a world in which everything is random. For all these reasons, medieval contingency did not cause anger and ressentiment and was not perceived as a threat that one had to cope with. The conspiratorial mindset does not attribute a soul to the world; it rather attributes to it an evil conspiring spirit, or a conspiring group that can be found at the root of everything. Here it is necessity—which is created in opposition to an equally unsettling contingency—that creates anxiety.

If the medieval person suffered from contingency, then certainly in a way that was very different from how, in the twenty-first century, the conspiratorial mindset suffers from contingency. Christians could attribute contingency to God. In the end, the medieval Christian had to accept the finite world as (divinely) contingent. If it was bad, she could escape from it only through salvation, that is, through a transfer into another world. Strictly speaking, in this situation, conspiratorial ideation was useless: as long as they were alive, the medieval man or woman simply had to accept the world created through God's contingency as a necessity.

Apart from that, the theme of contingency was only present in very abstract ontological and cosmological discussions and would rarely affect the ethical feelings of the general populace. Most probably, contingency left medieval people just as indifferent as it did ancient people. Contingency was either beyond good and evil or, if it was evil, it could conveniently be circumvented by embracing God. The only possible conspirator was Satan, and the ordinary citizen saw no need to invent complex theories about his machinations.

Today, the idea of a contingent god whose deeds must be seen as necessary is reflected in science. As mentioned in Chapter 4, while natural processes are contingent and follow necessary laws, it is impossible to say why *these particular* laws are necessary and not others. Science has no answer to these questions; it can only spell out the necessary laws. In other words, for science, contingency *is* necessity, just as in the Middle Ages, a contingent God *was* necessity. Despite newer developments in quantum physics and chaos theory, in general, science has not really moved beyond Democritus, who replaced divine necessity with natural necessity.

Modernity

The late Middle Ages and the early Modern Era in Europe witnessed important crises due to religious, social, and economic changes. The Black Death, overpopulation, and religious wars had destabilized many valid worldviews. Initially, incomprehensible phenomena could be relatively easily replaced with "comprehensible" ones by attributing them to Satan or to the intentions of certain outsiders such as Jews or witches. In medieval Europe, there was still a predominant belief in providence; only when this belief waned would humans assume new responsibilities. "The Middle Ages came to an end when, within their spiritual system, creation as 'providence' ceased to be credible to man and the burden of self-assertion was laid upon himself," writes Hans Blumenberg (1985: 138).

Linked to providence was the belief in a stable cosmos and the vision of a centralized universe whose micro and macro aspects were entirely controlled by God. At the end of the Middle Ages, this belief would be lost in parallel with the belief in providence, which indicates a strong shift from the necessary to the contingent. This shift happened gradually. Major crises of belief, first sparked by Copernicus, then later, in the seventeenth century by Galileo, let humans lose their central place in the world (see Koyré 1962: 10). After Galileo, there still was "God" or an "Absolute Being" that could function as a center and guarantee a necessary order, but this center was no longer physical-concrete and only metaphysical-abstract, that is, less strongly related to real life. Newton's worldview and the work of modern science would make any centralized universe appear as an idealistic illusion. Basically, Newton shows that the world as a calculable object of science has a mathematical center but no "real" center. "Newton split our world in two [by] substituting our world of quality [...] in which we live, and love, and die, with another world in which there is no place for man," comments Koyré (1968: 23–24). The universe had become a mathematically computable entity, which meant that the concrete human life world no longer seemed to be part of it. Gone were the days when Christian thinkers could explain the universe through biblical cosmology in which "God placed the Heavens 'above' and fashioned humanity from the elements that rested 'below'" (Sauter 2019: 29). Space, even if it still contained God, was an idealized and—most importantly— open-ended system. At the same time, the world and the cosmos appeared more necessary than ever as Newton's thinking was mechanical and deterministic: everything was determined by natural laws, which left practically no room for contingency. This is precisely the conception of modern science: the universe follows necessary rules, even though the existence of the universe itself cannot be traced to necessity.[6]

All this contributed to the fact that in the eighteenth century, the style of conspiratorial ideation would change. The baseless theories that we find today are modern phenomena whose characteristics developed in parallel with the Enlightenment. Furthermore, the change came with the generalization of education. The early eighteenth-century peasants did not yet have a sufficient number of elements to construct a complex theory that was appealing, nor were they likely to have the abstract thinking skills to combine these elements in an attractive fashion. They had superstitions and folk cultures but not the literacy to create a modern conspiracy theory. With schools and, later, modern media and the internet, masses of people could hone their "conspiracy skills."

In the Middle Ages, accusations of scapegoats such as outsiders, Freemasons, and Jews abounded, but the outstanding period for unwarranted conspiracy theories in Europe (as well as in the United States of America) begins around 1750, that is, with the Enlightenment. There was the "famine plot" (pacte de famine) and the theory that the French King and the aristocratic "elite" had conspired to raise the price of bread (the Flour War), which contributed to emerging revolutionary activities. Early globalization

---

6 See Botz-Bornstein 2015b: 88–89 where the points made in the above paragraphs are explained.

played a role too. The proliferation of international banking cartels and secret societies inspired a new, broader, and more complex kind of conspiratorial thinking. Theories, some warranted, most unwarranted, emerged. First, banking cartels and secret societies would be linked to Jews. After the French Revolution, the culpability would be shifted onto Freemasons and Jacobins (Freemasons and Jacobins were often believed to have mutual interests). In France, the intellectuals, that is, the *philosophes* who prepared the Revolution in philosophical terms, would be considered part of the conspiracist horde and linked to Freemasons and Jacobins. Obviously, the *philosophes* had indeed conspired against the monarchy, which put them on par with Freemasons and Illuminati (see Bieberstein 1976). Finally, it was possible to see the entire Enlightenment movement as a conspiracy. Philosophers and Illuminati were key figures of such theories, which initiated a pattern that would later be expanded until it reached the specter of a socialist world conspiracy, a specter that would remain popular until the 1960s.

All this went hand in hand with a spirito-political crisis that was equally spurred by the revolutions. So far, Europe had been dominated by a firm awareness that the king, emperor, and a metaphysical God would forever govern peoples' destinies. However big the occurring confusions and misfortunes, they could not affect the symbolic reality of the "God and Emperor" duality. The French Revolution played a significant role in the shattering of this belief. Although the resulting confusion turned out to only be temporary because a new emperor would soon crown himself in front of the pope in Rome, the ideology behind it continued to spread, influencing numerous later revolutions such as the German Revolution of 1848.

In any case, 1789 is the starting point of the unequaled proliferation of modern conspiracism. To the common observer, the French Revolution was simply too important and too unexpected to be attributed to "normal" causes. We have many examples of unwarranted conspiracy theories. In 1797, the Jesuit priest Augustin De Barruel published his *Memoirs Illustrating the History of Jacobinism,* whose first volume was subtitled "The Antichristian Conspiracy," and for the whole nineteenth century, Abbé Barruel's book became the manual for everything concerning myths of secret societies. In a style bursting with enthusiasm and agitation, Barruel explains in his *Memoirs'* preface:

> Strong in the facts, and armed with the proofs shown in the following Memoirs, [...] we shall demonstrate that, even to the most horrid deeds perpetrated during the French Revolution, everything was foreseen and resolved on, was combined and premeditated: that they were the offspring of deep-thought villainy, since they had been prepared and were produced by men, who alone held the clue of those plots

and conspiracies, lurking in the secret meetings where they had been conceived, and only watching the favorable moment of bursting forth. (Barruel 1799: xii)

Explaining historical and political events was no longer, as it had still been in the Middle Ages, the sole job of political or religious authorities; now, educated common people could create relatively complex theories about politics and history too. In the Middle Ages, the authorities had created numerous absurd "theories." However, in pre-Enlightenment times, authorities could control not only the flow of knowledge but also, to a considerable extent, the gullibility of the population. Now, the new Enlightenment culture pumped vast amounts of knowledge into various strata of its societies and also allowed autonomous thinking. This had many positive effects, but a side effect was that popular "stupidity" could develop its own dynamic, often generously fed by badly digested facts or by what would today be called fake news. A hundred years before Barruel, Locke had written in his *An Essay Concerning Human Understanding* that "we should make greater progress in the discovery of rational and contemplative knowledge, if we [...] made use rather of our own thoughts than other men's to find it" (Locke: 84). Locke encouraged autonomous reasoning but also, unknowingly, the kind of theorizing unreason that would later invent pseudo-scientific theories.

In the nineteenth century, the boom in indefensible conspiracy theories is, to a considerable extent, due to yet another Enlightenment effect, which is the split of society into two groups: the secularists and the remaining religious people, each accusing the other of conspiracies. A famous secularist subgroup are the Freemasons who were almost constantly accused of fomenting anti-religious conspiracies. Later, another factor entered the conspiracy game, which was yet another inheritor of the French Revolution: terrorism. Terror acted against conspiracies, but it was often also based on conspiracies.

From the nineteenth century onward, technology had a considerable impact on the spread and character of unwarranted conspiracy theories. Advanced applied sciences began providing more signs, traces, and images, and allowed people to see things that had so far gone unnoticed. It also helped preserve signs that would otherwise have gotten lost. Soon, laboratories began working for the police. In parallel, new communication methods left behind more signs and traces, some obvious, some encoded, which required interpretation. This process continues to this day. Media provide an ever-increasing abundance of documentary images, which can enrich the imagination of conspiracy fantasies.

As mentioned in Chapter 2, Enlightenment thought had firmly believed that with the progress of science, superstitions and obscurantism would disappear. This belief was strongly linked to another conviction: as science progresses, *coincidences* will disappear, and the world will be explained in terms of necessity only, thus strongly reducing unfounded conspiracist speculation. The strongest supporter of this idea was the early nineteenth-century mathematician and determinist thinker Pierre Simon Laplace, who declared in his *A Philosophical Essay on Probabilities* that coincidences are illusions because it is an "illusion of the mind" to assume that things can determine themselves without motives (Laplace 1902: 2/French: 3).[7] Laplace joins the pre-Socratic Democritus, for whom coincidence was simply a euphemism for lack of knowledge. Like Democritus, Laplace moves away from the Aristotelian understanding of coincidence, which the Stagirite expressed in his *Physics*: contingent or accidental events such as *endechomenon, tyche, automaton*, and *symbebekos*, are not merely subjective perceptions without substance but *are* something, because they are *not* merely hypothetical or possible (*dynaton*). According to Laplace, making events dependent on coincidences is due to ignorance, and "a sound philosophy" ("la saine philosophie," 2/3) makes all coincidences disappear. Laplace mocks Epicurus's "blind coincidence" and predicts that in the future, superior education will illustrate the necessary reasons for everything. Failing to acknowledge necessary reasons is irrational, superstitious, and represents a pre-scientific way of seeing the world. It is like attributing events to wonders.

Nineteenth-century science also supported this conviction in the realm of cosmology. In astronomy, scientific knowledge was thought to make contingency disappear because all random events would be integrated into the necessity of an overarching cosmos. Laplace writes: "All events, even those that on account of their insignificance seem not to obey the great laws of nature, are as necessary a consequence of these laws as the revolutions of the sun. Ignorant of the bonds that link them to the entire system of the universe, we have made them depend on final causes, or on chance [...]" (2/2–3). For Laplace, finality or chance is a false dichotomy. It is the bonds "in between" elements that create a coherent system because they follow necessary rules.

It can appear that this science attempts to cosmologically restore the theological certitude that had been lost through the "decentralization" from the late Middle Ages onward. However, this philosophy of nature is not rational but merely rationalizing. In his *Exposition du système du monde* (1796), which concentrates on cosmological questions, Laplace links the regular course of planets to political order. Such thoughts, which appear mystical and astrological

---

7 The text, published in 1814, goes back to Laplace's lectures at the Ecole Polytechnique from 1795.

today, were relatively common among serious early nineteenth-century thinkers. The step into cosmological mysticism is not so unusual if one considers that Laplace's book was published only sixty-eight years after that of another rationalist thinker, Newton, who defended very similar views in his *De mundi systemate* (*The System of the World*, posthumously published). Cosmological rationalization was particularly common among thinkers with socialist tendencies. The socialist philosopher Charles Fourier, in his *Théorie de l'unité universelle* (1822), attempted to establish unity by linking heavenly harmony and social order, and Auguste Comte tried to transform the power of scientific laws into a spiritual power capable of guiding society (see Comte 1851–54). Similarly, the socialist philosopher Louis Auguste Blanqui, in his *Eternité par les astres* (1872), developed a theory of eternal return based on astronomical speculations.

Enlightenment rationalism did not kill all irrational thinking, because often Enlightenment thought was only rationalizing. The frantic "rational" search for necessity can lead to irrationality, which is also a recipe for conspiracy theories. It is not without reason that Blanqui had strong conspiratorial tendencies. According to Pipes, "Blanqui coined the phrase dictatorship of the proletariat and devoted his life to achieving it through conspiratorial means; toward this end, he wrote books, went to jail, fled to exile, and fought governments" (1997: 78).

Even today, the conspiratorial mindset likes to talk about the "order of the universe" that is controlled by evil powers. The link that Keeley sees between conspiracism and cosmological order has historical roots going back to the nineteenth century: "Conspiracy theorists are some of the last believers in an ordered universe. By supposing that current events are under the control of nefarious agents, conspiracy theories entail that such events are *capable of being controlled*" (58). Furthermore, the entire Enlightenment "world system" project can be understood as a step toward animism as it has been explained in Chapter 4: the universe is alive, it is not just a contingent accumulation of facts, and there is sense and meaning in everything.

For eighteenth-century determinists, it was the rejection of *necessity* that denoted ignorance. They perceived it as an attitude of the uneducated masses. Today, the pattern has been inverted: the prominent social problem linked to ignorance is the rejection of *coincidence*, which can lead to conspiracism. Surprisingly, and different from what was the case in the past, this paradigm of ignorance is not only common among popular masses but also among the elite. Computation, algorithms, and the preponderance of what Nassim Taleb calls "standardized minds" have become a real social problem. Standardized minds (whom Taleb depicts as serious-looking businesspersons in dark suits) are constantly "theorizing, explaining things, or talking about random events with plenty of 'because' in their conversation" (2007: 39). They are rationalizing just as nineteenth-century determinists were linking the course of the planets to political order or creating theories of eternal return. All this is only a few steps from unwarranted conspiratorial thinking. The scientific mentality that became visible for the first time in the works of nineteenth-century determinist thinkers, is today present in the works of "necessity seeking" individuals who are strongly drawn to bell curves and rankings. Taleb writes: "Before Western thinking drowned in its 'scientific' mentality, what is arrogantly called the Enlightenment, people prompted their brain to think—not compute" (129). The problem is that the "formal thinking" patterns that first migrated from the natural sciences into the economic sciences and then— regrettably—into all human sciences, are only interested in certitude and not in uncertainty or contingency. In economics, Taleb calls these thinking patterns "mind-closing models" that are delusional because they create an "imaginary world, one that lent itself to their mathematics" (283). The protagonists of standardized minds contribute to the late Enlightenment's perfect world model that was described in Chapter 2. This model meets strong opposition from those who find no place in this utopia; however, the latter are, just like their opponents, opposed to contingency. They subsequently invent their alternative anti-contingency theories.

Though Taleb is generally right, it is nevertheless misleading to accuse Platonic theorizing of all evils. The problem is not theory in itself but rather the fact that these theories are unwilling to consider contingency. Theory means speculation, which should be naturally inclined to integrate contingency. Practical thought, or what Taleb calls "down-up" thought, is not necessarily superior. It can be as prone to necessity obsessions as theoretical thought. Mind-closing formal thinking patterns should rather be contrasted with practical reason (*phronesis*). *Phronesis* would be a more useful method in economics, medical science, philosophy, and other realms of life, especially in education.

The Role of the Disease

Conspiracies (though not necessarily conspiracy *theories*) have mainly existed in the realm of politics. There have always been groups of individuals who conspired against a center of power. However, though exaggerations and mystifications could occur, this rarely led to the modern model of unwarranted conspiracy *theories*. The mass psychotic model of ungrounded conspiracy theories emerged with revolutions but even more clearly with the epidemics that befell nineteenth-century Europe. Bad urbanization fostered an ever more rapid spread of diseases. The factor that galvanized the growth in modern conspiratorial thinking was that, more than ever, disease was mixed with politics. The French Revolution had created panic in the upper echelons of power, and to link the spread of diseases to subversive elements had become a common *modus explanandi*: Do revolutionary ideas not spread like bacteria, exponentially contaminating entire populations? It is worth noting that bacteriology developed in the nineteenth century too. But even before, that is, right after the French Revolution, the mix of sanitary crises and political intrigues led to increasingly threatening theories that were mainly launched by conservative circles. The fact that many epidemics had been introduced from the outside helped to consolidate a conspiratorial mindset: leprosy had been brought in by Roman soldiers from Egypt, China, and India, and the Black Death came from China. Parallels between the rapid spread of diseases and the equally rapid spread of political ideas were taken seriously. Mass diseases and mass political movements emerged simultaneously and were soon confounded, which accelerated the production of rumors and phantasms. By the early twentieth century, diseases like cholera and typhus had been largely brought under control. One efficient measure was the construction of canalization systems in cities. Bacteria were now underground, and there, under the ground, was also the idea of the conspiracy. Conspiracies were relegated to the subconscious of citizens, where they fermented and became a part of modern culture.

Chapter 7

EVOLUTION, MERITOCRACY, AND FAKE SCIENCE

Back to Contingency

For Plato, human reason "sees" abstract ideas and concepts that are necessary, whereas concrete objects and appearances of objects, as long as their existence is not explained through reason, are contingent. Real is only what can be rationally explained. Laplace's determinism continued to build upon these convictions. But despite the popularity of this powerful paradigm, science and philosophy never entirely neglected the idea of contingency. On the contrary, it remained a relevant philosophical topic during a time span ranging from Aristotle to Descartes. As mentioned, Aristotle was opposed to any deterministic denial of contingency: coincidences were not just subjective perceptions but real. Aristotle even created an ontology of contingency in which an aggregative totality called "the world" was composed of both necessary essences and contingent beings. For centuries, contingency would be discussed along these lines, and most of the time, this happened in theological contexts. It is only after Descartes that contingency would disappear from major philosophical debates—though not because it had been scientifically solved, but, paradoxically, because science and philosophy had abolished divine determinism. Contingency was worth targeting only as long as it represented the opposite of providentialism. Once philosophy was de-theologized, the modern world was freed from contingency much as it would later be freed from God. For the historians of philosophy Graevenitz and Marquard (1998), the intellectual history of contingency is therefore a major philosophical episode that ends with Descartes. In the aftermath of this long episode, contingency could still be seen as an antidote against *scientific* determinism. However, compared to earlier theological projects, these new discussions remained relatively marginal. It would only be with the rise of Darwinism and other important scientific theories such as atomic theory in the nineteenth century (which put forward the coincidence) that discussions of contingency once again became more prominent. In the twentieth century, relativity theory and chaos theory theorized contingency in their own ways. None of these sciences ever claimed to have solved the problem of contingency; they merely reformulated it in different fashions.

The Greeks did not accept cosmological contingency and believed that the universe had always existed as an eternal and unchangeable being. As has been shown above, in the Middle Ages, the theory of *contingentia* held that, though the world was created out of nothing, it was still sustained by a divine will. Modern cosmology set a completely different tone. To say that the world order is contingent and emerged is the opposite of saying that it is created. There is neither purpose nor divine providence in emergence. If the world emerged in nature, we must admit contingency. The "emergence instead of creation" paradigm became plausible in the nineteenth century through the advancement of the natural sciences, especially in biology through the theory of evolution. A similar contingency shift happened in other sciences, including astronomy. Probability theory and the science of statistics sought to stem the tide of contingency. Curiously, today, the work of statistics can even be seen as a new "determinism."

The theory of evolution holds that selection and mutations have discernible causes, but these natural events are contingent because many chains of causality can collide. Darwin stresses in *The Origin of Species* that "for a large class of problems about species and interacting groups, answers must be sought in the particular and contingent prior histories of individual lineages, and not in general laws of nature that must affect all taxa in a coordinated and identical way" (Darwin 1859: 314, quoted in Gould 2002: 1335). The nineteenth century was overwhelmingly deterministic, but, mainly through Darwin, this deterministic spirit faded. Initially, Darwin's achievements could be misinterpreted in terms of determinism,[1] but in the end, contingency won out.

In the twenty-first century, contingency became even more deeply anchored in biology than during Darwin's time and had effects that are reminiscent of those that quantum theory or chaos theory had earlier had on physics. Molecules are not consistent but change or are even destroyed through interaction with other molecules, atoms, or ions, or through the addition of energy. In this context, any exact transmission of genetic material turns out to be impossible. Mutations, determined by coincidences, are the

---

1 See Gould: "Darwin's own commitment to contingency has been underemphasized, or even unrecognized, by his later followers (largely in their own attempt to win more prestige for evolution under the misconception that science, in its 'highest' form, explains by general laws and not by particular narrations). I am scarcely alone in identifying this central (and, in my judgment, entirely laudable) aspect of Darwin's view of life" (1336).

rule. Evolutionary biologist Veiko Krauss explains that genomes are unstable because they must be "constantly multiplied in order to save at least one copy. As the necessary process of copying of the DNA is multiple times more prone to changes than the mere conservation of an original, genomes will multiply mutations through their necessary multiplication" (Krauss 2014: 12). DNA is not eternal. More than selection, the driving force of evolution turns out to be genetic mutation, an idea that was already contained in Lucretius's concept that nature cannot create anything without the clinamen (see preceding chapter). In order to subsist, DNA must be multiplied. One effect is that genomes are always blurred and cannot be clearly determined: "The absolute limitation of a certain gene to some DNA is not possible" (26).

Meanwhile, the decentralization of the universe continues. The Big Bang did not burst outward from a central point of detonation but every point in the universe expanded equally (Odenwald 1998: 54). The universe is homogeneous and isotropic (the same observational evidence is available by looking in any direction in the universe). Within this universe, the appearance of human life seems to be a mere coincidence, meaning that it could also not exist. Any idea of a universe containing an inner reason is unsustainable. However, to this day, the critique of necessity and the defense of contingency is not a merely technical enterprise but, certainly because of its ancient religious roots, it has also remained quasi-metaphysical. Quentin Meillassoux holds that "the critique of ideologies, which ultimately always consists in demonstrating that a social situation which is presented as inevitable is actually contingent, is essentially indissociable from the critique of metaphysics, the latter being understood as the illusory manufacturing of necessary entities" (58).

Secularization and Disenchantment

At the beginning of the nineteenth century, science attempted to establish determinism as the only correct way of thinking. At the end of the same century, determinism eroded. In the early 1900s, accepting contingency could be seen as modernity's distinctive civilizational paradigm. A good example is Freud, who values the admittance of chance as the most modern of all attitudes, as he explains in his book on Leonardo da Vinci. Any rejection of contingency and any desperate search for necessities signify a relapse into religious worldviews and mythology:

> If one considers chance to be unworthy of determining our fate, it is simply a relapse into the pious view of the Universe which Leonardo himself was on the way to overcoming when he wrote that the sun does

not move. We naturally feel hurt that a just God and a kindly providence do not protect us better from such influences during the most defenseless period of our lives. At the same time, we are all too ready to forget that in fact everything to do with our life is chance, from our origin out of the meeting of spermatozoon and ovum onwards. (Freud 1963: 186)

Ironically, Freud develops his own brand of determinism when he tries to spell out (sometimes rather obsessively) the invisible laws of psychological life.

The rejection of any emergence and the insistence on creation (not only of the world as a whole but also of micro phenomena that are contained in the world) characterize deterministic theories adopted by theologies. They exclude coincidences on the ontological level: the world and everything contained within it did not emerge but must have been created by divine agency. The link with unwarranted conspiracy theories is obvious. It is for this reason that another Viennese thinker, Karl Popper, famously categorically equated conspiracy theories with belief in divine agency. For Popper, unwarranted conspiracy theories are "just a version of this theism, of a belief in gods whose whims and wills rule everything. It comes from abandoning God and then asking: 'Who is in his place?'" (Popper 1969: 123). For the conspiratorial mindset, evil men and powerful pressure groups are in "his place."

It is enlightening to view the emergence of the coronavirus in this context. If the coronavirus is due to a coincidence produced by nature, then this contradicts Aristotle's idea that "nature does nothing by coincidence." There is a reason, but the reason could be epistemologically hidden. The conspiratorial mindset uses its imagination to link certain events to a reason. Why do viruses take shape in nature at a certain time and in a certain place? Did human interference really play no role? However, even if human interference did play a role, the event can still be an accident. There is a clear parallel with religious explanations of the creation of the world, in which the universe has not—coincidentally and without necessity determining its form—emerged in nature; God created it.

Unwarranted conspiracy theories resemble myths, and they are essentially political or scientific myths.[2] Though many baseless conspiracy theories are instantaneously created, others develop, like myths, over long time periods. Various groups adopt and readopt motives like FEMA concentration camps or population control and develop them like memes. The conspiratorial

---

2 I insist that I am not saying that conspiracy theories *are* myths, but that *unwarranted* conspiracy theories *resemble* myths.

mindset replaces contingent events with fake necessities, for example, by attributing a coincidence to a heterodox order only known to the initiated. While Enlightenment philosophers managed to deprive myths of their scientific power, the conspiratorial mindset attempts to equip its "myths" with pseudo-scientific powers.

After World War II, the advancement of unfounded conspiracy theories seemed to have been temporarily halted but would soon reemerge, only to become more complex and more "scientific" than ever before. During the Cold War, it was easier to attribute conspiracism to entire regimes, each of which was seen as plotting to take over the world. Already before the two World Wars, it had become fashionable to blame big countries for one's own misfortune. Within the new Cold War logic, which opposed *ideologies* to each other rather than pragmatically acting countries (Marxism sees capitalism as a conspiracy, etc.), simple accusations could more conveniently be transformed into theories about conspiracies. Unwarranted ones necessarily emerged. The existence of secret services like the CIA and the KGB would also accelerate such ideation. Secret services make political actions more "secret" and thus more easily attributable to vague necessities that *cannot* be spelled out. In this universe of hazy motivations and clouded requirements, contingency, which might have often been the only "reality," would be buried under a spiderweb of networking conspiracists led by ideologies.

Throughout the entire "modernization" process of the last two hundred years, cosmological and theological decentralization have always progressed in parallel. From the late nineteenth century onward, secularization abolished even the abstract notion of God. "God is dead" was not just Nietzsche's war cry but, in Germany, it had been circulating in writings by diverse thinkers such as Philipp Mainländer, Eduard von Hartmann, Julius Frauenstädt, and Julius Bahnsen. What sets Nietzsche apart is that he, on top of his atheism, most consistently accepted the idea of an intrinsic coincidence in theology and cosmology. According to Jacques Bouveresse, Nietzsche and Charles Sanders Peirce (who designed experiments introducing artificial randomization) are the only great thinkers who dared such a leap into modernity, and this already in the nineteenth century (Bouveresse 1993: 11).

During Nietzsche's time, the belief in a necessary order was shattered by certain events that could appear highly "coincidental" because they could not be traced to necessary causes. It concerned, for example, the failed German Revolution of 1848 or the economic crash of 1873. Consequently, the nineteenth century witnessed a boom of unwarranted conspiracy theories that looked very much like our contemporary ones. Typical targets of alleged and real conspiracies were Christianity, Protestantism, Jews, democracy, liberalism, socialism, free enterprise, and the achievements of revolutions.

In the twentieth century, some people suggested that the next most useful step would not be the reestablishment of old necessities but, on the contrary, a further plunge into the most radical contingency. Contingency was seen as liberating. Many intellectuals, among them prominent figures such as Georg Simmel and Max Scheler, interpreted the First World War as a chance to break away from the necessities imposed upon humanity by modern civilization. The war was a moving existential experience capable of freeing individuals from fixed schemata, standardizations, and dull routines (see Joas and Knöbl 2013: 134). Italian Futurists announced this break with necessities and determinism in the most dramatic fashion by presenting the concept of *random* violence as a useful force through which humans can escape the constraints of civilizational necessities. Violence for its own sake, or a war for its own sake, were not goal-oriented activities and therefore most capable of incorporating contingencies. Both Left and Right found this peculiar solution attractive.

Meritocracy and Contingency

A very important modern phenomenon is meritocracy, which developed in parallel with economic liberalism. Both liberalism and meritocracy strive to overcome contingency by trying to replace the random conditions to which humans are subjected by birth with the more plausible and "necessary" laws of the market. A commercial product is successful because the economy desires it, which means that its success follows the "necessary" laws of the market. Equally, in meritocracies, achievements are thought to "necessarily"—not randomly—deserve merit. The problem is, as will be shown below, that "market necessities" and "merit necessities" are not as absolutely necessary as they appear to be. Still, modernity manifests a strong drive to establish necessities through both the market and a meritocratic system. In earlier times, finding necessities had been the task of religions, and it is correct to say that the liberal market economy and the meritocratic systems that are attached to it function like new religions.

Modernization means disenchantment, which modern humans, once they recognized that they were thrown into an arbitrary existence without God, did not openly combat but rather avoided by eagerly turning their environment into the "perfect" world model described in Chapter 2 of this book. It is a world in which everyone is liberated, democratic, tolerant, and ranked. This world is best represented by a utopian post-industrial society, which, strictly speaking, no longer produces anything "real," instead favoring services, most prominently "expert" procedures and "ceremonies" intended to inform us about the nature of quasi-everything. This is an enchanted or reenchanted world that earlier ages would perhaps have identified as a bewitched fairytale world. The late modern lifeworld with its science, excellence, organization, self-help books, and perfectionated meritocratic system appears unreal precisely because it follows the rules of "self-made necessities." Its machine keeps running, perfectly and smoothly, not in order to combat hunger or fend off enemies lurking at the border, but merely in order to sustain its own ethical standards. By doing this, it pursues a civilizational agenda that had already been current in the Middle Ages, though it then operated through the medium of religion. Now this agenda has become the most intense and palpable in modern democracies. With an enthusiasm that can appear quasi-religious, one strives to overcome spiritual uncertainty by means of worldly certainty. The main enemy is no longer hunger or foreign armies, but contingency, which is not a "real" danger but more like an invisible disease. Contingency is a virus that must be feared. And the conspiratorial mindset is one of the most conspicuous manifestations of this fear.

Another item that occupies a prominent place on the same agenda is the politics of victimization, which is strongly rooted in feelings of resentment. Those who did not get any merit, though they believe they deserve it, *claim* merit and hope to receive it by appealing to the sense of guilt that the necessity-creating elite usually eagerly cultivates within itself. Phenomena like "wokeness" are closely linked to these meritocratic developments. Meritocracy is very much a guilt-coping device. Wokeness has a peculiar way of influencing society, which becomes clear when we compare it with other victimization movements. Terrorism, for example, though also having its roots in self-victimization and resentment, does not appeal to meritocracy's sense of guilt and simply tries to destroy the meritocratic system altogether.

There is yet another phenomenon that has supported the spectacular rise of meritocracy: the "society of statistics" that emerged in the nineteenth century under the economic umbrella of liberalism. Probability theory, genetics, and various other methods capable of calculating chance, all of which will be analyzed in the next chapter, contributed to the thriving of meritocracy. From the middle of the nineteenth century onward, everything was going to be measured: intelligence, achievements, and, of course, merit itself. Liberalism and meritocracy share this requirement to measure, which is one reason why they always go hand in hand. The instruments of measurement are usually derived from the economy. Liberal capitalism sees humans as surplus *producers* and surplus *consumers*, and it distributes merit or sanctions accordingly.

The necessities of the market become absolute truths. As capitalism advances, its actors will no longer be employees working in a company but freelancers forced to constantly sell their human capital on the market. The worker submits not to company rules (that could be contingent to some extent) but to the necessary rules of the market. In the end, society adopts the structure of a huge company guided by an economic rationality based on what the market sees as logical and necessary. This belief goes so deep that one even presupposes that human beings mainly act according to such necessary economic forms of reasoning.

With industrial capitalism, the enterprise of creating an ideal world based on necessities had already acquired extraordinary dimensions. Later, the post-industrial world would transform these "real" necessities into "self-made" necessities. The link with religion has always been extant.

First, this concerned the industrial society. Assured by its impressive material productivity, capitalism did not overturn traditions in order to destroy an ancient religious world order, but, on the contrary, it simply aspired to reach God's necessities in another fashion. This is at least how Max Weber describes the relationship between secularization and capitalism in his unfinished manuscripts *Economy and Society* (1919–1920).[3] Disenchantment and modernization are protective mechanisms meant to make us forget the godlessness of secularization. This means that capitalist culture and lifestyle are not *against* feudalism and religious values, but that they emerge from pre-capitalist traditions and even try to maintain these values. Only economically, but *not* culturally, is capitalism against feudalism. The most important modern value derived from feudal and religious traditions is "merit," which modern society recasts by creating a highly ethically oriented version of meritocracy within liberal economies.

Today, some parts of the population contest this project; they are mainly those who are unable to get any merit. Though the main purpose of meritocracies is to overcome the injustices of feudal societies or class societies, more than ever, meritocracies are resented as hypocritical, as Michael Sandel has well shown in his *The Tyranny of Meritocracy* (2020). In principle, one contests necessity and refers to contingency. For example, one believes that the upper 1 percent of society have in reality received their so-called "merits" by chance, that is, by being born in the right place. Some individuals become immensely rich by speculating on the stock exchange. In the most charitable interpretation, we can say that they knew how to handle contingency more efficiently, but does this really deserve merit? The recent bitcoin boom has transferred "anti-meritocracy" feelings to an even more general level. Many conclude that in post-industrial capitalism, "real" work, that is, work that earns you profits "necessarily," is no longer appreciated, which creates large-scale resentment. This time, there is no religion or other master narrative that can help accommodate the anger that emerges when facing contingency. One

---

3 *Wirtschaft und Gesellschaft*, 203–21 and 492–503. See also Schluchter 2009: 97–100.

rather takes refuge in populist politics that questions meritocracy, and then the drift into the conspiratorial mindset is but a few steps away. Meritocracy is depicted as a big *necessary* conspiracy.

Of course, from the beginning, the perfect world scenario of meritocracy has been suffering from an immense flaw. Its first aim was to combat contingency, that is, the contingency of birth. However, if everybody battles for merits, will not, once again, those who are "born in the right place" obtain all merit? In this scenario, contingency has not been eliminated but merely endorsed by merit. Merit will even create new and persistent class divisions that can now be ethically justified. As they are due to merit, they can no longer be contested by pointing at inequality. As a result, a merit-based authoritarianism will arise. For Mauro Boarelli, therefore, "the age of merit coincides with the age of inequality" (Boarelli 2019: 106).

Milton Friedman and Friedrich Hayek rethought liberalism in terms of "neoliberalism" because they recognized that uncontrolled capitalism, even though it preaches the ethical principle of merit, can only lead to injustice. Though many people believe that Friedman's and Hayek's theories suggest an unbridled "war of all against all," when looking closer, this was rather the kind of liberalism that they wanted to avoid. The original neoliberalism they conceived was a reaction against the exaggerated individualism of liberal laissez-faire economics. In "Neoliberalism and its Prospects" Friedman describes the nineteenth-century model of liberalism, which held that the state could only do harm, as a "negative philosophy." For Friedman, laissez-faire "underestimated the danger that private individuals" represent (Friedman 1951: 91). There is no reason to suppose that market redistributions reflect a person's merit. In order to have an ethically justified meritocracy, one needs equality of chance. The destinations that various competitors attain will be very different, but at least the starting points need to be equal. And for this to happen, the state must interfere. In particular, Friedman criticizes the old Chicago School idea that the state can only do harm and holds that "important positive functions […] must be performed by the state" (Friedman 1951: 91). These meritocratic liberals suggest that meritocracy should always come in combination with state control and the establishment of equality. Once the race has begun, the state should stop interfering, but before the race, everybody must be allocated equal starting positions. In principle, this adjustment is not only *not* part of the liberalist package as we know it, but it even goes against it. This becomes clear when one considers that important stabilizations of retributions based on merit would necessarily lead to the destruction of the market. Liberalism claims to be about the necessity of the market, which it attempts to maintain by excluding the contingency of birth. But by actively interfering in the market to avoid the contingency of birth, it contradicts its own "liberal" principles of non-interference. It might introduce equality sparingly, but a paradox remains in place. The neoconservative Irving Kristol very well understood that the only reason for such amendments to competition is a pronounced contingency adversity, as he wrote in a critique of Hayek in 1970: "Professor Hayek's [believes that] men cannot accept the historical accidents of the marketplace—seen merely as accidents—as the basis for an enduring and legitimate entitlement to power, privilege, and property" (Kristol 1970: 9). Of course, the neoconservative version of liberalism is in no way better in this respect: it does not accept contingency either and instead justifies the coincidence of birth as a necessity.

What Hayek and Friedman originally launched under the name of neoliberalism punctually introduces equality but not egalitarianism. Liberals are no egalitarians. They do not see equality as the natural state of human beings. The only thing that is natural is competition with its resulting inequalities, but to enable fair competition, one needs some amount of equality. There are thus two major problems: by establishing equal chances and equal points of departure for everybody who participates in the race, one equalizes and flattens the market, which can create resentment. Second, like the rightist version of liberalism, this version can only lead to centralization and authoritarianism. Ludwig Marcuse described in his *One-Dimensional Man* (1964) how the market leads to homogenization, uniformity, and an excess of hierarchy. The introduction of a helping hand for those who have weak starting points does not contradict this process but even reinforces it. Victimism will crop up because the "socialist" part of neoliberalism supports self-victimization. Even the least favored need to be helped to deploy their capacities, and if this does not happen, they will be seen as victims.

The paradox can only be solved by going beyond left and right. The solution is neither to allocate equal starting positions nor to let meritocracy run "freely" without state intervention. The solution is simply to abolish meritocracy, that is, the generalized race, altogether. The alternative is neither a reinforcing of the "neo" in neoliberalism nor a neoconservative rejection of it. Rather, one must no longer see the market as a race but as a game dominated by contingency. Instead of insisting on—often imaginary—necessities (of the market), and instead of amending competition by introducing a supplementary amount of necessity through rules, it is better to abandon the competition altogether. Paradoxically, this would lead to *real* liberalism. By establishing fake necessities, neoliberalism reestablishes an ethics of feudalism. It has been shown above that this is, according to Max Weber, an intrinsically capitalist program. A real liberalism can only be materialized when risk, uncertainty, and contingency are constantly accounted for. *If* the state interferes, it should happen in order to guarantee that everybody has his own track, meaning it should combat the idea that everybody competes with everybody, which is how neoliberalism is understood today. State interference is necessary to separate competitors from each other in order to guarantee each individual's contingency.

Already in 1999, the Italian philosopher Pierluigi Barrotta wrote a book (*The Demerits of Merit: A Liberal Critique of Meritocracy*) that criticizes meritocracy in a way reminiscent of what Sandel would express twenty years later. More clearly than Sandel, Barrotta formulates the idea that meritocracy is not an integral part of liberalism but rather against liberalism, because liberalism always wants (or rather should want) diversity. To guarantee this diversity, one must, first of all, abandon the idea that everybody partakes in the same race, as well as the idea that everybody needs equal starting points. There should be no unified race in which everybody follows the same rules. Real market liberalism proceeds not through the production or the evaluation of merits but through the adoption of new ideas that are always risky and submitted to contingency. Saying that market selection is linked to merit signifies an ethicization of capitalism that goes against the principles of contingent action. Liberalism is not anti-meritocratic, but merit should not be seen as its driving force: liberalism's driving force is diversity. Merit-based liberalism, with its competition, unified merit scales, and forced comparisons where everybody is compared with everybody, reduces diversity. In other words, as Barrotta concludes, merit and market are incompatible (22).

It boils down to saying that liberalism should foster not competition but competence, which is a concept that Christopher Lasch, who was a fierce critic of liberalism, saw as essential even to sport (Lasch 1979: 104). We can also conclude with Michael Young (who may have written the first critique of meritocracy already in 1958) that the antithesis of inequality is not equality but difference. According to Young, in school, children should be allowed to

> develop at their own pace to their own particular fulfilment. The schools would not segregate the like but mingle the unlike; by promoting diversity within unity, they would teach respect for the infinite human differences which are not the least of mankind's virtues. The schools would not regard children as shaped once and for all by Nature, but as a combination of potentials which can be cultivated by Nurture.
> (Young 1958: 170)

Meritocracy and Religion

Meritocratic thinking is based on religion inasmuch as it "reflects the belief that the moral universe is arranged in a way that aligns prosperity with merit and suffering with wrongdoing" (Sandel 2020: 35). Just like Popper and Weber, Sandel explains ethico-economic developments as continuations of religious thought: "It might seem that contemporary meritocracy emphasizes human agency and will, while the biblical version attributes all power to God"; however, "contemporary meritocracy gives rise to harsh attitudes toward those who suffer misfortune" (35), attitudes that are not different from God's punishment. This means that those who do not believe in meritocracy's merits are subjected to damnation. While Popper talks about conspiracy theories, Sandel talks about meritocracy, but the link between the two is obvious. Many theorists of conspiracies see themselves as those who have been "damned" by meritocratic society. These theories can be warranted, but often they are not.

The fiercely meritocratic work ethic that the Puritans and their successors had brought to America, and on which Sandel concentrates his study, had already laid, at a relatively early stage, the foundation for the "perfect world" we know today, and which I have described in Chapter 2. Puritans have always emphasized the connection between God and merit: "In the presence of God, humans are seen to earn and therefore to deserve their fate" (Sandel 2020: 35).[4] Between worldly merit and heavenly grace, between worldly punishment and divine damnation, the conspiratorial mindset invents a third avenue that conceives of damnation as a punishment inflicted by hidden powers. Further, it also acknowledges the possibility of salvation that it thinks will one day be announced by a truth-teller such as QAnon or perhaps President Trump. The problem is that all three, the religious, the meritocratic, and the conspiracist way of looking at the world, repress the idea of contingency. For all three, everything *always* happens for a reason. Those who find neither religious, nor meritocratic, nor unwarranted conspiracist explanations plausible are rejected. They are said to believe that things happen for the wrong reasons. Contingency is rarely seen as an option. I find the strategy that Sandel highlights in meritocratic thinking equally well implemented in religion, pseudoscience, and the conspiratorial mindset. It concedes nothing to luck and always finds necessary reasons for our fortune and misfortune.

The frantic adherence to "rational" explanations that see only necessity is not only current among high-flying traders and celebrities that both Sandel

---

4 Sandel also points out that the notion of salvation by works "was already present in the background—both in the Catholic emphasis on rites and sacraments and in the Jewish notion of winning God's favor by observing the law and upholding the ethical precepts" (39).

and Nassim Taleb prefer to criticize.[5] The necessity syndrome can be found in all population groups, and it is a very generalized trait of decadent meritocratic societies; and among its worst outcomes is the conspiratorial mindset. No such decadent meritocratic ways of thinking would exist had para-religious anti-contingency thinking not been ingrained in Western cultures over the course of centuries.

In meritocratic societies, the exclusion of contingency leads to a political stalemate. Egalitarians hold that the rich are undeserving, whereas conservatives insist that they are deserving. Not so differently, a typical religious paradigm postulates that believers deserve happiness, whereas non-believers deserve punishment. Finally, the conspiratorial mindset holds that a system designed by evil powers distributes privileges unequally. The problem is that all three are moralizing. A more "ludic" perspective that puts contingency at the center of a system would lead to the conclusion that "merit" need not be an undisputable value. It is only supported within systems that have been invented for the very purpose of merit, that is, for their own sake. Through the idea of merit (accompanied by reward or punishment), meritocracy, religion, and the conspiratorial mindset import an ethical aspect into the economy, with the result that the central ideal, that of winning the game by earning a maximum of merit, can no longer be questioned. Instead of disputing the value of "winning," one attempts to amend the system that distributes the merit. This, once again, mainly signifies a neutralization of contingencies, as John Rawls very well explains in his *Theory of Justice*:

> Those who have been favored by nature, whoever they are, may gain from their good fortune only on terms that improve the situation of those who have lost out. The naturally advantaged are not to gain merely because they are more gifted, but only to cover the costs of training and education and for using their endowments in ways that help the less fortunate as well. [...] the basic structure can be arranged so that these contingencies work for the good of the least fortunate. [...] no one gains or loses from his arbitrary place in the distribution of natural assets or his initial position in society without giving or receiving compensating advantages in return. (Rawls 1971: 101–2)

---

5 See Taleb: "One may argue that the actor who lands the lead role that catapulted him into fame and expensive swimming pools has some skills others lack [...]. I beg to differ. The winner may have had some acting skills, but so do all of the others, otherwise they would not have been in the waiting room" (2001: 182).

Though the above-described approaches, meant to improve the human condition, vary in their concrete applications, all of them insist that justice can only be attained by overwriting an ungraspable, elusive contingency with more essential necessities. I suggested above that everything could be done otherwise. Of course, the solution is not financial capitalism. Financial capitalism is not a positive phenomenon and should not be accepted as a viable socioeconomic system because it basically *is* gambling. However, I hold that as long as it *does* exist, financial capitalism should be recognized as a genuine gambling activity and nothing else.[6] The same goes for many other lucrative professions where success depends to a large extent on luck, that is, on birth or, less traditionally, on an advantageous algorithm on Google or YouTube.

Social theories, just like socioeconomic attitudes, rarely integrate ludic views of society. Instead, one prefers to essentialize merit, the scientific pertinence of algorithms, God's will, or conspiring powers. The proponents of the latter think that the winner does not deserve his gain because the system is unjust. These theories are not always unwarranted. It is certainly true that some games are bad, but they are not bad because they contain contingency. Many of them are only bad because contingency is not recognized as such. In some cases, one could even induce *more* contingency into the game instead of reifying a fake necessity aspect. One could do so, for example, by modifying algorithms. Sandel writes: "If everyone knew such inequalities had nothing to do with people's merit, the rich would be less proud and the poor less resentful than they would otherwise be" (Sandel 2020: 133). Instead, just like the religious cultures of the Middle Ages, one prefers to describe the world in terms of necessity and pretend that contingency does not exist.

Sandel presents an example from the Old Testament in which Job complains to God that he has been so unfortunate in his life and inquires why he has deserved such treatment. In his response, God turns out to sympathize with the logic of contingency much more than with the logic of merit and punishment and points out that "not everything that happens is a reward or a punishment for human behavior […]. All rain is not for the sake of watering the crops of the righteous, nor is every drought for the sake of punishing the wicked. It rains, after all, in places where no one lives—in the wilderness, which is empty of human life" (Sandel 2020: 36). Sometimes things just

---

6 Sandel suggests such a game-based view: "I do not morally deserve my superior pay and position, but I am entitled to them under fair rules of social cooperation. And remember, you and I would have agreed to these rules had we thought about the matter before we knew who would land on top and who at the bottom. So please do not resent me" (141–42).

happen. In other words, Job should recognize that for him, there is only a "that" and no "what." All there is, is the "It rains," in the Heideggerian sense; we should not say "there is rain." In the latter option, we will be concerned with the why, the merit, and the justice of the event. The rain that falls on the fields is a Heideggerian "Being-event" that just happens. It is not inserted in some grand economico-religious narrative: God's rain is pure facticity. Job wants to know the why of the what, and God tells him that he should accept whatever happens as these are just accidents, which suggests that there is no ethical theory hidden in God's actions.[7] Subconsciously, Job was looking for a conspiracy: "There must be a reason for all this." God instructs him that he should simply accept his fate as facticity.

The Discreditation of Science

In the twenty-first century, both the growth of pseudoscience and the over-scientification of everyday life maintain a peculiar relationship with another widespread phenomenon: the discreditation of "real" science. In the United States, since the 1970s, especially conservative and far-right individuals have become increasingly distrustful of science, as is most obvious with regard to topics like climate change (Lewandowsky et al. 2013b: 1). However, as has been explained, even advocates of supernatural and paranormal modes of thought do not declare science as such to be bankrupt. For the conspiratorial mindset, it has become easier than ever to find scientific support for their fancy ideas. Usually, the conspiratorial mindset and "paranormalists" do not give in to simple mysticism. Fundamentalist religions underwent a similar "scientific" turn. As a matter of fact, this scientifico-religious paradigm emerged not in the context of mystically minded religiosity and traditionalism, but precisely from the encounter between religion and modernity and the attempt to reconcile opposing ways of thinking. This happened not only in Christianity and in the West. The Islamic religious reformer Muhammad 'Abduh (1849–1905) sought to explain that Islam—contrary to Judaism and Christianity—is entirely compatible with modern science, and used Western thought, spanning from evolution to Comteian positivism, to prove his point (see Büssow 2016: 148–49). Here science was used to justify religion, which would become a common paradigm in radical religious thought. Today, a creationist is similarly likely to explain that evolution is wrong not because the Bible or the Qur'an present different views, but rather because "scientists"

---

[7] This departs, of course, as Sandel points out, from the theology of merit that informs Genesis and Exodus.

have supposedly proven evolution impossible. He will use pseudo-scientific arguments to support religious beliefs. Fasting during Ramadan is healthy, nutritionists have proven pork to be unhealthy, and the holy scriptures contain an amazing amount of modern *scientific* knowledge [...] Not a litany of religious teachings, but of "scientific" theories, will follow. Things become even more explicit in alternative religions, as with the UFO cult of the Raëlians, whose leader claims to have communicated with extraterrestrials, and who announce in their messages that "Science at last replaces religion."

This transformation of *religious* culture into a *pseudo-scientific* culture happened in parallel with the rise of the conspiratorial mindset. The two are closely correlated. Like contemporary fundamentalism, the modern conspiratorial mindset does not preach outright irrationality but rather attempts to create an alternative rationality that superficially follows the patterns of real science; however, this science is methodologically sloppy and disregards facts.

Finally, it should be noted that this peculiar science project does not first emerge in the twentieth century and that it can be traced to the Enlightenment. Contemporary fundamentalisms, diverse as they are, also recuperate old ideas of "natural religion," "natural theology," or "Deism" that European philosophers had formulated in the seventeenth century against the idea of revealed religion. Enlightenment theologians were the first to seek to establish the existence of God on the basis of observed *natural facts*. Natural religion was also a favorite topic of Kant, which this philosopher most clearly exposed in his *Religion within the Bounds of Bare Reason* (1793). Already in his *Critique of Practical Reason*, Kant had declared that God, or the existence of an immortal soul, though both cannot be empirically proven, are simply necessary postulates of reason. For natural religion, the supranatural is thus natural, and God can be found in nature. Animism, which I compared above with unwarranted conspiracy theories, is based on very similar convictions.

Chapter 8

THE LOSS OF UNITY

Through the death of God and the gradual disappearance of theological determinism, modern humans gained more liberty to shape their world. Their lives were neither predetermined, nor were humans considered victims of what the Middle Ages could still see as "satanic powers." As philosophy—and with it, all theoretical thought about necessity and contingency—became "detheologized," humans could feel as they saw fit. Compared with former times, life was less mightily determined by inherited expectations: a new horizon of possibilities opened up, which provided a hitherto unknown freedom. At the same time, it brought about a dramatic loss of order.

Contingency is the "air" that Marx famously speaks of in 1848 in the *Communist Manifesto* when announcing that in modernity "all that is solid melts into air": "Constant revolutionizing of production, uninterrupted disturbance of all social conditions, everlasting uncertainty and agitation distinguish the bourgeois epoch from all earlier ones. All fixed, fast-frozen relations [...] are swept away, all newformed ones become antiquated before they can ossify" (2012: 38). Baudelaire echoes this view in 1863 when framing modernity as "the transient, the fleeting, the contingent" (2006: 403). The ever-increasing speed of change creates contingency.

On the one hand, contingency had become more prominent than ever because God's will no longer established necessity; on the other hand, contingency was felt and feared less because a larger variety of psychological and technical coping mechanisms had become available. To some extent, the lost order could be pragmatically reestablished by eliminating a big chunk of contingency from public and private life. The above-described post-industrial "perfect world" model represents the latest version of this anti-contingency utopia. From the nineteenth century onward, technology began to compensate for the loss of theological landmarks and created the sober modern certitudes that everybody in the industrialized world is now used to. Insurance companies helped in the handling of accidents, and applied science, with its capacity to foresee the future and to prevent disasters (one can think of meteorology or earthquake foreshock detection), helped reduce contingency.

Vaccinations protect against coincidentally contracted diseases and epidemics. In daily life, much bad fortune can now be prevented through more precise and professional planning. This planning is increasingly supported by modern technology of communication that continues to be improved to this day: thanks to cell phones, messaging apps, and GPS, fewer appointments have been missed "by bad luck."

While Pascal and Galileo had already calculated probabilities, a real theory of probability arrived relatively late in mathematics. One of its earliest protagonists was the mathematician Moritz Cantor in the nineteenth century. In the twentieth century, mathematicians like Richard von Mises developed probability theory as a separate branch of mathematics. As it evolved out of gambling theory, this theory "tamed" randomness by transforming it into relative determination. A century before Mises, mathematicians Daniel and Jacques (Jakob) Bernoulli had already established the "logarithm" and began collecting data on births, deaths, and marriages. Laplace would improve this (see Laplace 1902: 265). Statistics could now work with increasingly larger data banks, with the result that apparently random events could look regular. It was now possible to positively know what is "normal." Durkheim made use of these insights in 1897 for his sociological studies of suicide. "Society became statistical," writes Ian Hacking (1990: 1). Standards would be established for various items, most importantly, perhaps, for intelligence. In 1905 Alfred Binet suggested a series of tests and a matching scale capable of measuring the intellectual level of humans. Through statistics, coincidence was no longer the opposite of certitude, and certitude would no longer be contrasted with the impossible. Science could calculate the "grey" zones in between, which was psychologically reassuring. The whole project would take place within the context of a "secularization program," through which it further contributed to the world's disenchantment. Anthropologist Talal Asad therefore points out in his book on secularism: "Responsibility is now held for events he or she was unaware of—or falsely conscious of. The domain in which acts of God (accidents) occur without human responsibility is increasingly restricted. Chance is now considered to be tamable. The world is disenchanted" (Asad 2003: 193).

Criticism of this statistical rationality emerged only much later. Is probability real, or, if it is, is it still real in light of a "really happening" accident? These are rather questions of late modernity or even of the "postmodern" age. Only once much belief in historical, evolutionary, or teleological metanarratives had been discredited could the narratives that statistics had created be criticized, too. For example, Ulrich Beck disputes "science's rationality claim to be able to investigate objectively the hazardousness of a risk [den Risikogehalt des Risikos]" (29/38). Beck's point is that a science that evaluates a risk does not grasp anything real, and that in the end, all statistics are based "on a house of cards of speculative assumptions and moves exclusively within a framework of probability statements, whose prognoses of safety cannot even be refuted, strictly speaking, by actual accidents" (29/38).

Meanwhile, in the twentieth century, the elimination of contingency would continue. Social systems and welfare programs provided cushions against the repercussions of the anarchic capitalist economy and the unpredictability of the market. "Genetic programs" would no longer be pronounced as metaphors but would be taken literally as scientific measures to prevent genetic coincidences. Technical control of procreation promised to reduce the "risk" implied by the coincidence of birth, and, as a result, genes would no longer be a matter of lottery. A new perspective on human existence, in which the individual is responsible for their fate and is the "maker" of their life, became commonplace. All this concorded with the meritocratic work ethics of capitalism. Whatever happens, happens because it was chosen in some way. Eventually, coincidence came to be understood as a lame excuse for not fulfilling one's duty. A perfect world model in which life coaches push individuals toward the realization of their utmost "personal development" becomes part of the meritocracy project that aims to eliminate all contingency. Your life's circumstances, beliefs, and constraints might be coincidental; what matters now is your "true self" that lies hidden at the bottom of your personality in the form of a necessity. And it is even your moral duty to live up to your necessary self's potential. New management philosophies, normally deeply rooted in meritocratic culture, create a corresponding concept of efficiency that does not accept coincidences, deviations from the straight necessary path, or even luck. All this often comes with rhetoric about happiness, positive thinking, and self-fulfillment. Above that, it is very much supported by (often questionable) "scientific" evidence based on statistics and measurements.

As a result, toward the middle of the twentieth century, much of the "problem of contingency" had disappeared from people's minds. Of course, except in certain cases of genetic engineering, contingency could never be replaced with causality. Chance had not been replaced with necessity, nor had the indeterminate been replaced with the determinate. Most of the time, contingency had simply been calculated more properly until it became a reality on its own; and as such it was found apt to replace the reality of causality. Chance was not abolished but only tamed, and within this culture of tamed chance people could live lives forgetful of the reality of contingency.

Looking closer, what happens from the late nineteenth century onward is odd and paradoxical. On the one hand, technology successfully combats the coincidence in everyday life. On the other hand, equally from the late nineteenth century onward, science seeks to establish the idea "that the world might be regular and yet not subject to universal laws of nature" (Hacking: 1). Science clears more space for chance than ever before. Hacking explains in his *The Taming of Chance* that "the most decisive conceptual event of twentieth century physics has been the discovery that the world is not deterministic. Causality, long the bastion of metaphysics, was toppled, or at least tilted" (Hacking 1990: 1).

While insurance companies used statistics to reduce indeterminacy, science fights deterministic ideologies and paints the picture of a physical universe in which everything is random. Henri Poincaré sees all scientific principles as incapable of reflecting reality because reality always contains contingency. Relativity theory and Monod's anti-animistic biological theories pursue similar goals in other areas (more on Poincaré and Monod will follow below). Hacking sees these strategies reflected in the physical sciences of the time, especially in quantum physics, but also in the quantitative psychology of Wilhelm Wundt.

How can these scientific developments be harmonized with the simultaneous elimination of contingency in society? Hacking sees a sort of counterreaction relationship between necessity-based statistics and contingency-based modern sciences, suggesting that "the more the indeterminism, the more the control" (2). Probably unknowingly, Hacking supports typically "postmodern" reflections on the non-founded character of reality and the creation of a new, simulated, or virtual reality in which everything is *apparently* necessary. Quite similarly to Hacking, Baudrillard writes that contingency has "plunged us into an abnormal incertitude" and that we tend to respond to this incertitude with an "excess of causality and finality" (Baudrillard 1983: 16). The perfect world model from which all contingency has been eliminated is such a simulated and virtual reality. And the modern conspiratorial mindset can be linked to such a counterreaction system too. The conspiratorial mindset, as it obviously plays out control against contingency, has its origin in this "postmodern" ambition to flee contingency and take refuge in a simulated reality.

In reality, contingency was never dead but had only been pushed into the background and suppressed in a quasi-Freudian way. There, in the background, it would linger until the day it was called up again. Partially, the call came from science, which had become so increasingly contingency-oriented that contingency could no longer be ignored by the broader public. The popular writings of neurologist Oliver Sacks and paleontologist Stephen Jay Gould stressed the importance of individuality and contingency in nature. Furthermore, a full and integrated genetic engineering of children turned out to be unrealistic, if not downright dystopian. Advanced DNA research increasingly drew a picture of a genetic lottery that distributes talents and abilities randomly. At best, nature could appear as an "interaction of random and deterministic processes, and of predictable and contingent influence" (Gould 2002: 28).

Since the 1970s, new risks and dangers, very different from those of earlier times, have arisen in parallel. Most of the risks humans face now are no longer due to underdevelopment but rather due to industrial overproduction, which gives these risks a new aura of absurdity. Are these risks really necessary, or are they not rather the result of some industrial gambling? Beck calls the new dangers *risks of modernization* (Modernisierungsrisiken) (Beck: 21/29), among which there is nuclear energy and pollution. In any case, risks have become more contingent. A disease like cancer, which could apparently be caught by coincidence, has moved to the center of medical attention. Unemployment could hit anybody, independent of precautions taken. Overall, modern humans no longer appear to be the masters of their fates but are once again victims of unforeseeable circumstances.

Economically, in the post–World War II world, despite the existence of stable geopolitical blocs until 1989, power was no longer stable, and instead became increasingly fluid. The profusion of multinational capitalism and finance culture introduced contingency into processes that used to appear, in the more limited national contexts of the past, as necessary and determined. Now, fewer things were controlled from inside, and outside forces could seemingly subvert existing patterns at any moment. Economic interests and political alliances seemed to have adopted autonomous existences as they followed laws that were difficult to apprehend. The outsized rewards of Wall Street bankers resemble lottery gains brought about by luck rather than the fruits of real work. Necessity-based meritocracy came to be severely questioned: it could no longer be taken for granted that "the best and the brightest are better at governing than their less-credentialed fellow citizens" (Sandel 2020: 98). Further, "real work" seemed to disappear and be transformed, according to David Graeber, into "bullshit jobs" (Graeber 2018). Late capitalism pushed not for productivity but rather for a disruption of labor, which stands in a strange contrast to the managerial "positive thinking" discourses that developed at the same time. The "personal development" programs that strive to maximize human capacities and personal experience in all domains of life appear absurd in the light of Graeber's more realistic findings and look almost cynical.

A strong symbol of the contingency economy remains the CryptoPunk project, which was evaluated at 5 billion dollars in 2020. CryptoPunk represents 100,000 realistic characters generated by an algorithm, that are subject to random rarity and an equally random flux of international speculators. Bullshit is not only on the side of the poor; the rich indulge in it in their own ways. Some gain millions with CryptoPunks by doing quasi nothing while the rest of us have bullshit jobs. The situation seems to require a profound revision of capitalist theories in terms of "contingency capitalism."

In any case, at the end of the twentieth century, contingency was back. It did not even need the scientific contingency narrative of chaos theory to be brought back with pomp and circumstance. Globalization, a speculative financial system, and an increasingly complex life world with a constantly growing number of choices and interconnections made the modern human aware of the power of coincidence. So-called "postmodernity," with its flattened hierarchies and collapsed oppositions, accentuated the sense of randomness. Who can still say "I am here, and it could not have been otherwise"? Through social media, interhuman relations became increasingly dominated by individuality, resulting in more random interaction. Logically, individuality leads to more fortuitous meetings. As a result, opinions and feelings became increasingly complex as it was no longer likely that a single opinion could fully represent a person. At the same time and paradoxically, opinions became personalized to the point that political parties no longer managed to represent the thoughts of larger groups. People had become increasingly aware of random circumstances and contexts. Progressive political ideologies such as communism, which are the direct inheritors of eighteenth-century mechanistic thinking, went bankrupt when faced with this new world of complexity and unpredictability. Likewise, political parties became more brittle. In the past, party members used to maintain *relationships* with other party members that were rooted in social contexts; today social life is determined by "floating" *connections*. "Connections" are looser and more random than relationships, and they also have a more secret ring than the latter. Revolutions are still possible, but instead of leading to a utopian scenario of a better world, most likely, they open onto an even wider spectrum of contingencies. The COVID-19 phenomenon summarizes much of this situation. It is highly random and leads to further randomization through individualization and social fragmentation.

Similar to Hacking, Ulrich Beck shows that in risk societies, authorities concentrate on downplaying risks and convincing people that contingency *can* be mastered. Mostly, they use the classical modern instrument of statistics. While, according to Meillassoux, any "kind of dogmatism which claims that this God, this world, this history, and ultimately this actually existing political regime necessarily exists [...] seem[s] to pertain to an era of thinking to which it is neither possible nor desirable to return" (58), the dogmatism of statistics is still permitted. Why? Because its purpose is to prevent contingency. The perception is that "there is no contingency because we have statistics." The logical inconclusiveness of this reasoning is often overlooked. Those who still insist on the importance of contingency, that is, on the randomness of gains and *potential* dangers, might even be declared out of touch with modernity, progress, and development. They are labeled alarmists.

Then there are those who point out not contingencies but imaginary necessities. They have fallen victim to a necessity dogmatism similar to that of statisticians, with the difference that they point out necessities that are entirely imaginary. They are the representatives of the conspiratorial mindset, who are alarmists when it comes to imaginary conspiracies, and who can be anti-alarmist when the danger is real. A random world order and random economic principles have contributed to the rise of gratuitous conspiracy theories. Keeley, in his article on conspiracism, points to the fact that the world is today "made up of an extremely large number of interacting agents, each with its own imperfect view of the world and its own set of goals. Such a system cannot be controlled because there are simply too many agents to be handled by any small controlling group. There are too many independent degrees of freedom" (Keeley 2006: 58). Those who do not accept this contingency or cannot bear it for whatever reason, often turn toward unwarranted conspiracies. According to Mathew Gray, "postmodernists often cite, as characteristics of postmodernity, societal structures and dynamics that could contribute to conspiracism by alienating or disorientating the individual" (Gray 2010: 25).

The new complexity creates insecurity, uncertainty, and stress. Some begin to shy away from urban environments because of this complexity. Obviously, accidents occur more often in cities than in the countryside. The modern *Gesellschaft* of deracinated individuals has become fleeting and contingent, as opposed to the permanent *Gemeinschaft* of which one is part simply because one belongs there. In the intricate contexts of cities, everybody could be an agent; everything that appears to be true could be fake. In movies, urban heroes cope with contingency because they are fast, keen-sighted, and cold-blooded. There is a sense that normal people are better off in the countryside. The rural community is perceived as law-bound and purposeful, as people still live in a state of innocence in an impeccable order. Institutions are stable, social relations are harmonious, and honest individuals fulfill their functions well. Anti-urbanism and anti-civilization lifestyles represent a way of coping with contingency; unwarranted conspiracy theories represent another. In their more developed configurations, both can represent a new civic faith.

Conspiracy and Science

There is, of course, one discipline that is still capable of tracing the random bits of actions and events to necessary sources, and explaining, in terms of necessity, at least part of what is happening in the world. This discipline is science. However, in the eyes of the conspiratorial mindset, science is problematic because it was precisely science that caused the loss of the center. The collapse of transcendent certainties and absolute values is very much due to the growing success of the life sciences in the second half of the nineteenth century. So is the advancement of contingency-oriented approaches toward nature that came with evolutionary science. If science is responsible for the lack of necessity from which the world now suffers, it must appear paradoxical that science should now try to explain the chaos that it created with its own hands. The conspiratorial mindset thrives within the ambiance created by this paradox. Science provides necessity, but at the same time, it is science that produced the world of contingency. Already in the narrative of Adam and Eve, the loss of unity and scientific fragmentation is attributed to the biblical temptation to eat from the "tree of science." Eating from the tree meant obtaining knowledge of good and evil and thus indicated a shift away from unity toward particularities. The temptation proposes an image of science and knowledge as fragmenting forces, as opposed to uniting theological systems. This shows that from the "beginning," knowledge and science were linked to contingency insofar as scientific knowledge always signifies an awareness of multiplicity, that is, of the distinctively contingent character of things. The Fall represents the first unfortunate contingency in the history of humanity, especially if we use the concept of contingency in its original theological sense that has been explained above. Paradise, the pre-scientific world, was a place without contingency; it was an original place very different from our actual life world. In paradise, there is absolute order: questions, illegal desires, and conspiracy theories of any kind are not forbidden but simply unnecessary. The acquisition of knowledge estranges humans from the awareness of an original central unity. Tellingly, Paul Virilio calls original sin the "original accident." The eating from the tree introduces contingency, which leads to the conclusion that "as soon as there is an invention, there is accident" (Virilio 2005: 87). Paradoxically, afterward, science did everything to retrieve the lost totality and order by establishing stable structures capable of explaining the world in terms of necessity.

Because baseless conspiracy theories develop within this epistemic paradox of modernity, they are also deeply paradoxical in and of themselves. As mentioned, the modern "decentralized" vision of the world as a fragmented patchwork of facts, values, and opinions is the work of science, as it abolished the belief in a centralized cosmos and in a God that hovered above all. The most consistent reaction to counter this development would be to reinstall a medieval, God-centered worldview in which all actions revolve once again around a powerful center. However, in general, that's not what unwarranted conspiracy theories do. Typically, the conspiratorial mindset does not refer to myths, ghosts, or angels, but rather to science (it doesn't prevent it from becoming a scientific myth). It embraces a vaguely scientific approach that is carelessly mixed with mystic and religious elements, as though it wanted to imitate the model of "scientific modernity" in an alienated and more disconcerting fashion. These "conspiracy scientists" who develop unwarranted theories are eager but bad scientists. Much like religious fundamentalists, they attempt to find modern scientific inventions in ancient scriptures. In the documentary *Behind the Curve*, which depicts the movement of flat-earthers (dir. Daniel J. Clark, 2018), Dr. Lamar Glover claims: "These folks are potential scientists gone completely wrong. Their natural inquisitiveness and rejection of norms could be beneficial to science if they were just scientifically literate. [...] So, every flat-earther shouldn't be held with contempt, but serve as a reminder of a scientist that could've been, someone that fell through the cracks. And we, as ambassadors of science, are called upon to do more." Very obviously, flat-earthers are thinking outside the box, and so does all unwarranted conspiratorial thinking. Harris thinks that they exhibit "a sort of higher-order epistemic vice—a cocktail of intellectual traits that jointly impede successful inquiry" (Harris 2018: 255). Fragmented and rambling as it is, this pseudoscience looks rather "postmodern," and not so much modern, let alone premodern. Though the conspiratorial mindset is generally opposed to a postmodern world of disorder in which singular elements float about randomly in a sphere of relativism, it does not point to a scientific alternative. Instead, it simply attempts to contradict the postmodern contingency by pointing to powerful and hidden macro rationalities, by which it believes the world to be dominated. Religions too, address some superrationality, but the difference is that, first, for religions, this macro rationality is conceptualized as "good" whereas for the conspiratorial mindset it is always "evil": not God but the chaos-seeding "Satan" is their object of interest. Second, the sheer abundance of indefensible conspiracy theories leads to disarray and not to a vision of a well-ordered world.

The main problem with the conspiratorial mindset is that it wants to overcome contingencies through assumptions that are entirely random, which is a paradox. It does not adopt an organic view of science capable of delivering some macro principles about, for example, the benefits of vaccinations, and instead embraces precisely the "negative" view of science that is reflected in the biblical narrative about temptation. To the tree of science, it does not oppose, for instance, God's unity but rather its own tree of pseudoscience, which "eliminates" contingencies by conjuring up diffuse necessities, that is, again, randomness.

Though many unwarranted conspiracy theories are religiously inspired, in the end, they do not combat the fragmented postmodern world from which they emerge, but merely duplicate it. The macro realities created by conspirators are not meant to serve as positive alternatives to the postmodern chaos. The conspiratorial mindset tends not to focus as much on traditional spirituality, contemplation, and quietude; instead, it produces disturbing pseudo-scientific theories about various evil macro structures that present the world in an even more fragmented light. In the Middle Ages, the retreat from the world of contingency into a quiet center of necessity could bring about peace of mind. God symbolized a unity that could be contrasted with the multiplicity of worldly phenomena.[1] The conspiratorial mindset amplifies fragmentation by spreading doubt about science and thus disintegrates the last remnants of order and coherence. It does not represent science as a consolidating movement but as a big, well-organized conspiracy that needs to be disbanded by inventing alternative theories.

Conspiracy and Determinism

Much has been said above about the determinism of Democritus and Laplace. When contingency is entirely excluded, the world finds itself described in terms of determinism. Determinism was materialist in the case of some Pre-Socratics, and the Stoics conceived of it as divine providence. Monotheistic religions would later embrace the idea of divine providence and see the divine will as necessary, which had to be accepted even when it led to situations that were uncomfortable for humans. Against this, Aristotle insists in his *On Interpretation* on the openness or contingent character of the future: whatever will happen in the future is not necessary.

The conspiratorial mindset does not represent radical determinism. Today, radical determinism is practically only maintained by religious fundamentalists who find, for example, the "disorder" created by evolution too random and look for a superior principle. For them, contingency does not even exist in natural development. Something like natural selection may well be considered to exist, but even that must follow the plan of a creator. Nothing in the world's patterns can be entirely random. Contingencies are controlled by God, which means that for religious people, just like in the late Middle Ages, all apparent contingencies *are* necessities. Jorge Luis Borges describes the desire to eliminate all contingencies, which can become a paramount principle in the reading of the holy scriptures. It can lead to the algorithmic rendering of the letters and numbers in those scriptures:

---

1 Even the uniquely fragmented concept of the Christian God, wherein the Father does not coincide with the Son, did not weaken the unifying force of God.

> They thought that a work dictated by the Holy Spirit was an absolute text; in other words, a text in which the collaboration of chance was calculable as zero. This portentous premise of a book impenetrable to contingency, of a book which is a mechanism of infinite purposes, moved them to permute the scriptural words, add up the numerical value of the letters, consider their form, observe the small letters and capitals, seeks acrostics and anagrams and perform other exegetical rigors which it is not difficult to ridicule. Their excuse is that nothing can be contingent in the work of an infinite mind. (Borges 1981: 244 and 246)

Cryptology seeks to find confirmation of present beliefs. The conspiratorial mindset borrows from this religious approach but presents it not as religious but as scientific. It uses codes, symbols, and numbers to reveal the existence of evil conspirators; and these necessities must be combated. Some amount of fatalism and determinism can result from these theories as they might lead to the conclusion that "we are victims of conspirators, and nothing can be done about it." But in general, this determinism tends to be moderate, because often the conspiratorial mindset is ready to fight against the evil system in some way. In other instances, ressentiment sets in, which creates the poisoned fatalism that Scheler describes.

Historically, determinism outside the realm of science has not been the privilege of religious philosophies, and, in the past, some secular models have been just as categorical about determination as religious ones. Early nineteenth-century determinism that evolved around Laplace has been mentioned above multiple times. Two generations later, Marxism developed categorical views about determinism. The history of historical materialism, which is heavily indebted to Hegel, is directed against the idea of contingency. Chronologically, Hegel falls right between Laplace and Marx-Engels. The fact that historical materialism is directed against the idea of contingency is surprising given that Hegel's "Absolute contingency" (see Chapter 5) eludes determinism. Despite this, Friedrich Engels extracted his "Dialectical Determinism" from Hegel, whose Absolute Idealism can also be interpreted as deterministic in a pantheistic sense. It is this alleged determinism that fascinated Engels. He admired the Berlin philosopher's "ability to make it appear that nature and history follow a pre-ordained course" (Lichtheim 1961: 253) and attempted to show that contingency is objective, meaning that it is merely a manifestation of necessity. This does not signify that the outcome of all our actions is mechanically predetermined. There are several possible outcomes, but they are only possible within a given set of parameters, which leads to "parametric determinism" (see Mandel 1989). Through his determinism, Engels installed certainty in Marxist thought and gave it the "unshakable conviction that the stars in their courses were promoting the victory of socialism" (Lichtheim 1961: 246). This presupposition, which echoes the cosmologies of Laplace and early French socialist thinkers, became dogmatic.

Deterministic positions like Engels's are marginal in the contemporary world. In the later twentieth century, historical sciences turned against teleological approaches and ideologization in history, and viewed history more in terms of limited problems. There are no laws in history. The unfolding of the lives of individuals and groups, of nations and institutions, has no finality and is impossible to predict. The proximity of this philosophical position to the conspiratorial mindset is striking. When the right course is predetermined, everybody who contradicts this natural course becomes a conspiring enemy. Victory and loss are seen as absolutes, which makes the narrative dramatic.

Combining Contingency and Necessity

Can the world be existentially contingent while essentially necessary? In the history of philosophy, this question has been answered in various ways, most of the time by depicting the world as an aggregative totality containing both contingency and necessity. Most philosophies, as well as monotheistic religions, instead of insisting only on necessity, attempted to coordinate contingency and necessity in relatively sophisticated fashions. This becomes most obvious in discussions of predetermination and free will. One way to overcome the necessity-chance opposition is to refer to the already mentioned concept of ontological contingency designed by Aristotle. Contingency exists *just because* whatever happens could also not have happened if the contexts had been different. However, this contingency does not exclude the idea of causality because, obviously, there always *are* certain determining contexts. Things are never entirely random because not *everything* could have happened. There is determination, but at the same time, the unfolding of events remains unpredictable.

Enlightenment philosophers acknowledged that reason is not simply the faithful reflection of abstract and necessary truths, but that it is at least partly constructed, much as human institutions are, according to random situations unfolding in the real world. Things are always *more or less* reasonable depending on place and time, which means that everything we deal with in our lives is neither entirely necessary nor entirely contingent. This did not, however, mean that everything is relative; most Enlightenment philosophers saw rather contingency and necessity as forming a well-functioning whole.

Such combinations remain problematic when it comes to the existence of God. How can we think of the coexistence of a necessary God and contingent beings? Theists will develop their own approach to combining necessity and contingency. They believe in a superior design, and even if the world sometimes looks random and as though produced by contingencies, God is presumed to know exactly what he is doing. The world's vast spectacle of contingencies might appear random, but God always watches from afar. As mentioned, even Einstein held this view and believed that the chaos and contingency that science perceives is only the surface of a deeper development. It shows that even a proponent of indeterminist physics can hold such a belief. Deep underneath, there is a necessary order, which is known only to God. God himself is necessity and not submitted to contingency.

This view might look similar to the earlier-mentioned fundamentalist one, which suggests guided evolution. The difference between the two depends on the proportions: How much latitude do we grant to contingency, and how much to necessity? Einstein takes a "liberal" view toward necessity because the necessary order he believes in can only be found "deep underneath," that is, it will be perceived only in a metaphorical rather than a literal fashion. It is not an order that a scientist can or should address, but only an order that a scientist can imagine and believe in privately.

The conspiratorial mindset sees the opposition of necessity and contingency as basically unresolved and suggests its own theories that eliminate contingency and exalt necessity. Having one's life totally under control might be more difficult today than in past époques. Our media-saturated world preaches individuality, but at the same time, it seems to make absolute individuality impossible. One always needs to accept some degree of manipulation. The conspiratorial mindset continues to dream of a self-reliant, self-determined individuality, which means basically two things: it abhors contingency, but it also does not want to be fully determined. Therefore, it creates theories that help to cope with contingency by detecting hidden determinations; at the same time, these help to get rid of unwanted determinations, as it does not want to be "determined" by governments and other "evil" powers. The unwarranted conspiracy theory is thus not only a contingency-coping device but paradoxically also a determination coping device.

Einstein thought of contingency as only the surface of phenomena that a scientist can perceive, and that deep underneath, there is a necessary order known only to God. But the natural sciences can also coordinate necessity and contingency another way. They might point to an order that is not established by an external force (God) but that emerges internally, that is, organically. Biological development is not just the result of random mutations, but micro mutations are controlled by necessary macro structures that are part of the organism. This macro-order is not absolutely necessary and remains subject to the influence of the micro elements. At the same time, the micro elements are not passive automata controlled by an environment, but they have their own dynamic, which permits contingency. The Greek *dynamis* translates into Latin as *potentia* or *possibilitas*. *Dynamis* is not the living actuality of Aristotle's *entelechia*, it is not the determined force inherent in organisms that pushes them toward self-realization; *dynamis* constantly plays with possibilities.[2] Micro-macro relationships follow an organic logic capable of integrating coincidence and necessity. Such views were explicitly advanced in the early twentieth century by "vitalist" or "holist" scientists such as Hans Driesch (1908), who wanted to overcome the mechanic biology of his teacher Ernst Haeckel,[3] as well as by Ludwig von Bertalanffy, Johannes Reinke, Paul Alfred Weiss, and Jakob Johann von Uexküll. Driesch assumed Aristotelian entelechy as an inherent vital principle in organic development; but this entelechy was not predetermined. It was mediated by the organism. Today such approaches can be found in biological neo-organicism (see Nicholson 2014), which holds that life develops neither as a random micro-order, nor as a predetermined macro-order designed by natural selection. In organic systems, contingency and necessity cooperate.[4]

Contingency signifies that events cannot be traced to general laws. However, every event happens within a context, which means that both the event and the context can go against the necessary rule. The conventional understanding of coincidence holds that single elements behave in ways that cannot be explained, but that the exterior circumstances still follow necessary rules. When this occurs, we speak of a system-interior coincidence. A system-*exterior* coincidence implies that the system behaves unpredictably, which might affect the elements, though the elements' nature will not be changed. The functioning of the macro structure is of course more important, and system-exterior coincidences tend to have more dramatic consequences. An organic view emphasizes the relationship between the single element (for example, a virus) and its environment. The coincidence is here not either internal or external but might have been produced by interferences between the two, which makes the localization of the coincidence's potential "necessary" sources more difficult.

In 1907, the Lamarckian biologist Félix Le Dantec explained that there are no laws of randomness but that, in theory, an explanation can always be obtained through a change of scale. Microscopic considerations can explain

---

2 Aristotle introduces this concept in *Metaphysics* IX, 8.
3 Haeckel represents a reductionist form of Neo-Darwinism and founded the "Monist League," which aimed to replace German churches with the evolutionary theory as a secular religion (see Rupke 2006: 180).
4 See Botz-Bornstein 2020 where I develop thoughts on this topic.

macroscopic "randomness" and vice versa (Dantec 1907). The "scaling" is an interesting idea, but it is not plausible that the coincidence would eventually disappear through scaling; it is simply no longer seen as such because it has been covered under necessity. Coincidences are single events that appear entirely random only when seen in isolation. The context can provide necessity. In historical science, this becomes more obvious. If the spatial and historical scale of the observed historical field is broadened, we *lose sight* of contingencies and see history as a determined narrative. We no longer perceive the fluctuations of single events that are subject to instantaneous reactions. Instead, we create stable descriptive and explanatory schemes in which the accidentality of single events is no longer visible. Conversely, historical events, which make perfect sense when embedded in their general political context, can appear as identical because their perception simply depends on the scale we employ. Paul Virilio's analyses point in this direction when he declares that war and accident are but one and the same thing; or that 9/11 was an accident (Virilio: 104). The accident is a coincidence, but it is still determined by large-scale reasons. Taking a large-scale perspective, one can say that with all the armaments and tensions built up in the international world during the Cold War, the breakout of a real nuclear war should be considered an accident. Had such a war happened, although it would be either coincidence or willful action that sparked it, in both cases it would be an accident.

Of course, making historical events look entirely random can lead to what Willman calls "contingency theories," which practically erase history by foregrounding the complexity of disconnected details, and which Willman presents as the inverse of conspiracy theories (see Willman 2002: 36). The rejection of necessities leads to relativism. For example, if one refuses to see that single economic ventures are directed by the sort of multinational capitalism that confers economic power to very few agents, then one is blind to a necessary system, with the result that one will naively accept all the vicissitudes of multinational capitalism. Vice versa, an over-emphasis of necessity would lead to a baseless conspiracy theory about multinational capitalism. Multinational capitalism is not a conspiracy; it has not been planned by evil powers, but merely emerged over time as it integrated lots of purely contingent options. Again, everything depends on how much we focus in on details and how strongly we affirm larger structures. Dantec was right in emphasizing the importance of scaling: what is most important is to find the right scale.

A historiography without contexts is superficial. Modern philosophers like Michel Foucault and Richard Rorty strive to discover contingencies in history and to see history through contingency. Foucault even describes history as the "place of absolute contingency" (though without referring to Hegel, see Foucault 1977: 144), which is naïve because it denies that history can have a sense. Foucault, the great lover of micro-events and deconstruction, sees the single element as vitalist and strong, which for him mainly means that this micro perspective is capable of deconstructing totalitarian necessary structures. Philosophers like Foucault, Deleuze, and Lyotard fight the specter of necessities that comes, for them, in the shape of totalitarianisms of all kinds. For example, Deleuze's rhizome is anti-totalitarian because it rejects the existence of necessary structures. A more "realistic" approach would try to combine micro and macro history. The change of scale affects both deduction and generalization and makes the coincidence more or less visible in the historical narrative. Raymond Aron speaks therefore, more appropriately, of the coordination of structure and individual action, which affects the performance of contingency (Aron 1984: 99).

The conspiratorial mindset plays with scales and invents systematic macro structures capable of explaining away coincidences, often even firmly insisting that coincidences do not exist at all. It acts as though coincidences were wonders and therefore impossible. It is an undiscussable truth that everything is caused by something and is thus due to a necessary source. The principle of insufficient reason says that nothing can be without a reason, and if there is no cause, the effect does not exist. An "absolute coincidence" in the sense of an event without a cause would not be possible because it would indeed be what we call a wonder. But coincidences are embedded in objective contexts, which means that they always *do* have a cause, but this cause does not always need to follow systematic rules. The conspiratorial mindset embeds single events into larger structures, plans, or projects and negates the contingency input of the micro-event, which leads to a distortion of reality. The conspiratorial mindset creates a pseudo-organic worldview in which everything is held together by a superstructure. At the same time, the macro conspiracy structure remains unconfirmed by the micro details, and therefore the whole construction is a pseudo-organism.

Ontological contingency approaches tend to see necessity and contingency as forming a whole. For example, as mentioned above, a war might break out through a fortuitous event, but if the international political situation was full of tensions, it allows us to say that the war "*had* to break out." Contingency and necessity do here not exclude each other. Similarly, theists (such as Einstein in the above example) believe in some unity of nature granted by God, which means that a virus can have been sparked by a coincidence, even if this can have happened within the framework of divine power. A secular scientific philosophy following an identical pattern would believe that nature is a big macro-organism following a necessary order and that an incident such as the coronavirus can alter, though probably not totally harm, the overall functioning of this macro structure. Should the balance really be disturbed by coincidence, it must be reestablished by bringing the organism back on track. The coincidence is not simply negated but is recognized as being embedded in a larger structure, which is not the "right" structure in the sense of a necessary structure, but a structure that cooperates with the coincidence. The conspiratorial mindset does not employ this unifying approach. It establishes a necessary structure that simply negates the coincidence.

In the above organic vision of biology, coincidences can also be beneficial if we adopt a macro perspective. A good example would be—apart from viruses or bacteria leading to immunization through vaccinations—a micro element such as a parasite that enters an organic system. Parasitism is a form of symbiosis in which one organism (the parasite) benefits at the expense of another organism, which is usually of a different species and called a host. Parasites disturb necessary orders by importing coincidences into systems. These systemic alterations can be malevolent but also beneficial and creative since parasites can create entirely new systematic constellations. Sometimes, systems that function only in terms of necessity are indeed too straightforward and rigid and suffer from a lack of communication between parts. In such cases, coincidences provoked by parasites can enable exchanges between various components. Parasites can even establish links between separate systems or activate other systems, for example defense systems, by creating tensions. They can push organic development from planned, rational, and telic (purposeful) patterns to more dynamic or "creative" patterns. From an "existentialist" (as opposed to essentialist) point of view, both parasite and host take part in the unified being of the organism: both are thrown into a web of possibilities and must function together. There is no mere coincidence and no mere necessity; both form a whole.

The conspiratorial mindset does not adhere to the religious option, but it finds the "nature" option just as unattractive because nature leaves too much space for contingency. As soon as news of the coronavirus had become public, the conspiratorial mindset decided that it could not have been produced by nature but only by an evil human organization. This shift from the natural to the artificial is characteristic. One needs to find man-made necessary structures.

What does the conspiratorial mindset believe in? An unwarranted conspiracy theory is neither a philosophy, nor a religious doctrine, nor science. It does not accept contingency, but it does not overcome contingency by finding some sort of necessity in the form of a natural or divine preestablished harmony either. Nor does it enact justifiable relationships between necessity and contingency (as do organic philosophies of nature), but it rather invents subrationalities, which are usually evil, and which are said to disturb a possible better order. What this possible better order is, is never spelled out; strictly speaking, it could be disorder. Unwarranted conspiracy theories concentrate on the evil order that some powers are trying to enact.

Contingency, Existence, Facticity

Some philosophies see only contingency and suggest a "contingency only" option. Stephen Hawking, when discussing Heisenberg's Uncertainty Principle, famously contested Einstein's claim and maintained that "Even God is bound by the Uncertainty Principle and cannot know both the position, and the speed, of a particle. So, God does play dice with the universe. All the evidence points to him being an inveterate gambler, who throws the dice on every possible occasion" (Hawking 1999). Uncertainty arises through the connection between particle and wave independent of the measuring methods. Hawking and Heisenberg reach their contingency-only stance, which still echoes Epicurus and Lucretius, by adjusting the scale to concentrate on particles, which express, in scientific terms, the existentialist position that particles (or single humans for existentialists) are thrown into a nonsensical, contingent situation with which they must cope. For Hawking, even God is subjected to this contingency. Nietzsche had already anticipated such a position by referring in the *Untimely Meditations I* to physicist Georg Christoph Lichtenberg (1742–1799), who believed that the world could be the work not of a supreme god but "of a subordinate being who as yet lacked a full understanding of his task, and thus an experiment. A novice's test-piece [Probestück] which was still being worked on" (1997b: 32/1988: 198). This god would be a tinkerer and not a creator. He would resemble a gambler who cannot fully control his actions. Similarly, Jacques Bouveresse distinguishes between a calculating god and an experimenting god (Bouveresse 1993: 67). Monod's microscopic and fortuitous elements with which nature "plays roulette" express the same idea, and it has been likened to existentialism.

In the Middle Ages, a god marked by contingency, that is, a god submitted to fortune and misfortune, would have been seen as a bad and weak god. From a modern perspective, a weak god makes humans stronger. When even God gambles, a belief in fate is no longer possible, and humans are responsible. When God gambles, humans have to take their destinies into their own hand. Hawking's concept of the gambling god can also be read as an inversion of Laplace's "demon" or "superior intelligence"[5] that knows everything. Laplace illustrated his idea of causal determinism through a demon who uses the laws

---

5 Laplace does not call it demon but "intelligence," which his interpreters later changed to demon.

of classical mechanics and is thus capable of calculating the past and future values of any atom (Laplace 1902/2009: 2/4). This demon would know the precise location and momentum of every atom in the universe, which makes coincidences impossible. Early nineteenth-century science already put an end to this concept. Some thermodynamic processes turned out to not be reversible: no demon would be able to trace these events to their source. In 1808, John Dalton concluded that gases must consist of tiny particles that are in constant, random motion. Gradually, the nineteenth century discovered that atoms *are moving unpredictably* whenever they are in close contact with other atoms. As any statistical determination for the smallest particles turned out to be impossible, one decided to reserve determinism for very large objects only. The anti-deterministic positions of quantum mechanics and chaos theory made it definitively clear that Aristotle's claim that "nature does nothing by coincidence" (*Of Heaven* 11, 291b, 13) was wrong. Quantum physics, above mentioned with regard to Hawking, describes the spontaneous disintegration of atomic nuclei with the result that entire microphysical systems become undetermined. The Greater Uncertainty Principle, which Heisenberg formulated in 1927, postulates that certain pairs of values (for example, the position and momentum of particles) cannot be measured with precision. A particle can be in different places at once, which is called a "superposition." Nothing can be predicted, not even by a superior intelligence. This suggests that objective reality does not exist: all we have is subjective perception. For quantum physics, uncertainty becomes part of a natural law. Everything could also be otherwise—but still there is a law. Similarly, chaos theory is not about total chaos; rather, it highlights a certain disproportionality inherent in basic functions, such as in population models where small inputs can have disproportionate responses. Math can grasp certain processes but has difficulties grasping others (usually long-term processes) that are due to an uncertainty anchored in nature. In principle, chaos theory still tries to "calculate" contingencies wherever possible, but it is aware of its limits. Nature is recognized as contingent, and the natural sciences, once they have recognized this reality, must create their own coping devices. A world without coincidences is a utopia: it is an ideal and cannot be real.

In all this, the parallel between this newest scientific worldview and existentialism remains strong. Most broadly speaking, existentialists like Sartre built on the Enlightenment view of the necessity-coincidence problem but decided to exclude any form of necessity to depict a world entirely ruled by coincidence. Before Sartre, Heidegger had expressed the paradigm of contingent existence through the concept of *Geworfenheit* (thrownness) into *Dasein*, taking up a paradigm that was important in the Middle Ages. Originally, the distinction between an all-encompassing Being and single beings had theological dimensions. Thomas Aquinas explained in his *Summa Theologiae* that Being does not coincide with beings because "Being is the actuality of every form or nature [...]. It follows then that being itself is compared with essence, which is distinct from it, as actuality is from potentiality" (I, q. 3, a. 4, ad 2). Being can be the actuality of being (*actus essendi*) or the composition of a proposition, but while we cannot know God or his essence through the actuality of being, we do know him through propositions. The proposition "God exists" is true for Aquinas, which means that though God is not an actuality, he can still be affirmed through a proposition. Heidegger takes the distinction between Being and beings that do not coincide out of its religious context and "detheologizes" the problem of being and existence. All beings participate in Being, but this participation is now unrelated to God. As a result, beings are "thrown" into being-there (*Dasein*), that is, they are thrown into an existence full of possibilities and contingencies. In § 31 of *Being and Time*, Heidegger declares that Dasein is primarily "Being-possible" (Möglichsein). Dasein is "what it can be, and in the way in which it is its possibility" (Engl.: 183/German: 191–92). This is not mere contingency, that is, an empty logical possibility, because, once again, not everything is possible. "Possibility as an *existentiale* [*Möglichkeit als Existenzial*]" is not a free-floating potentiality for Being in the sense of the "liberty of indifference [Gleichgültigkeit der Willkür]." The *Möglichkeit als Existenzial* is rather "the most primordial and ultimate positive way in which Dasein is characterized ontologically" (ibid.).[6] It is against this background that Dasein can also be experienced as a burden (see §§ 29 and 58 of *Being and Time*), and the awareness of this potential can create a "mood" (Gestimmtsein) comparable to melancholy, though it is a melancholy of the creative kind rather than of the depressed kind. In *Die Grundbegriffe der Metaphysik*, Heidegger calls it "creative melancholy" (schöpferische Melancholie) (1983: 270).

It is notable that the term "facticity" as a "basic constitution" (Grundverfassung) of *Dasein* appears here, more precisely in § 12 of *Being and Time*, for the first time in Heidegger's work. *Dasein* must both be a "Faktum" and be of a world. Earlier, Heidegger had mentioned facticity orally in his lectures on Augustine. Agamben draws attention to the fact that one of the first appearances of "faktisch" is in the 1921 summer course on Augustine and Neoplatonism, which Otto Pöggeler and Oskar Becker have summarized:

> Here Heidegger seeks to show that primitive Christian faith (as opposed to Neoplatonic metaphysics, which conceives of Being as a stets

---

6 "[...] die ursprünglichste und letzte positive ontologische Bestimmtheit des Daseins."

Vorhandenes and considers *fruitio dei*, consequently, to be the rapture of an eternal presence) was an experience of life in its facticity and essential restlessness (Unruhe). As an example of this "factical experience of life" (faktische Lebenserfahrung), Heidegger analyzes a passage from chapter 23 of Book 10 of the Confessions, where Augustine questions man's relation to truth. (Agamben 1999b: 187/Ital 2005: 296)[7]

After Heidegger, Sartre assumes an atheist (though not entirely materialistic) position and holds that the world's development is random, though it remains possible to find a reasonable way of living within an absurd world by inventing goals and objectives within limited contexts. In this optic, the "whole" is not needed: we have only individual situations within which we must solve particular problems. Sartre's first novel *Nausea* had been developed out of a philosophical treatise that was initially called *"Factum de la contingence"* and was supposed to explain that human beings are basically alone in the world without any landmarks of necessity. For Sartre, this finding is not negative because contingency provides a chance to break with oppressive systems and thus brings us existential liberty. The hero of *Nausea*, the historian Roquentin, notices that his relationship with ordinary objects changes, that he feels a strong disgust toward everything. This "existential unwell being" [*mal-être existentiel*] is due to his insight that "history speaks only of what has existed, but never can an existing thing [un existant] justify the existence of another existing thing" (1972: 32–33). Phenomena are subjective, they have no meaning in themselves and depend on our "way of seeing." In other words, there is no transcendence, which makes any metaphysical search for necessities impossible and leads to the conclusion that "l'essentiel, c'est la contingence." Later, in his *Notebooks on Ethics* (written in the 1940s though only published after his death), Sartre jots down sentences like: "The passage to pure reflection must provoke a transformation: of my relation to my body. Acceptance of and claiming of contingency. Contingency conceived of as a chance" (Sartre 1983: 12).[8]

---

7 The winter course of 1921–1922 in Freiburg, which bore the title "Phenomenological Interpretations of Aristotle," was to a large degree also dedicated to the analysis of what Heidegger would later call "factical life" (das faktische Leben), and which would later become Dasein (see Agamben) (1999b: 186 / 2005: 289).
8 For Rorty, Sartre is still a metaphysician because he fails to develop a truly ironic perspective of existence: "A metaphysician like Sartre may describe the ironist's pursuit of perfection as a 'futile passion,' but an ironist like Proust or Nietzsche will think that this phrase begs the crucial question" (Rorty 1989: 99). For Rorty, Sartre still tries to discover "a secret," which is not the case for Proust and Nietzsche.

Existentialism is the late result of transformations that had taken place since the Enlightenment. The fixed order of the universe and, in parallel, the order of society had been called into question. Both would be depicted as unstable and as submitted to contingency, and there were basically three ways to react to this: (1) the religious person attributes the contingency to a higher order; (2) the conspiratorial mindset looks for alternative necessities; and (3) the existentialist sees contingency as an opportunity. Sartre conceptualizes contingency in terms of liberty and responsibility, suggesting that there is no liberty without contingency and that we can take advantage of contingency by framing it for our purposes. Whereas both monotheistic religions and the Enlightenment tradition had sought to establish a harmonious coexistence of contingency and necessity in order to make life livable, Sartre's existentialism negates necessity altogether. At the same time, he manages to outline a reasonable life project within a fully affirmed contingency. His radical anti-determinism leads Sartre to the notion of "facticity," which signifies that the lifeworld is just there, in front of us, without any necessary determinations. Facticity here overlaps largely with contingency, with the difference that the contrary of contingency is necessity or regularity, whereas facticity has no counterpart. Facticity is a situation in which necessity cannot even be constructed or thought of as an alternative. It is thus an absolute contingency in Hegel's sense. Contingency is not merely "fact," but is constantly measured against regularity, which leads to a peculiar experience of the contingent. The coincidence can appear unusual, funny, or grotesque; accidents can make us sad, and chance can make us happy, and usually, we are astonished when encountering a coincidence. In contrast, facticity is a sort of "predetermined contingency" that does not surprise us and is simply noticed. In this sense, it is a contingency that contains its own coping mechanism.[9]

To see facticity like this is a modern paradigm that emerged with science. Any idea of facticity could at earliest surface toward the end of the Middle Ages, where, as Blumenberg explains, reality "comes to be seen as 'fact,'" that is, as "a contingent state of affairs." Since now the "bad aspects of the world no longer appear as metaphysical marks of the quality of the world principle or punishing justice," they have to be seen simply as facts, though they do not necessarily need to be accepted (Blumenberg 1985: 138). Since

---

9 Agamben insists that, contrary to Sartre, for Heidegger, the proper trait of facticity is not *Zufälligkeit* but *Verfallenheit*: "Everything is complicated, in Heidegger, by the fact that Dasein is not simply, as in Sartre, thrown into the 'there' of a given contingency; instead, Dasein must rather itself be its 'there,' be the 'there' (Da) of Being. Once again, the difference in modes of Being is decisive here" (Agamben 1999: 187/Ital 2005: 295).

the *factum* is something that is made, one can also choose to oppose it. It would take several centuries for philosophies that deal with facticity in a "creative" fashion, that is, by interpreting it within complex contexts of necessity and contingency. Heidegger is one of the philosophers to develop this option. Contrary to Blumenberg, for Heidegger, facticity means that things are the way they are, but that there is no necessary reason. Facticity does not concern single facts; rather, it always looks at life as a whole. Blumenberg criticizes that Heidegger, all while integrating contingency into an ontological analysis, neglects the fact that humans tend to avoid any awareness of contingency. But existence is always shaped by both contingency and contingency avoidance (see Blumenberg's unpublished habilitation, 1950: 7–12). In defense of Heidegger, I would say that Blumenberg's suggestion points more to an anthropological than a philosophical approach.

In modernity, the world becomes malleable through facticity because there is no necessary meaning attached to things. Sartre would probably have called the coronavirus an absurdity, not because it is more absurd than other things, but simply because *everything* is absurd, and we must find reasonable ways to live within such contingent constellations. For him, the coronavirus would come wrapped in a package of facticity; and consequently, it would not have surprised him. The virus exists without a reason; it is a coincidence, and, in that case, for the existentialist, unfounded conspiracy theories that look for necessary reasons are not required. The absurd is merely what cannot be traced to any rational system. It does not imply that the existentialist would reject a warranted conspiracy theory.

Sartre and Hawking (and to a lesser degree Heidegger) perceive the futility of all carefully laid-out schemes that attempt to explain the world. In a mix of disparate eventualities, no total logic can be established. However, contrary to the conspiratorial mindset, they do not try to create an alternative logic. Nor do they establish "contingency theories." Rational plans and real life can never be matched; rational plans will always come up short in the face of real life, which is why play and improvisation are often the best options, and this is even true for God. In the end, this playing activity can be a source of truth and reality.

Not having to deal with absolute necessities can also be a relief, and modernity has embraced this opportunity gracefully. Blumenberg analyzes how, in early modernity (Neuzeit), people opted against the pressure of the absolute that theology had imposed upon them for centuries and decided to concentrate on the future. This produced considerable scientific progress. The future is full of possibilities and contingencies, and science represents a modern way of gaining distance from the power of God, providence, and other necessities. Already in the Middle Ages, many overcame the notion of gnosis, this belief in the divine nature of humans capable of delivering them from the constraints of earthly existence. As mentioned, in modernity, science and scientific thinking become a means to cope with a contingent world by developing various techniques of survival and social improvement. If this world is freer than the world of theological absolutism, it is only because it permits ontological contingency. But this contingency will have to be mastered by constantly developing new techniques. The modern way of life is a means to distance oneself from necessity; but it is also a means to show that one can handle contingency properly. Quantum mechanics and existentialism are the most elaborate expressions of this civilizational development. The conspiratorial mindset opposes this most general project that had already started in early modernity. At the same time, the conspiratorial mindset does not want to go back to premodern times; it pushes the modern development in a direction that can only be called "postmodern."

Chapter 9

FRENCH PHILOSOPHY OF CONTINGENCY

While German biologists experimented with organic models, France produced an anti-deterministic intellectual current called "la science du hasard" (the science of the coincidence). A related anti-deterministic philosophy had emerged earlier in the nineteenth century, but in the early twentieth century, about three decades before the publication of Sartre's *La Nausée*, it would reach its climax. Sartre was indirectly influenced by this philosophy, mainly through Bergson, who was loosely linked to this science of coincidence. What was really more of a French *philosophy* of contingency (instead of a *science* of contingency) is interesting because it represents a rare example of a rationalization of contingency. While Engels had rationalized history to the point of letting the mystery of contingency disappear under the glaring light of determinism, these French philosophers adopted the opposite approach. They depicted the world as a manifestation of contingency and demystified it to the point of making it coterminous with reality. As will be shown below, this is directly opposed to the conspiratorial mindset, which cancels coincidence and mystifies necessity. The French philosophy of contingency is vaguely reminiscent of Hegel's speculative idealism, which sees chance as a necessary event and conceptualizes it as an "absolute contingency" (see above). Coincidence is real because, without it the world could not be (see Henrich 1971: 164n8).

I introduce the French *science du hasard*, which is representative of a French Renaissance of philosophy that happened around 1900, not only because it is a rare example of the rationalization of contingency in the Western world, but also for another reason: this philosophy, which has, most of the time, been seen as a philosophy of science, bears resemblances to Eastern philosophies of contingency that will be presented in Chapter 11. The main idea is that contingency is real and that necessities are only abstractions. Despite its name, the French "science of the coincidence" had no intention of being primarily in the service of science, and rather deemed itself to be in the service of life in more general terms. Emile Borel, the initiator of French statistics and (despite his purely mathematical expertise) a prominent representative of this philosophy, wrote in his book *The Coincidence* [*Le Hasard*, 1914] about the aims of this new "science": "The science of the coincidence can indeed claim, no more and no less than any other science, to administer our actions; it can, according to the role of science, make it easier for human beings to reflect upon their actions before carrying them out" (1938a: ii, my trans.). Borel's point is that contingency is real, whereas determinism can only be realized on an abstract level, a stance that differs from the classical Western (Platonic) attitude toward contingency, which opposes not only the necessary to the contingent but, in parallel, the real to the ideal, and the rule to the fact. Is the necessary just following a rule without being a fact? Is contingency a fact just because it does not follow a rule? Do absolute necessities exist at all? Is contingency not always present in all necessity? If necessities are never absolute, they cannot be called real, and the only thing real is the contingency. French philosophy of the coincidence revolves around these questions.

From Boutroux to Virilio

The philosopher of science (and Bergson's teacher), Emile Boutroux, attacks in his doctoral thesis *De la Contingence des lois de la nature* (1874) the determinism to which he believes contemporary French philosophy and science to be submitted. A firm opponent of materialism, Boutroux insists that relations between things cannot be established in terms of static but only of dynamic laws. Nature constantly evolves, and natural processes can constantly change spontaneously and without any predetermination. Boutroux emphasizes the complexity of the natural world and insists that mathematical and quantitative procedures cannot grasp this complexity because nature is always moving and incomplete. Boutroux's work can appear to represent a unique link between the *Naturphilosophie* of the German Romantics and the theories of his brother-in-law, the mathematician Henri Poincaré, who saw scientific principles as incapable of reflecting reality because reality always contains contingency. Poincaré's philosophy will be presented below. For Boutroux, contingency is reality whereas necessity is only appearance. Similar beliefs in the "concreteness" of coincidence were also formulated, at the same time, by the French philosopher Alain, who declared his preference for betting at horse races over engaging in more abstract forms of gambling. Contingency is linked to human activity, life, and labor, and in Alain's opinion, it should be conceptually removed from the abstract, mathematical forms of the *jeu d'hasard* (1920: 81). Today, Nassim Taleb expresses related ideas when he suggests that thinking about randomness should always be a "way of thinking" rather than merely a mathematical method (2001: 41). Mathematical intuitions should always be combined with realism and not contain excessive abstractions. Taleb makes this perceptibly clear when comparing gambling with real-life contingency and when he suggests that "the sterilized randomness of games does not resemble randomness in real life" (2007: 286).

Before Boutroux, other French philosophers of science such as Charles Renouvier (1815–1903), Jules Lachelier (1832–1918), and Jules Lagneau (1851–1894) had attempted to pull philosophy away from Laplace-style determinism as well as Cartesianism. Renouvier suggests in his *Essai de critique générale* (written between 1854 and 1864) that contingency is not imaginary but is found in the phenomenal world (Vol. 1). Drawing on Kant though severely reinterpreting him, Renouvier holds that contingency is a requirement for human freedom, thus already anticipating later existentialist thoughts. Comte's mechanical determinism had prevented the world of science from coinciding with the world of life. Idealistic and schematic conceptions had also been imposed upon French science by the mathematician and economist Antoine Augustin Cournot (1801–1877), who proposed mathematical tools for the understanding of philosophy and the economy. Furthermore, determinism entered the human sciences more broadly through Hegel, Marx, and the deterministic historian Hippolyte Taine (1828–1893). The latter philosophers concentrated mainly on history: similar to what Freud would later do with regards to psychological life, they sought to spell out invisible laws of history.

Boutroux targets Cournot as well as Taine when claiming: "Man wanted to be able to arrange phenomena not according to the order in which they appear to him but to the order in which they depend on each other" (1908: 2). According to Boutroux, although science can merely establish links between the phenomena it observes, it should never fall victim to the illusion that all these phenomena are subordinated to some "real" order. The order is a mere abstraction and not real; the only thing that is real is contingency. Science should cease proceeding in an abstracting manner and instead "discover the contingency that exists in the world" (36). Abstract theories can find punctual causal links, whereas the overall framework remains contingency. Also, relations between things can only be established in terms of dynamic laws because action is always a becoming (95). Boutroux expresses this same idea by suggesting that science must stop treating phenomena as "things as such" (choses en soi, 32). Boutroux initiated a philosophical program that Bergson would later extend in his own original way, developing in *L'Evolution créatrice* (1907), the vision of a free and contingent dynamism opposed to the categories of a mathematical philosophy for which everything is determined by necessity.

The "science du hasard" is also linked to Henri Poincaré, who died in 1912 after having been the main protagonist of a French philosophy renaissance. "Conventionalism," which was Poincaré's philosophical trademark, asserts that scientific principles are not reflections of the "real" nature of the universe but only convenient ways of describing the natural world, whereas the real world always contains contingency. Scientific principles are only a language that does not reflect reality. This view anticipates the philosophical criticism of language that became common in post–World War II philosophy, for example, Wittgenstein's, which holds that language is always already essentialized and cannot grasp reality. Earlier, the idea that language does not reflect reality was at the center of continental philosophy of language (Hamann, Herder, and Humboldt), and in the twentieth century, it was developed by Heidegger and modern hermeneutics. In epistemology, Poincaré's ideas match those of later historians of science such as Thomas Kuhn and Quentin Skinner, who expressed the same kind of skepticism toward scientific problems that are merely linguistic. These theories do not suggest that language is senseless, but rather that while language can help us make predictions about certain limited phenomena, it does not reflect reality. According to Rorty, Skinner paid attention to "the vocabularies in which sentences are formulated, rather than to individual sentences, [which] makes us realize, for example, the fact that Newton's vocabulary lets us predict the world more easily than Aristotle's. [However, this] does not mean that the world speaks Newtonian" (1989: 6).

In three books published between 1903 and 1908,[1] Poincaré presents new ideas about the uncertainties of science and explains that even geometrical axioms are not self-evident truths because they cannot be empirically established as unequivocally real. He regrets that for the longest time throughout human history, mathematical truths were seen as "so absolute that even the Creator is fettered by them"(1905: xxi). Similar to Hawking, Poincaré looks at the dynamic components of life, not only in society but also in nature, and he finds contingency. Rather than perceiving a phenomenon such as evolution as mechanical, he concludes that it must be organic. Nature is not a hierarchically organized universe but an organism that is also capable of integrating contingency. Contingency can create not only freedom within nature but even, strangely enough, spirituality. Already in 1868, Félix Ravaisson had called this emerging philosophical current "realisme spiritualiste" (1868). Six decades later, Emile Bréhier (1928) would dub it "positivisme spiritualiste."[2]

The idea of contingency as a concrete, existential event rather than as a merely calculable entity is still present in Paul Virilio's writings on the accident as a product of "real contingency." As mentioned in Chapter 3, the

---

1 *La Science et l'hypothèse* (1903); *La Valeur de la science* (1903); *Science et méthode* (1908).
2 Bréhier refers here, above all, to Boutroux and Lachelier.

accident is the event that is most unlikely to happen, but *when* it happens, it looks more necessary than anything else, which is why the accident is always "more real" than reality. For Virilio, the "accident" becomes a metaphysical model of existence, which becomes clear when he affirms that for him "everything that constitutes the world has experienced an accident, and this *without exception*. This colossal dimension of the accident surpasses us, and that's why I am so passionate about it" (34). This is not an Aristotelian reasoning that sees substantial reality as absolute and the accident as relative; on the contrary, here the "accident reveals substance" (107).

The Coincidence in Biology

Given the link that the "science of the coincidence" has with nature and biology, one can expect parallels with what happened in German scientific circles around the same time. I earlier mentioned Driesch, von Bertalanffy, and von Uexküll. However, despite obvious similarities, there were not many exchanges between both camps, which is partly due to the two World Wars that had severed communication. In France, German thought would often still be depicted as mechanistic. Earlier in the nineteenth century, there had indeed been the idealistic *Naturphilosophen* grouped around F. W. J. Schelling who searched for a divine design in natural patterns (or in Goethean archetypes). This was still a brand of determinism by which most of the nineteenth century had been overshadowed. Arthur Schopenhauer and Eduard von Hartmann were the inheritors of this Romantic *Naturphilosophie*. However, at some point, biologists like Driesch and Reinke formulated a new teleological approach that concentrated on living organisms, which they called "neovitalism." This thought is in many respects similar to that of their French colleagues, even though it went almost unnoticed in France. Vice versa, Germans were not much aware of this new output of French philosophy and acknowledged it only once Bergson had become popular.[3] In 1908, Driesch (1908b) publishes a positive review of Bergson's *L'Evolution créatrice*, in which he insisted on the useful amalgamation of biology and philosophy. Much later, Max Horkheimer would write a review of *La Pensée et le mouvant* (1934). After World War II, very few French authors reacted to the work of German biologists and physicians such as Driesch, Uexküll, or Kurt Goldstein. Georges

---

3 Two books by Boutroux were translated into German by Isaak Benrubi: *L'Idée de la loi naturelle dans la science et la philosophie contemporaines* and *De la Contingence des lois de la nature*. German: *Über den Begriff des Naturgesetzes in der Wissenschaft und in der Philosophie der Gegenwart* (Jena: Diederichs, 1907); *Die Kontingenz der Naturgesetze* (Jena: Diederichs, 1911).

Canguilhem applauds, in 1947, in an article on contemporary French philosophy of biology, the work of the neo-vitalists Driesch and Reinke because they consistently question mechanism. But he also regrets that a dynamic philosophy of life had not taken root in France. According to Canguilhem, the reason for this failure is its strong Cartesian heritage. In the Cartesian system, life "has been granted no ontological originality. Understood by reason and contained in matter, life poses no particular theoretical problem and even more so, it contains no mystery" (324).

Maurice Merleau-Ponty creates, in his *Phenomenology of Perception* (1945), a sort of phenomenology of organic life. In 1946, Raymond Ruyer (1902–1987) publishes *Éléments de psychobiologie,* and later also original studies on cybernetics and "neofinalism." Apart from that, it appears that for French philosophers, the analysis of organic life as an accumulation of coincidences remains incompatible with philosophy. The reason for this paradigm is not necessarily an inveterate Cartesianism. When Borel and Boutroux speak of a "science of the coincidence," one needs to understand the intrinsically curious character of this concept. For any science, a position of contingency is difficult to assume because science's *raison d'être* is to explain why things happen. In some way, Borel's as much as Hawking's line of thought is difficult to follow *in scientific terms.* If contingency is real, then this reality is not the reality that science usually talks about. Was Boutroux's book on the "contingency of natural laws" (*De la Contingence des lois de la nature*) not devoted to an oxymoron from the beginning? Any scientific law must be based on some sort of necessity. Contingency, especially when seen from the point of view of modal logic, is different from probability. Probability follows laws that can be spelled out, but contingency has undefinable laws. Eventually, Boutroux suggests that the laws of nature are no laws, or at least no static laws, because in nature, necessity (finality) and contingency (spontaneity) are always combined. Nature is evolution and its laws change in time:

> The laws of nature have no absolute existence; they simply express a given phase, a stage like a moral and aesthetic degree of things. They are the image, artificially obtained and determined, of a model that, in essence, is living and movable [d'un modèle vivant et mobile par essence]. The apparent constancy of these laws is based on the inherent stability of the ideal that one has of it. (Boutroux 1916: 195/French 1908: 155).

Still, Borel's *Le jeu, la chance et les théories scientifiques modernes* would appear in 1938 in a Gallimard series entitled "The Future of Science" (L'Avenir de la science).

Can science ever grasp the contingent reality that these thinkers have tried to conceptualize over decades, or are we not rather in the realm of philosophy or metaphysics by definition? Marcel Conche speaks of a "metaphysics of the coincidence," which he sees as initiated by Democritus, but he quickly points out that this is "not a work of science but of thought" (2002: 4). Opposing itself to providentialist metaphysics, the "metaphysics of the coincidence" aims to explain the world through coincidence, but, obviously, it cannot do so scientifically. Reality might be contingent while science's task remains to describe it in terms of necessities. Only philosophy can develop an analytical approach that is not based on a "necessity of laws," a norm of thought, or even on probabilities, and which is only based on contingencies that cannot be reduced to formal laws.

It has been said at the beginning of this book that coincidence is the event, and contingency is the concept. Science, especially mathematics, can very well deal with (calculate) coincidence as a more or less probable event, but it cannot talk about the concept of contingency, for the simple reason that the latter is philosophical. After all, the French philosophers called their movement the "science of the coincidence" (science du hasard) and not the "science of contingency." This science can, as Borel had pointed out, "administer our actions [...] according to the role of science [and] make it easier for human beings to reflect upon their actions before carrying them out" (1938a: ii). *Scientifically*, contingency can only be apprehended when it is mixed with necessity, as happens in living organisms. Here some amount of necessity emerges through the interdependence between micro and macro elements. In this sense, Gould points out that "the science of contingency must ultimately be integrated with the more conventional science of general theory" (Gould 2002: 47). However, when laws are *purely* contingent, we leave the realm of the natural sciences.

It is thus no surprise that in France, the spirit of the "science of the coincidence" would not enter the research area of biology but rather that of French existentialism as well as modern art. Already Nietzsche suspected that only poets could truly appreciate contingency; and as Rorty sarcastically remarks: "The rest of us are doomed to remain philosophers. We are doomed to spend our conscious lives trying to escape from contingency rather than, like the strong poet, acknowledging and appropriating contingency" (1989: 28).

Surrealism inherited much of the science of the coincidence's potential, as is well demonstrated by André Breton's confession that for him the strongest of all images would be the one that presents the "highest degree of arbitrariness [le degré arbitraire le plus élévé]" (1924: 47). Both Surrealism and Dada stage art production as a chance event. Automatic writing, Marcel Duchamp's readymades (1913), Hans Arp's collages from 1916, and sketches by André Masson self-consciously play with coincidences. Similarly, the Russian Formalists' "disautomatization" (*ostranenie*) enables new expressions and new ways of perception and interpretation by taking into account the coincidence.

Philosophy can philosophize about contingency, but science can deal only with coincidences. The clash between Jacques Monod and Henri Bergson can be traced to the difference between coincidence and contingency. Monod finds that Bergson's vitalism (which he sees as animistic) is purely spontaneous and undirected, which is precisely why human reason, for Bergson, cannot grasp the evolutionary state of life. Philosophy can conceptualize this spontaneous movement, for example, by calling it an *élan vital*, but it must rely on instinct for an appropriate understanding, which is ultimately unsatisfactory for science. Monod writes:

> Contrary to almost all other vitalisms and animisms, that of Bergson predicates no ultimate goal. He refuses to put life's essential spontaneity in bondage to any kind of determination. Evolution, which identifies with the vital element itself, can therefore have neither final nor efficient causes. Man is the supreme stage at which evolution has arrived, without having sought or foreseen it. (1971: 26/French 1970: 40, trans. modified)

Science can detect coincidences and describe their functioning within a social or natural context, but contingency such as it is represented by the *élan vital*, cannot be grasped scientifically. Science comprehends only what is determined, that is, what goes from A to B for a certain reason. At present, contingency is most important in biology, a development that is very much due to Stephen Jay Gould's works on the contingency of evolution. Gould's research can be seen as a continuation of the French "science of the coincidence" as it stresses "the centrality of historical contingency in any theoretical analysis and understanding of evolution and its actual result" (2002: 37). For Gould, "the science of contingency must ultimately be integrated with the more conventional science of general theory" (47). It is desirable that in the future, this research will have an impact on social and historical sciences.

Bergson profoundly influenced Sartre and arguably led the existentialist philosopher to the formulation of the concept of nothingness (see Richmond 2007 and Somers-Hall 2017). Beyond that, Sartre's account of imagination seems to be indebted to Bergson's logic of multiplicities. In *The Transcendence of the Ego*, Sartre's first philosophical work, the author praises Boutroux's criticism of Kant because Boutroux had recognized that Kant's transcendental consciousness depends "merely" on necessary conditions of our empirical existence (see Sartre 1966: 14–15). Contingency remains an important theme in Sartre's future philosophy. On the one hand, contingency must be borne (Michel Kail even talks of Sartre's "Stoicism of contingency," Kail: 170). On the other hand, Sartre describes bad faith (*mauvaise foi*) as an attempt to escape the contingency of life, that is, as a desire to lazily rest within necessities instead of taking advantage of contingencies. For example, for the ill athlete, "his illness is an excuse for not realizing his possibilities as not-ill, but it is not one for his possibilities as ill, which are just as numerous," Sartre writes in the *Notebooks on Ethics* (1992: 448/French 1983: 323). This is not fatalism (putting up with illness) but coping with necessities by seeing contingencies: "It is not a question of adapting oneself to one's illness [d'adopter sa maladie], of installing oneself in it, but living according to norms in order to remain a man" (ibid.). This attitude strongly contrasts with the "anti-existentialism" of the conspiratorial mindset, which strives to find an essential reason for *not* looking at other possibilities within the new necessity (the illness). The conspiratorial mindset will most likely ascribe the illness to an overwhelming power; at the same time, it will not abandon the athlete's former existence because there is no reason to give in or negotiate with these evil powers. A conspiratorially minded athlete will stick to his "essence as an athlete" as if it were God-given; and they will resent the conspiracy that prevents them from assuming this essence.

The conspiratorial mindset is also diametrically opposed to the approaches favored by Boutroux and his colleagues, which are approaches that exalt contingency and deny determination. At the same time, they are opposed to Engels' determinism. Cartesianism, Comte, Engels, and the conspiratorial mindset all deny contingency, but only the latter *mystifies* necessities instead of spelling them out clearly, which sets the conspiratorial mindset against both determinism and the philosophy of Boutroux & cie. Both determinism and the science of contingency want to understand coincidence through reason. Both determinism and anti-determinism want to demystify science, history, and even art by pointing to reasonable structures. However, only the conspiratorial mindset negates the coincidence by ascribing the fortuitous event to a mystified necessity. It declares everything to be determined, but rarely explains the determining cause in terms of reason. The coincidence is not real, but the aspiration to realism that is proper to determinism is likewise absent.

Chapter 10
THE AESTHETICS OF CONTINGENCY

Classical Western (Platonic-Aristotelian) philosophies tend to split the world and everything that exists in it into two sections. According to Rorty, Kant "splits us into two parts, one called 'reason,' which is identical in us all, and another (empirical sensation and desire), which is a matter of blind, contingent, idiosyncratic impressions" (1989: 32). Reason reveals necessary structures whereas contingency is ignorance and blindness. It has been mentioned that already Epicurus tried to overcome this opposition by seeing coincidence as a *rational* explanation. The division of the world into necessity and contingency became one of the most inveterate principles of Western thought, and the last chapter demonstrated how the French "science of the coincidence" acted against it.

Contingency and Creativity

The necessary-contingent opposition is related to the Platonic opposition of the real versus the appearance. In the *Republic* (6: 509d–511c), especially in the *Allegory of the Cave* (Book VII: 514a–517a), Plato differentiates between perceptible and intelligible phenomena and explains how the ever-changing realm of physical objects (particulars) is separate from the invisible and eternal universals, that is, from ideas or "forms." The latter we perceive through reason (*noesis*) or—with regard to mathematical objects and abstract ideas—through intellect (*dianoia*). Physical objects, which are more random than reason-based ideas, can only be cognized through opinion (*doxa*), practical reason (*phronesis*) or trust (*pistis*). Images and appearances of objects occupy an even lower level of cognition than physical objects. Reason "sees" abstract ideas and concepts that are necessary whereas concrete objects and the appearances of objects remain more contingent. When it comes to images in art, we can even judge them by using taste rather than reason.

The light of reason illuminates the world of objects and appearances and shows necessary ideas; thus, and only thus, randomness disappears. Causal determinists like Laplace would merely reformulate this same idea at the end of the eighteenth century. The coincidence is not real but only a dream or an appearance that we perceive because we are scientifically incompetent. As sciences progress, the unreal world of coincidences will be replaced with the real world of necessity.

What does this mean for art? The Platonic distinction between the real and the apparent has been dominating the Western philosophical scene for millennia. Concepts and ideas are real and necessary, whereas objects (and especially images) are random and contingent. Can art ever be a necessity recognized by reason, or is it forever bound to remain irrational and inessential? Can art only subsist within the shadows of contingency, unaffected by the light of reason? Art is already an appearance; and beyond that, it integrates contingency into its expressions. Coincidences are important with regard to the production as well as the perception of art. Though multiple attempts to create a "science of art" (aesthetics) have been launched, especially since the eighteenth century, it remains obvious that reason cannot fully illuminate art. Reason cannot fully replace art's intrinsic contingency in terms of necessity. From a scientific and necessity-seeking point of view, art remains ontologically inferior and therefore eternally obscure. Be it *symbebekos*, the scholastic *accidens*, *hasard*, or *Zufall*: most often, the coincidence signifies a diminution of essence.

The problem with art is that it also expresses essences. Art can convey essential insights into life and the world. How can this be coordinated with the (apparently inessential) contingency to which art is also subjected? Does art have a particular way of dealing with contingency?

This book has already described various ways of combining necessity and contingency. The problem of free will, for example, usually handles the necessity-contingency problem by relying on a concept of ontological contingency. Enlightenment philosophers combined necessity and contingency by seeing reason not as an abstract power but as an entity constructed within random situations. Organic philosophies find that all order emerges internally and is not imposed upon by external forces. In another vein, Arthur Schopenhauer, in the Appendix to the first volume of his *The World as Will and Representation* (1859), establishes that "everything which is actual [wirklich] is also necessary" (2010: 493/German 1998: 592). Schopenhauer's aim is to develop the notions of necessity, actuality, and possibility in the light of the principle of sufficient reason (der Satz vom Grunde). Eventually, he finds that all three coincide. Not only does possibility presuppose necessity, but vice versa, necessity presupposes contingency: "Every object of any sort, e.g. everything that takes place in the actual world, is always simultaneously necessary and contingent: *necessary* in relation to the one thing that is its cause; *contingent* in relation to everything else" (493/592).

However, the ontologically interesting mix of necessity and contingency does not lead Schopenhauer to the conclusion that the coincidence is real and objective. Contingency merely *contributes* to actuality; as such, contingency remains a subjective perception: "Contingency [Zufälligkeit] proves to be a merely subjective phenomenon that arises from the limitation of the horizon of our understanding, and is thus just as subjective as the optical horizon where the sky meets the earth" (497/596).

Once again, the coincidence is not real, but merely something that is "seen" subjectively. Like the Greeks who had integrated contingency into ontology, Schopenhauer combines reality and illusion, suggesting that the subjective-objective way is how we normally perceive the world. Likewise, both the Greeks and Schopenhauer always find contingency to be ethically and anthropologically irrelevant. Schopenhauer's originality is that he does not conclude that the coincidence could be something other than an illusion; he refers to contingency as an "optical" phenomenon. Not only *can* it be seen, but it is always seen. As long as we have an aesthetic view of the world (which we practically always have), we perceive contingency. Not only is the aesthetic contingent, but contingency *is* aesthetic. This does however mean, once again, for Schopenhauer, that contingency should be excluded from the scientific and ethical realm.

Art, Nature, and Liberty

The Platonic reality-appearance dichotomy can be linked to yet another dichotomy: the one that opposes art to nature. It is the insistence on necessity as *the* real part of the world that leads to concepts of "essence," "foundation," as well as "nature." Science can best illuminate nature as long as it believes nature to function along necessary rules. It has been shown above that at least since Darwin, these assumptions about nature are no longer valid. This means that, while the twentieth century overcame a certain necessity-oriented determinism in science, in aesthetics, the contingency-necessity dichotomy still remains intact and can be represented through the following pattern:

contingent vs. necessary
apparent vs. real
art vs. nature

When reflecting on art, this system yields a variety of parallelisms. Nature is real because it is not contingent, whereas art cannot be real because it is not inscribed in the realm of necessary nature. Reason is on the side of both the necessary and the real, whereas contingency is unreal because it cannot be grasped by reason. Reason apprehends necessary structures—or at least probabilities—whereas the purely contingent part of the world escapes reason, which puts art in a peculiar position. According to Canguilhem, "reason is regular like an accountant whereas life is anarchic like an art" (1947: 327). If reason is already so structurally different from life, it is unlikely that it can ever appreciate art.

Part of the problem is the misconception that nature has an intrinsic, goal-oriented necessity; another problem is the misunderstanding of the relations between necessity and contingency in the realm of art. There is a strong link between contingency and creativity; art *needs* contingency because art is an assertion of liberty. Coincidences shape many human activities, but they are most important for creativity because in creative actions, the system, the logic, the ideology, or the theory, all of which claim to be based on necessities, must be enriched by fantasy. And fantasy is always subject to coincidences, which applies to creative *productions* as much as to the *experience* of art. Contingency is an aesthetic quality capable of expressing artistic uniqueness, a uniqueness that the formal method of science has difficulty grasping. There is no necessary rule in art, but artists like to break rules. In artistic productions, more than in any other activity other than gambling, we are aware that every manifestation, every stroke that we see on the canvas, *could* also have been done otherwise. Similarly, in fiction, literary invention is up to the writer: he could have invented whatever he wanted. Not only are we aware of contingency, but we admire it. Longinus said that "what is useful or even necessary for man is at his disposal. Yet, what he admires is the unexpected" (*On the Sublime* 35, 5).[1] In art, we admire the unexpected, which becomes particularly clear not only in crime novels but also in aesthetic phenomena like the sublime or the uncanny (for example, in horror movies) and in Surrealism or Dadaism. Here art turns out to be the opposite of gambling. Though both are very much contingency-based, in a game, the gambler hopes for *the expected* (as it helps him win) and fears the unexpected (the potential loss). Any formal game (and not merely "play") in which winning is no longer the purpose becomes a work of art: deprived of a purpose (the winning), it becomes aesthetic.[2]

The real problem is that, at the same time, aesthetic beauty can very much appear determined by necessities. The slightest modification or the slightest change to a line in a drawing can turn out to be disastrous because now the

---

1 *On the Sublime* is a Roman-era Greek work of literary criticism of the 1st century AD. Its author is unknown but is conventionally referred to as Longinus or Pseudo-Longinus.
2 A game that has really become art would be one in which all players aim to get even. It would not be a game, but a ritual.

line is no longer where it *should* be. Paul Valéry rightfully held that "L'art est non-hasard - par définition" (Valéry: 17), which can also mean that in art, randomness becomes a necessity. Art is an adventure as opposed to a planned trip, but the random events appear as necessary *for this particular adventure*. What distinguishes the adventure from ordinary traveling is that, in the former, random experiences are part of the project. They are necessary for the trip to be an adventure; and the trip as a whole even appears necessary *as an adventure*. In conclusion, in an adventure, contingency has become a necessity, and necessity and contingency form a unity. A further observation is that the adventure also becomes more real through contingency. We can think of adventure tourism where travelers desire to have experiences that are "more real" and more "authentic" than those that can be made during trips in which everything follows the necessities of a preconceived plan. In parallel, art becomes more real through contingency, too. More precisely, art is more real than "regular" or factual life not merely because it contains contingency, but because art creates reality out of contingency, just as the adventure vacation is more "real" because it is improvised. Similarly, a writer *creates* necessities by freely choosing a certain framework for their events with the result that single events, which could also be otherwise, begin to make perfect sense within the set plan. Often, they even make more sense here than they would in real life, which precisely confirms Valéry's idea. Hegel had defined art along very similar lines in his *Lectures on Aesthetics (Vol II)*, which Henrich summarizes like this:

> While in the natural contingent being elements coexist irregularly through the right of the coincidence, in the work of art it is essentially the case that the power of necessity shines through the fortuitous parts that are only related among each other. This has the result that these parts gain, precisely through the being that was first contingent, the appearance that they cannot be otherwise; the unity of the idea breaks, concretely, through the contingency of the exterior.[3]

Even artistic expressions like Surrealism and Dadaism, which play with absolute coincidence and have broad and floating limits of plausibility, produce

---

3 "Denn während im natürlichen kontingenten Seienden durch das Recht des Zufalles die Elemente in Regellosigkeit nebeneinanderstehen, ist das Kunstwerk wesentlich dies, daß an den an sich zufälligen, nur auf sich bezogenen Teilen die Macht der Notwendigkeit zum Scheinen kommt, so daß sie gerade in ihrem zunächst zufälligen Sein den Anschein des Nichtandersseinkönnens gewinnen, in dem die Einheit der Idee durch die Kontingenz des Äußerlichen anschaulich durchbricht" (Henrich 1971: 171).

this kind of aesthetic necessity. The surrealist writer develops a sort of facticity in which contingency is supposed to be accepted—within the work of art—as a necessity. All writers of fiction do this to some extent, but in Surrealism, the outcome is most dramatic. Surrealists produce an aesthetic necessity within an environment of absolute absurdity and randomness.

Art produces its own necessity and is therefore less liable to external necessities laid down, for example, by nature, politics, religion, or the economy. As a result, throughout history, contingency could thrive better in the realm of the aesthetic because here it was protected from the strong appeals to necessity that Western philosophy, religion, and science have been issuing for two millennia. Science, apart from the purely theoretical speculations of the Greek materialists, absorbed the idea of chaos and contingency only at a very late stage. In biology, a perceived reproduction and multiplication of structures only made the idea of randomness scientifically relevant around the nineteenth century, while physics considered contingency noteworthy only in the twentieth century through a change of paradigm in the form of indeterminate physics, quantum mechanics, and chaos theory. Only in the 1920s did quantum physics suggest a coincidence-based concept of math and physics, and only in the 1980s did chaos theory begin to study apparently random behaviors within systems. In comparison, in art, chaos has always existed: it accepted contingency when science and religion still tried to explain the world as a necessary creation.

Before quantum physics, randomness was mostly considered only apparent and not real, simply because in complicated systems the causes could not be known. Only relatively recently did science discover an intrinsic unpredictability in natural phenomena, which led Stephen Hawking to conclude that even God is bound by the Uncertainty Principle. Only late in the history of science could randomness receive the status of reality. When even God is gambling, this means that there is nothing beyond contingency, and consequently, the contingent world must be seen as real. In contrast, art has always tended to know that its expressions are intrinsically unpredictable, that they cannot follow preestablished necessities (for example, they cannot simply imitate reality) and that art can create its *own* "necessary" reality, and that it does so "randomly." Consequently, Stephen Jay Gould thinks that the natural sciences can learn from the literati because even "scientific reality" is "bristling with possibilities, and nudgeable by the smallest of unpredictable inputs" (2002: 1341).

Of course, all this concerns only "good art." Bad art operates with necessities, rules, and stereotypes, and it has been explained in Chapter 5 that this rule-following attitude will most likely lead to kitsch. Propaganda art or too quickly created commercial art follows "necessary" rules and thus eliminates a large amount of the contingency that is required for creative productions. The too quick and too consistent acceptance of commercial, political, scientific, or religious necessities can easily lead to kitsch. No autonomous "aesthetic" necessity is created. Kitsch is indeed very often realistic and insists, in a formulaic fashion, on necessary ways to proceed aesthetically. "Good" art should not follow these kinds of necessities because, in art, necessity arises *from contingency*. Consequently, any aesthetics that integrates contingency into its works is anti-kitsch.

It is interesting to note that with regard to the *activity* of science, coincidence has never been entirely excluded. Even at a time when it was still believed that the universe of science always followed necessary rules, the aforementioned Lichtenberg could point out that "all inventions are due to the coincidence [Zufall], some more, others less, because otherwise any reasonable person could sit down and make inventions just like one writes letters" (1776–1779: 1195). The scientist does not *only* follow methods established by necessity, but their scientific discoveries and decisions also depend on creativity, that is, on contingency. In Lichtenberg's conception, the advancement of science is partly due to contingency, which brings it closer to art.

Aesthetics and contingency always go together. Already, Aristotle saw contingency as a component of an aesthetics that is essential to the artistic production of tragedy. In tragedy, the coincidence comes forth through the narrative. Usually, coincidences collide with necessary ethical obligations. It is here, in the realm of the aesthetic, that Aristotle expresses a pattern that comes very close to the "contingency as reality" concept of the French philosophers presented in the last chapter. According to Aristotle, within certain aesthetic experiences (and especially within those experiences that are determined by the tragic), we become aware of contingency as an aesthetic quality. And in tragedies, this contingency can be experienced as a moment of truth about life. Victor Goldschmidt analyzes this aspect of Aristotle's concept of the tragic as follows:

> There is thus coincidence in our life, there is this obscure cause which, as the first book of the *Physics* attempts to explain—within the limits of what science is able to explain. [The discourse] forces itself to conclude that coincidence is caused only "accidentally." Tragedy, however, can make this cause intelligible, it can submit it to criteria that defy science and that are also pertinent for the development of fables: […] This is what Aristotle calls the wonderful. (Goldschmidt 1982: 404, my trans.)

Creativity transgresses the boundaries of necessary systems and integrates coincidental and imaginative elements that acquire the status of an aesthetic necessity within the fable, the tragedy, or any work of art. In artistic renderings of life, there is always a cooperation of necessity and contingency, whereas in real life, coincidence and necessity tend to be carefully kept apart, for example, when it comes to the cohabitation of the individual citizen (the coincidence) and the state (the necessity). Democratic political systems attempt to coordinate both forces, but this project requires many rules and policies because here we are in the realm of ethics.

The Aesthetics of Life

As the last paragraph indicates, the contingency-necessity pattern does not only concern art in the strictest sense but also the "art of life," and thus ethics, or at least a mixture of ethics (which is about the right actions) and aesthetics. In general, to say that something is "aesthetic" can attach a certain amount of contingency to an achievement, to an event, or even to a person's entire life. For example, when we become aware of how much in our lives depends on chance and not on necessity, when we recognize that our lives are not as goal-oriented as we had perhaps once thought them to be, and when we take an "ironic" and more distanced view toward our lives, then we might say that life is "like a work of art." "Life is like a work of art" expresses the fact that life does not always evolve along the firm tracks of (genetically, ethically, meritocratically, or economically established) purposefulness, but that it can also appear as playful, as though it were an artistic production or an adventure. We recognize the contingency of decisions; just as we recognize the contingency of birth, race, and merits.

Sartre's thoughts on contingent existence have recently been recognized as an antidote to racism. Mabogo More, in his book *Sartre on Contingency: Antiblack Racism and Embodiment,* argues that the notion of contingency is very useful in combating racism as it makes us recognize that "whatever exists, need not exist, and that therefore it can be changed; that the fact that one is born white or black without their choice, has no moral weight at all in treating others as though they are responsible for what they are" (More, blurb). Life is meaningless as long as we only look for transcendental truths that lead *beyond* contingency. The meaning resides rather in the contingency of events. Similar to a work of art, an entire life can dramatically *gain* in meaningfulness and "sense production" once we look at it aesthetically, that is, once we detect and accept the amount of contingency that was invested in its "production." It does not mean that we simply attribute everything to chance; on the contrary, the idea is rather to recognize how randomness has been turned into an aesthetic kind of necessity. For example, when we see a part of our life as a story or as an adventure, any apparent randomness can become an "aesthetic necessity." What happened had to happen *because* the course of events was supposed to be a story or an adventure.

Sartre describes in *Nausea* how apparently random experiences take on meaning as soon as we see them as narratives. Antoine Roquentin, the protagonist of the novel, has had an adventurous life and now looks at his past actions, as well as at other people's actions, with irony and from a distance. Experiences are made of instances, but all those instances will become meaningful once experiences begin forming an adventure. Seen as an *aesthetic* structure, bits of experiences that were once random move toward an end. This does not mean that Roquentin's life had a *telos* or was predetermined by God. The coincidences remain coincidences because otherwise the adventure character would not be sustained. Through a "life as art" perspective, the most meaningless life becomes meaningful and necessary, but the acceptance of contingency is a precondition. The aesthetic perspective requires a distance that remains impossible as long as we stick to preconceived, telic, or divine necessities. Normally, we do not have this perspective while in the middle of it but only afterward. Sartre's adventurer says:

> Something is beginning in order to end: adventure does not let itself be drawn out [ne se laisse pas mettre de rallonge]; it only makes sense when dead. I am drawn, irrevocably, towards this death which is perhaps mine as well. Each instant appears only as part of a sequence [pour amener ceux qui suivent]. I cling to each instant with all my heart: I know that it is unique, irreplaceable—and yet I would not raise a finger to stop it from being annihilated [s'anéantir]. (Sartre 1969: 42/French: 60)

Things used to be chaotic, but *retrospectively*, everything looks coherent. The adventure is like an artistic slice of life. A few pages later, Roquentin describes how life becomes art as though it was a novel:

> Nothing has changed and yet everything is different [tout existe d'une autre façon]. I can't describe it; it's like the Nausea and yet it's just the opposite: at last an adventure happens to me and when I question myself *I see that it happens that I am myself and that I am here; I am the one* who splits the night, I am as happy as the hero of a novel. (Sartre 1969: 56 French: 82, italics only in the French version)

Roquentin sees parts of his life as a finished narrative with an inner necessity. To do so, he first had to take a distanced view at life. In adventures, we are aware of contingencies. As an aesthetic experience, the adventure comes close to a game; and to *become* an adventure, the sequence of events only needs to be seen as such. Purposeful structures, like those determined by ethics or religion, are replaced with aesthetic structures. As it avoids all ethical weightiness, the adventure has the "lightness" of a game. Normally, adventures are not supposed to have a lasting impact, and they are spontaneous and punctual by definition. As we say, "it was *only* an adventure […]"

The Ethics of Merit

In and of itself, life is not logical or rational, and the shift from necessity to contingency implies a shift from ethics to aesthetics, strangely, in order to see what life "really" is. In and of itself, life is not ethical. Vice versa, the shift from aesthetics to ethics can imply a shift from contingency to necessity. Ethics is about rules, whereas aesthetics plays with contingencies. Like science, ethics hates contingency, first of all, because contingency disables any discourse on reward and culpability. Sandel writes that ethics, just like religion, "prompts the successful to believe they are 'doing God's work' and to look down on victims of misfortune" (2020: 50), and adds that such ethical thinking can be found across all political spectrums, not only among religious conservatives. Any ethicization of life is only possible when contingency is at least partially negated. The pressures emanating from meritocracy that so many people today experience as overwhelming are due to the fact that the "aesthetic option" has become less available. When everything is seen in terms of merit, "life as a work of art" becomes impossible. According to Sandel, "viewing health and wealth as matters of praise and blame is a meritocratic way of looking at life. […] everything that happens is a reward or punishment for the choices we make and for the way we live. This way of thinking celebrates a thoroughgoing ethic of mastery and control and gives rise to meritocratic hubris" (50). In other words, the ethics of mastery kills the aesthetics of life.

Were I to decide, as an academic, to write my articles only in order to gain "merit" (as it is now officially called in universities), that is, to gain points for my end-of-the-year evaluations rather than because I am truly interested in certain questions just for the sake of it, I would have overethicized my professional life. To amend this meritocratic life system means to introduce contingency. Winning or losing "merit" should not matter as much as it does today; veering off from the merit path should not immediately show on a merit scale. Academics must have some leeway to pursue interests that are off the merit highway. An ethicized society turns all areas where aesthetic play used to be possible into ethically supported work. To say that this is the logic of capitalism is missing the point; it is rather a Puritan religious ethics. The reason is that capitalism is not about ethics at all; it is not even about how to have a good life. Capitalism is simply about the accumulation of wealth.

Nor has capitalism ever suggested that stepping out of capitalist logic and freely deciding to earn less would be unethical by definition or lead to a bad life. Stepping out of the merit system cannot even be sanctioned in terms of ethical merit. Accordingly, Barrotta writes: "There is no demerit in owning or deciding to cultivate rapidly growing talent on the supply side or rapidly decreasing talent on the demand side (one can think of teachers or certain artisanal works)" (1999: 31). It is not unethical to lose a game or step out of a game; you simply lose. Even the neoliberalist Friedrich Hayek rejected the claim that people who succeed in the liberal economy deserve it *morally*. He "rejects the very idea that the money people make should reflect what they deserve" or that "economic rewards reflect people's merits" (Sandel 2020: 126). Contemporary meritocracy ethicizes capitalism by creating a mixture of economic theory and religion.

There is a flagrant link between this ethicization and the conspiratorial mindset. The project of frantically looking for ethically supported necessities, despite the fact that a more distanced and "aesthetic" view would be more beneficial for having a "good life," has helped to create an immense apparatus of baseless conspiracy theories. Just like meritocracy and neoliberal capitalism, unwarranted conspiracy theories force reality into ethically motivated narratives. The conspiratorial mindset disregards the aesthetic-ironic aspects of situations that are submitted to contingency and describes them in terms of necessity. Already Hofstadter saw *ethical* zealousness at work in the conspiratorial mindset and even believed it to be its driving force. The conspiracy theorist's "sense that his political passions are unselfish and patriotic, in fact, goes far to intensify his feeling of righteousness and his moral indignation" (2012: 4). Basically, the conspiratorial mindset is a lack of "life art" or the incapacity to see life's playful dimension. The conspiracy theorist is not only an alienated scientist but also an alienated ethicist.

Algorithm and Conspiracy

When dealing with creativity, the Western mind will usually reserve a prominent place for contingency. There is, however, in more recent times, a strong tendency to rationalize creativity in order to find necessary rules even in the realm of art. As in many other domains, the algorithm has become the principal tool employed to replace contingency with necessity. I will show in this section that the algorithm is, like the unwarrantable conspiracy theory, a contingency-coping device.

An algorithm is a self-contained mathematical operation used in data processing and automated reasoning. In automatization, everything follows necessary rules and there is no space for contingency by definition. (I agree that algorithms are not entirely automatized but often "disautomatize" themselves on purpose by carefully introducing randomness into their calculations. Sometimes random options appear on YouTube, which represents an artificially installed "adventurous" selection of items.) Of course, applying this technique in the realm of art is problematic. On principle, contingent transformations, which can be read as metaphors for creativity, are not predictable. Despite this, algorithms are used to predict musical trends and even to compose pieces that follow the "necessary" rules of these predicted trends. We see that the conspiratorial mindset is not the only instance that abhors contingency and tries to find necessities at all costs. Music producers and radio directors desire to know which song will please which listener, and which song can interest investors. In a way, they believe that the consumers "conspire," and that this conspiracy exists in the form of a necessary rule hidden beneath the chaotic and contingent reality of the music market. And they try to detect this rule through algorithms.

Of course, as some have pointed out, the system has its limits. Franck Madlener, the director of the French music research institute IRCAM, holds that artificial intelligence "ignores the disruption which is part of the artist's business. One can determine schemes and metrics, which create or follow certain tendencies, but there will always remain a contingent and chancy part. Be assured, AI will not compose the hit of tomorrow" (Carpentier 2021). When songs are calculated, a suprapersonal and supraindividual algorithm absorbs ingenious ideas, on-the-spot metaphors, and all those elements that usually surprise and amaze us in art.

Statistics show that individual and personal events or decisions follow inexorable laws similar to the laws of nature. However, these general laws are established *after* the collection of data about individual facts. It is, of course, tempting to turn the system upside down and suggest that these laws can predict individual actions. This would suggest that statistical laws do not merely describe (contingent) human behavior, but that they are laws in their own right, similar to objective laws about natural phenomena. This is like putting the conclusion before the premise, which is also typical of the conspiratorial mindset. Brotherton writes: "The reality is that our brains often work in reverse. The conclusion comes first, then our brain seeks out and shapes the evidence to fit what it already believes" (2015: 217). As mentioned, in statistics this is called confirmation bias, and in psychology it is called *positive test strategy or biased assimilation*: we interpret ambiguous events in light of what we already believe. In logic, it is called fake reasoning. Much religious thought functions along these lines, of which Ziauddin Sardar provides the clearest example when writing that "in most non-western cultures truth is a priori given; in Islam [...] its source is revelation. In western perception, truth is arrived at by some act of observation and mathematical formulation; it is known only a posteriori. Thus, while non-western cultures start with a set of basic axioms, western civilization is forever searching for truth, something to believe in" (2003: 340). Instead of proceeding from premise to conclusion, Sardar suggests writing the "a priori" conclusion down first, and then searching for premises that match the conclusion. The inquirer is not concerned with finding the right answer but rather with an ulterior goal that is extraneous to the question. For believers, this circularity reinstates the validity of the argument. Algorithms do nothing other than follow this religious pattern of reasoning; and narcissism functions along the same principles. The aim is to find the individual truth suggested by the algorithm, that is, to find the truth one wanted to find. The narcissist's input confirms the proximity of such reasoning with kitsch: here, too, a ready-made aesthetic truth is supposed to be repeated and confirmed.

The drive to eliminate contingency in order to optimize outcomes does not only concern art but, again, also life as such. The philosophy behind the religious algorithmization of everything is that our lives, bodies, conversations, food, and sleep become measurable and that the right calculation of their data will make our lives more efficient. In order to have the "best life"—that is, the best lifestyle in terms of health, ethics, and aesthetics—life should be optimized by spelling out necessary rules that are supposed to lead to happiness. An ideal life partner can be identified with the help of algorithms. The problem is that contingency is an integral part of human life and that happiness can also come about through the *right handling* of contingency and not only through its religious elimination. One might find a suitable partner by chance and against all rules of necessity.

The enthusiastic use of algorithms by which our era is so strongly marked is due to the "fear of the uncertain" or the "fear of the coincidence" that Nietzsche already recognized as a major civilizational force of modernity (1970: 132). Western civilization has been evolving on this path for millennia. For Nietzsche, "culture means to calculate, to learn how to think causally, how to prevent, and how to believe in necessity" (ibid.). At the same time, Nietzsche sees that a potential weariness (Überdruß) with security, beliefs, laws, and calculability can engender the desire for coincidences. In a world in which everything is predetermined, we might desire uncertainty and suddenness, be it only because such elements provide a kind of thrill (Kitzel) that a precalculated world of necessity lacks.[4] Gambling as a social institution has the purpose of producing such thrills, and art can serve a similar purpose.

---

4 See Nietzsche in the posthumous fragments 1887–1888 (KGA 8:2): "Nun stellt die ganze Geschichte der Cultur eine Abnahme jener *Furcht vor dem Zufall*, vor dem Ungewissen,

Everybody sees the absurdity of algorithmically calculating the winning chances in a game of roulette. In art, such calculations are no less absurd, but they are less obvious when applied. Similarly, the careful calculation of one's entire life is just as absurd, though the "contingency reduction devices" that have been presented in Chapter 7 (insurances, vaccinations, genetic engineering, etc.) are constantly trying to bypass the reality of contingency through calculations. Algorithms represent the latest version of such quasi-religious devices, and we will see below that life coaching and the rise of personal development strategies in companies and private life, are other manifestations of the same practice. Calculating artistic expressions and leaving nothing to chance, even in art can be considered the peak of this development.

Nietzsche's reevaluation of values (die Umwertung aller Werte) also concerns the "values" of contingency and necessity. When affirming that civilization moves toward security and the gradual elimination of coincidence, Nietzsche points to the decadence of such a civilization of necessity. For him, this is the civilization of the weak, and those who look for thrills in contingency are always stronger. The civilization of necessity is representative of naïve optimism. In contrast, gamblers and those who take risks and thrive within contingency practice a "pessimism of strength" (Pessimismus der Stärke), which is, for Nietzsche, the "highest culture." Meaningfulness derived from necessities is always boring. Strong people find senseless evil (das sinnlose Übel) more interesting and can even enjoy absurdity. In former times, necessity was guaranteed by God; now other necessities have replaced God. According to Nietzsche, strong people remain more thrilled by "a worldly disorder without God, a world of the coincidence in which the terrifying, the ambiguous, the seductive is essential."[5] As mentioned, authors like Simmel, Scheler, or the Italian Futurists who read Nietzsche preached a similar break away from the necessities that modern civilization imposes upon humans. They saw the First World War as an experience that enabled the thrill of contingency.

It is not difficult to guess what Nietzsche would have said about algorithms. The algorithm is emblematic of the rules followed by the weak who fatalistically submit to necessities. Paradoxically, those who employ the concept

---

vor dem Plötzlichen dar. Cultur, das heißt eben *berechnen* lernen, causal denken lernen, prävenieren lernen, an Nothwendigkeit glauben lernen. [...] Ja, es ist ein Zustand von Sicherheitsgefühl, von Glaube an Gesetz und Berechenbarkeit möglich, wo er als *Überdruß* ins Bewußtsein tritt, - wo *Lust am Zufall, am Ungewissen* und *am Plötzlichen* als Kitzel hervorspringt" (132).

5 "[...] so entzückt ihn nun eine Welt-Unordnung ohne Gott, eine Welt des Zufalls, in der das Furchtbare, das Zweideutige, das Verführerische zum Wesen gehört" (132).

of necessity intend to combat what they call the "fatalism of contingency." Like *phronesis* in ancient times, algorithmic calculation is advertised as expert knowledge of how to behave in contingent circumstances. It is seen as a strength rather than a weakness, which is a paradox because, as has been shown above, normally determinism is the result of a strong belief in necessity, and contingency liberates us from this determinism. In the world of algorithms, this paradigm is flipped: it is through reasonably calculated necessities, rather than contingencies, that freedom is found. For the engineers of necessities, accepting *contingencies* means precisely to fall into fatalism, which runs entirely counter to Sartre's and Nietzsche's ideas of contingency as liberty and strength. For algorithm engineers, a well-calculated probability has become an essence to which we should submit our existence, instead of, as Sartre urges, imposing our own existence upon the world and only determining essences *afterwards*. Through algorithms, we accept our own essentialization via quantification and construe this procedure as an act of freedom because what has been quantified are *our own* choices. The profile that the algorithm has derived from our browsing history is supposed to lead to authentic statements about our preferences. However, such assumptions of authenticity are only viable as long as we believe that choices are always necessary. How much of our browsing history is due to contingency? The algorithm is a superb example of how contingency is transformed into necessity; the problem is that it does not transform our lives into art but merely into a scientifically established entity. Against this, real life (as opposed to life constructed by algorithms) is much more like art. In real life, contingency, and especially the right handling of contingency, can lead to more authenticity and originality. But this authenticity *emerges* and is not *created*. Algorithms are machines that *create* authenticity, which means that they apply the model of creationism to real life.

Finally, the conspiratorial mindset shares a similar belief: it holds that everything has been necessarily created and that nothing can coincidentally emerge. There is a huge hub of creationist and "anti-emergence" thinking in contemporary culture that manifests itself on various levels. Brian Keeley makes the connection between over-rationalization (through algorithms) and the conspiratorial mindset clearest: "We should be careful not to over-rationalize the world or the people that live in it. Rejecting conspiratorial thinking entails accepting the meaningless nature of the human world. Just as with the physical world, where hurricanes, tornadoes, and other 'acts of God' *just happen* [...]" (2006: 59).

As they do with creativity, algorithms also computerize symbolization, figures of knowledge, as well as the registration of knowledge, which means that contingency has been considerably reduced in these thinking processes.

What gets lost most flagrantly is the expectation of the unknown. The future does not emerge but is *created* according to the rules of a machine-produced, static regularity. The algorithmization of the world is thus a sort of creationism. Algorithms contain self-sufficient necessities that must be called fake as opposed to real for the simple reason that the real always contains more contingency than algorithms typically allow. In other words, algorithms transform our lives into kitsch lives in which a single rule and a single truth tend to establish "the real," and in which few nuances can be considered. Nuances will be calculated as probabilities, that is, as sub-rules of the necessary.

Carl Bergstrom (an evolutionary biologist) and Jevin West (a computer scientist) have identified, in their recent *Calling Bullshit: The Art of Skepticism in a Data-Driven World* (2021), a social phenomenon that they call "new-school bullshit," which involves statistics and algorithms. This cultural phenomenon

> uses the language of math and science and statistics to create the impression of rigor and accuracy. Dubious claims are given a veneer of legitimacy by glossing them with numbers, figures, statistics, and data graphics. New-school bullshit might look something like this: "Adjusted for currency exchange rates, our top-performing global fund beat the market in seven of the past nine years." (2)

The phenomenon they describe is a sort of scientific kitsch presented in the language of math and statistics.[6] I referred to bullshit in Chapter 5 as a more generalized version of the aesthetic phenomenon of kitsch. For Bergstrom and West, "the algorithms driving social media content are bullshitters" (29), which confirms the claim that algorithms create a kitsch world. YouTubers can be like sophists who operate with rhetoric, "likes," and clickbait titles, and might insist that these items express truths. They might be ethically and even scientifically correct, but these sophists neglect the common good that can only be found in the "art of life," which always contains contingency.

As mentioned, the above way of using sophisticated calculations in real life thrived around the turn of the nineteenth century. Statistics calculated "normality," which permitted society to evaluate its own achievements mathematically. Robert Musil found that "the slightest decision requires today the competences and the intelligence of a Leibniz" (in Bouveresse 1993: 57). Algorithms began even earlier, with the Bernoulli brothers, and the young Leibniz had already established, in his *De Arte Combinatoria*, an alphabet of human thought (an idea first presented by Descartes) and attempted to

---

6 On the relationship between kitsch and the philosophical notion of "bullshit" (established by Harry Frankfurt), see Botz-Bornstein 2015 and 2016.

understand all possible concepts as mere combinations of some more basic concepts. Characteristically, Leibniz gave this technique the name "art": *De Arte Combinatoria*. Everything thinkable can be expressed through the combination of basic elements, and the combinations can be calculated. *De Arte Combinatoria* provides a logic of creative invention that manifests many parallels with contemporary algorithms (see Rieger 1997). Cartesianism as well as Comte's mechanical determinism—which Boutroux criticized in 1874 when insisting that mathematical and quantitative procedures cannot grasp the real world—would build further on these mechanistic premises prevalent since Descartes. Descartes's "animal = machine" paradigm, defined in Part V of the *Discourse on Method* (1637), explains animal behavior in terms of the necessities dependent on the disposition of the animal's organs. No contingency can interfere with this mechanics. Viewed through the lens of critical nineteenth-century French "Science of Contingency," algorithms appear similar to those idealistic and schematic conceptions that Cournot and Taine used when analyzing history. Just like these deterministic historical schemes, the orders of algorithms are abstractions. They might provide a convenient way of *describing* life, but they cannot grasp it, let alone predict it. Therefore, Boutroux insists that science must "discover the contingency that exists in the world" (Boutroux 1916: 36), which is precisely what one could tell algorithm designers today. Despite their pretension to establish the best possible *real* life, algorithms work in the realm of appearance, which is, today, almost an intuitive truth given that much of the "real" life they help produce takes place in virtual reality. Meetings are virtual, relationships are online, and so on. But real life *should* still be experienced as unpredictable and as something that cannot be produced by algorithms. Real life is simply more "aesthetic" as it contains contingency.

The ambition to create idealistic and schematic models of life is not unique to certain YouTube users; the latter share this ambition with the conspiratorial mindset. The parallelism is strong: looking for a certain set of information online in order to validate what one already believes is precisely the posture of the conspiratorial mindset. Modern information technology accelerates this process. Instead of considering various possibilities, one wants confirmation, and one wants it quickly. Both algorithm designers and the conspiratorial mindset cannot bear contingency and seek to spell out necessary rules at any cost. Nietzsche would have identified them as weak protagonists of a decadent culture of necessity.

Once we admit that reality is a matter of contingency, we must conclude that algorithms operate similarly to unwarranted conspiracy theories because they construct necessities that do not reflect reality. This process leads algorithms to repeatedly recommend similar content to people, which coincidentally leads algorithms to encourage groundless conspiracy theories: once a conspiracy video is viewed, YouTube suggests more videos of the same kind, and the spectator falls down a rabbit hole. The freedom that has been acquired in modern or "postmodern" societies has led to new constraints, imposed upon us not by dictators or a capitalist system but by technology. The conspiratorial mindset is part of the same development because it fights contingency and looks for necessities that are not inscribed in the real world at all, but which can be put there by the human mind. According to Dominique Cardon, social indeterminism has led to a new determinism, or a behaviorism of new calculation techniques (2015: 68). The same social indeterminism has led to the proliferation of unwarranted conspiracy theories that are desperately searching for determination. What is needed is not a Cartesian mechanism that explains the world in terms of necessary rules or an *Arte Combinatoria*, but rather a real-world *phronesis* that helps us find our way amid contingencies. This might not always be as safe as following the "necessary" rule of the algorithm, but it represents a way of life that *needs* to be adopted if one wants "real life." "To be intelligent means to find one's way [se débrouiller], to try, to grope, to be mistaken," writes Alain (1920: 81). To live means to have the right to make mistakes, to be lost, to take risks, to lose time and money, to marvel at something one doesn't really understand, and to shoulder the responsibility for mistakes one has made.

The Aesthetics of Gambling

The combination of contingency and necessity, or the ambition to overcome both in order to act naturally and be creative, relates to aesthetic actions. Contingency is real: it can create disasters or lead us out of painful conditions. Despite this, contingency remains an abstract term that is difficult to grasp in terms of real life. It might lurk behind this or that event, but how will we even know it was there in the first place? Through play, contingency becomes concrete and can be better handled. As mentioned in Chapter 9, Alain declared that he prefers betting at horse races to more abstract forms of gambling (1920: 81). He wanted contingency to be linked to human activity, life, and labor, and not just be an abstract and mathematical concept. Play is a real-life activity and can be a bodily activity; it is shaped by different "ways of doing" and it even has a style. To a large extent, a game's style is determined by the right handling of contingency and necessity. In play, finding the right balance between the natural and the artificial is very much linked to a mastery of the necessity-contingency dichotomy.

The right handling of contingency and necessity also has ethical implications. Ethics is usually about what should be done out of necessity, but paradoxically, the assumption of such necessities only makes sense as long as we admit that contingency exists. Aristotle can present the "right action" as a moral problem only because there is contingency in life. If human life took place in a world in which all actions were necessary, it would be absurd to talk about moral questions at all. This becomes clearest when we think of an action that we only enjoy because it is determined by coincidence: gambling. Gambling would lose its attraction if contingency were replaced with necessity. The number of right actions is relatively limited, but they cannot be *necessarily* followed and must be found while reckoning with contingency. At the same time, the gambler does not simply submit himself to contingency by considering it as an absolutely unforeseeable force; he rather tries to deal with it in a creative fashion by combining (sometimes illusory) necessities with contingencies. Contingency does not exist abstractly here as the contrary of necessity, rather necessity and contingency have been (apparently) relativized, and this is precisely the attraction of gambling. The creativity of the gambler lies in the fact that he does not calculate his chances beforehand. A non-creative approach toward gambling would calculate algorithms and thus transform contingency into necessity. Professional statisticians do indeed visit casinos to make profits. They are not only scientific but also utilitarian, looking for businesslike efficiency, which is beneficial to them but not to the game (and the casino). In a Kantian "aesthetic" sense, the game should have no exterior purpose.

The same can be said about the gambler who consistently plays their "lucky number" in a roulette game to (erroneously) enhance his perceived sense of control. In reality, he only *loses* control by the very fact that he plays a number that will most probably never come. His "control" is an illusion, just like most control is an illusion in gambling; but in their case, the illusion is too obvious. We would deliver the same comments about the gambler who, when the odds are clearly stacked against him, believes he can transcend bad luck by holding on to a belief that destiny selected him for victory. Real gambling, which tries to benefit from contingency without transforming it into necessity, requires a certain psychological profile. We can say that the gambler needs to be "cool." The concept of coolness also includes ethical notions and good gambling is a matter of aesthetics as well as ethics. Coolness means to stay calm under stress (see Botz-Bornstein 2010). It is unethical to submit gambling to excessive (economic) rules of necessities; and a bad gambler (especially a bad loser) can be characterized as an unethical person.

It becomes obvious that not only does the bad gambler adopt the posture of a conspiracy theorist, but the conspiracy theorist also adopts the posture of a bad gambler. There is a behavior that can be called "inverse ressentiment": instead of only resenting his bad luck, the bad gambler applauds himself when he is lucky and does not recognize his luck for what it is, believing it to be a necessity. We can quote Nassim Taleb, who depicts in his book *Fooled by Randomness* several narcissistic characters (who are mostly dressed in black business suits), and who have in this book been called kitsch characters. They advertise chance as necessity:

> One may argue that the actor who lands the lead role that catapulted him into fame and expensive swimming pools has some skills others lack, some charm, or a special physical train that was a perfect match for such a career. I beg to differ. The winner may have had some acting skills, but so do all of the others, otherwise they would not have been in the waiting room. (2001: 182)

The good gambler who has the right ethico-aesthetic attitude assumes responsibility for their losses and does not accuse imaginary necessities of the loss. They are supposed to keep a straight face even when losing and accept the game's contingency. A good gambler does not say, when losing, "why does this happen to me?" From an existentialist point of view, they could have avoided the loss they suffered by not gambling in the first place; once they decide to gamble, they are accountable. The same goes for the winner. Seeing necessity in contingency is unethical as well as an aesthetic mistake.

In gambling, the one correct ethico-aesthetic attitude is that of moderation. The good gambler is supposed to avoid fanaticism as well as exaggerated pride. In the end, it is only a game. Putting up with contingencies, which is the only demeanor that makes sense when gambling, requires an anti-conspiracy psychological profile. This does not mean that the good gambler is insensitive and does not care about loss. They should simply have no regrets and no ressentiment. Fanaticism and exaggerated pride are often the results of ressentiment.

The cool attitude of the gambler can also be called tragic irony. There is an awareness of loss, but an ironic distance created by the simultaneous awareness that "everything is only a game" helps the good gambler get over the losses. The good gambler does not see loss as a disaster, disappointment, injustice, or conspiracy. They are neither optimistic nor pessimistic but simply assume the facticity of life. This is only possible because they do not believe in absolute truths or absolute necessities: such things do not exist in games. The good gambler does not entertain a "best world" utopia in which they will always win, but they are always aware that contingency can change the situation at any moment.

Chapter 11

CONTINGENCY IN EASTERN PHILOSOPHIES

This final chapter explores the ways in which Eastern philosophies avoid the obsessions with necessity that are so common in Western philosophy and culture, and which have led to a conspiratorial mindset, among other things. More consistently than Western philosophies, Eastern philosophies have tried to see the world in terms of contingency, or rather, as a realm in which the contingency/necessity dichotomy has been overcome. These views contrast most clearly with conspiracist ways of thinking, as the conspiratorial mindset's main occupation is to construct permanent and rigid identities, beliefs, foundations, and opinions. The purpose of these constructions is to create security. Eastern philosophies acknowledge that contingency can be difficult to bear, but the contingency-coping devices they offer are usually different from Western ones. Instead of replacing contingency with necessity, they recommend seeing necessities as non-essential. The conspiratorial mindset would certainly be the textbook example of a person in whom Buddhist teachers would try to instill an awareness of impermanence.

Strangely, the conspiratorial mindset can at times sound vaguely "Buddhist" as it tries to bring relief from the so-called real world or asks us to "awaken" to a reality that remains hidden from ordinary people. Such a Buddhist air seems to permeate the conspiratorial mindset because, on top of it, it preaches that the conspiracy must be borne like karma. But it is precisely non-Buddhist, because it is a non-dynamic perception of destiny or karma, or a view that refuses to see the contingency of time and history. The conspiratorial mindset cannot overcome its destiny and declare its shaping forces to be non-essential, but rather reifies destiny through ressentiment, and perhaps even to the point of seeking revenge.

Buddhism

Buddhism is traditionally rooted in doctrines of impermanence (*anitya*), emptiness (*sunyata*), no-self (*anatta*), as well as in conditioned or dependent arising (*pratitya-samutpada*). It teaches us to let go of such supposed necessities, as we tend to cling to them in the form of rigid images of our selves, or of fixed conceptions of how we think the world should be. The Buddhist philosophical view is that everything is impermanent, conditional, and thus contingent. Buddhism does not presuppose the existence of a god who controls the destiny of humans, with the result that, a priori, concepts of possibility and contingency can enter this philosophy more freely than in monotheistic religions and cultures. There is not even a god in the form of *contingentia*, on which all contingency reposes and which, in Medieval Europe, could represent the world's contingency *as* a necessity. Buddhism suggests an anti-essentialism in which contingency plays an important role as "dependent arising" or "dependent origination" signifies that all phenomena are interdependent and thus, principally, contingent. Impermanence means that all things change, which further supports a contingency-oriented view. Finally, the idea of "no-self" expresses the fact that the world does not have what Rorty calls a "core-self" and therefore no absolute necessity.

Karma as a principle of cause and effect is not deterministic but rather exists within constellations of impermanence and conditioned arising. Contingency is incorporated into karma. We can be liberated from karma through an act of personal choice; but this liberation remains strictly linked to the realization of the relationships between history and time. Only once we recognize the contingent state of a world in which everything is only temporary, will we be delivered from those tensions, anxieties, and ressentiments that make us suffer, that is, from our karma.

For Buddhism, our being in the world is purely fortuitous: certain conditions came together, and we thus happened to be; it could just as well have been otherwise. Being surprised at our own existence and at the existence of the world is a Buddhist sentiment that Western philosophies (Heidegger, for example) sometimes mention but rarely see as central. Because of contingency, everything, including our own existence, is fragile. Crises such as the one caused by coronavirus make us realize the fragility and impermanence of our lives. Nothing has a permanent soul or essence. However, it is also because of this very contingency that we are capable of determining our existence and of transforming the world. Buddhism aims to create a particular psychological profile: we should always be mentally prepared for contingencies.

This does not mean that Buddhism is relativistic. On the contrary, Buddhism looks for that which needs no explanation. Necessities need explanations, while contingency cannot be explained. Buddhism arrives at a generative "nothingness" that is purely contingent, which Hindu thought calls the Brahman without qualities, and which, in Western thought, might come closest to Plotinus's One. In Buddhism, it is called *sunyata*, which functions as a denomination of reality. Contingency reveals the voidness of reality in its most extreme form. Contingency is the nature or the true form of the being of reality, and the necessities we perceive are deceitful appearances similar to dreams or illusions.

Contingency is also cosmological because the universe has no beginning. There is what Nietzsche would call a purposelessness of the eternal cosmos. Nagarjuna, the second-century Indian Mahayana Buddhist philosopher, never referred in his cosmological teachings to a supreme non-contingent principle and thus held that the universe is contingent. As with the Greeks and the Chinese, the universe has always been there as *anādi* (beginninglessness), and it is irrelevant to ask when, how, and why it began (see Nagarjuna 2015: 33 and Stcherbatsky 1936: 34). Within the universe, nothing has self-existence because everything is interrelated.

Buddhism's special approach toward contingency becomes clearest when it strives toward a transcendent or intellectualist liberation from time. The ordinary experience of time is that of continuity, which presupposes that instants have a concrete existence. Through continuity, time can be perceived as being composed of periods or units, but these are only illusions. Only by saying that time is purely contingent and does not exist as a necessity in any form will we be liberated from a mathematical concept of time. When existence is a dynamic and continuous movement, time cannot be static and follow necessary mathematical rules. Like existence, time must be radically understood as "lived time." Dōgen, the thirteenth-century Japanese founder of the Soto school of Zen,[1] sees time therefore as "contingent lived-time" (Heine 1985: 4). If time is statically conceived of as an accumulation of time-points that are "piled up" on one another, there is only necessity; but time should not be based on a necessary structure of succession. In contingent lived-time, we can still distinguish between past, present, and future, but simultaneously, "all time" appears as a whole. Within these constellations, contingency will not manifest itself in separation (not even temporarily) from a world of necessity, meaning that contingency is not simply inserted into a world that is still controlled by a necessary logic. Instead, the world itself is declared to be contingent, as says Dōgen in the *Shobogenzo*: "Life is a stage of time and death is a stage of time, like, for example, winter and spring. We do not suppose that winter becomes spring or say that spring becomes summer" (Dōgen 1972: 103). This indicates the complete discontinuity of time. Life is

---

1 The Soto school (Sōtō-shū 曹洞宗) is the Japanese line of the Chinese Cáodòng school of the eighth century. The Japanese brand of the sect was not really founded but rather imported into Japan in the thirteenth century by Dōgen Zenji.

absolutely life in and of itself but not because the becoming or the transition would be relative in contrast to the absolute life. There is not even becoming, because becoming still indicates a shift from the possible to the actual. Dōgen's Zen Buddhism does not try to put time "in order" according to new criteria. Instead, it attempts to grasp the existential condition of the world and of human beings in a direct way as a "fullness of time" (Abe 1985: 64) recognizing that time *is* discontinuous and submitted to radical contingency. And only within this time can Buddha-nature manifest itself.

In other words, Buddhism strives to attain an "existential presence" in which everything is experienced as fluid, which accords with the concept of impermanence (*anitya*). Everything is changing. Normally, we can perceive change only when the present is assumed as constant and stable. Therefore, here, existence and time must be based on an "absolute contingency" that is not viewed in opposition to necessity. When there simply *is no time*, any opposition of contingency and necessity stops making sense. The liberation from time is supposed to lead to the intemporal eternity of Nirvana. Nirvana is unconditioned; it is beyond conditions and causes, and because it is beyond time, as an absolute contingency, it also exists *beyond* contingency. Again, this does not mean that time is relative. The present is still the present and the past is still the past.

In Western terms, Buddhism, with its transcendental atemporality, is not Aristotelian but rather on the side of Stoicism. When we have an awareness of contingency, we know that time does not develop progressively, with one instant producing the next instant. This view excludes any conspiratorial thinking based on resentment. Resentment is always directed against the past, but in contingent lived-time, no resentment toward the past is possible.

The fact that contingency and necessity form a whole, that they *aufheben* (sublate) each other in an absolute contingency, is difficult to grasp for the intellect. Often, Japanese art and aesthetics attempt to depict this constellation visually. Influenced by Buddhism, traditional Japanese art strives to express transiency and the passage of time by highlighting imperfection, incompleteness, asymmetry, irregularity, and suggestiveness in its expressions. Weathered and worn aesthetic items underscore a contingent, perishable, conditional existence. Such artistic devices permit a complex handling of contingency. The mere affirmation of contingency would lead to fatalism and abandonment, which is what Zen Buddhism tries to avoid. Correspondingly, in Japanese art, contingency will often be shown against a background of necessity, which can be considered an aesthetic expression of contingency qua necessity. Robert Wicks has given a list of how contingency and necessity can be found combined within one aesthetic expression:

(1) the uneven ceramic teacup that is set against the simplified, polished architectural setting of the tearoom; (2) the sparse decor of a Zen meditation hall that is accentuated by the contingent bodily appearances of the meditators; (3) the rough and jagged rocks of the dry landscape garden, as they are set against the even, perfectly raked field of gravel [...]. (2005: 97)

Without the complementarity of contingency and necessity, contingency would be understood as an essence to which the spectator must submit themselves. However, paradoxically, contingency will here rather be perceived as "mere contingency" as it appears, within a single aesthetic expression, coupled with necessity. At the same time, such an expression also avoids the relativism that essentialized versions of contingency could evoke.

Contingency in Language

Like Daoists, Buddhists struggle with questions surrounding the relation between language and experiential reality. By concentrating on necessity, the human mind manages to distinguish essences, which it will reify, most of the time, through language. For example, it invents words for black and white in order to grasp realities of race but forgets that racial reality is contingent and far more complex than simply *either* black *or* white. Categories such as black and white are shaky because, in real life, one can *coincidentally* change into the other within shifting contexts. It has been shown above that Wittgenstein and continental philosophy of language held that language cannot grasp reality because language is always already essentialized or "necessitized." Henri Poincaré found that even geometrical axioms are not self-evident truths but only linguistic expressions that do not correspond to anything real. All this matches with Buddhist as well as Daoist criticism of language, which is constantly aware of reality's contingency input, an input that language cannot grasp. As a result, most often, these Eastern philosophies conceive of language only as a means to a nonlinguistic end. Ultimately, truth is "beyond words and letters." The mind constructs a reality through language and forgets that concepts, categories, and names can only grasp those things that are supposed to be necessary. In Zen Buddhism, the *koan* can lead to liberation from language. What matters most is a pre-linguistic immediacy to be grasped in the form of a concrete experience. According to Masao Abe, "not relying on words or letters" implies a "return to the source prior to words and letters, that is a return to Buddha's Mind as the source of the Buddhist Scripture" (1995: 174). Non-linguistic and non-conceptual thinking avoids necessary structures and can, eventually, lead to a perception of the world as contingent. This language skepticism, or this distrust in any final vocabulary, comes close to the sort of skepticism that Rorty designates as ironist. Borrowing an expression from Sartre, Rorty calls language skeptics "meta-stable" as they are "never quite able to take themselves seriously because always aware that the terms in which they describe themselves are subject to change, always aware of the contingency and fragility of their final vocabularies, and thus of their selves" (Rorty 1989: 73).

Daoism

Daoism has a similar attitude toward the realization of contingency as it directly links, similar to Buddhism, contingency to the phenomenon of existence. It is possible to imagine the above-mentioned good gambler as a reedition of Zhuang Zhou from the famous Daoist "Butterfly Parable" in the *Zhuangzi* (Chuang-tzu). Zhuang Zhou is "acting happy with oneself and with wishes gladly fulfilled" because, for him, being a butterfly or being Zhuang Zhou is a matter of contingency. Zhuang Zhou does not search for necessities (let alone for conspiracies) that have turned him into one or the other. His life as a butterfly/non-butterfly is more like a game that must be played; and it is "just" a game because, in the end, winning or losing does not make much of a difference to him. Whatever the outcome of the transformation, the result will be accepted. For Daoism, the world is in a state of constant transformation (*hua* 化) from which all necessary essences are excluded, which is well shown by the Butterfly Parable. The parable is the last text to appear in a chapter called "Adjustment of controversies," which has also been translated as "The Equalization of Things" or as "The Smoothing out of Differences." Zhuang Zhou does not know whether he is a butterfly dreaming that he is Zhuang Zhou or whether Zhuang Zhou is dreaming that he is a butterfly:

> Once, Zhuang Zhou fell into a dream-and then there was a butterfly, a fluttering butterfly, self-content in accord with its intentions. Acting happy with himself and with wishes gladly fulfilled. (Trans. Moeller 1999: 446)

Zhuang Zhou being a butterfly is entirely contingent; it is not a necessary essence because his being is in *constant* transformation. The contingent being can be defined as that which does not have a sufficient reason in itself or as that which is nothing by itself, which is precisely what Zhuang Zhou appears to be in the parable. Daoism derives a certain purity of action and of being from this concept of transformation. Necessities can create images of the world in which the world appears as a difficult place to live in; a place full of constraints, threatening schemes, and conspiracies. Daoism wants to get rid of such necessities. It does not mean that constraints, threatening schemes, and conspiracies are non-existent. Daoism wants to get rid of the unwarranted ones. The problem is that people have plenty of unwarranted necessities (conspiracies) rooted in their minds, which sets limitations. The *Zhuangzi* says: "With everything people encounter, they become entangled; day after day, they use their minds in strife [...] sweating and laboring to the end of their days" (Ch. 2, trans. Watson 37–38). These people are not aware of contingency. "Acting happy with oneself and with wishes gladly fulfilled" is only possible when the contingency of existence is fully assumed. The conspiratorial mindset does the opposite as it "uses its minds in strife," which gets it ever more entangled in apparent and unwarranted necessities.

Both Daoism and Zen Buddhism administer a mortal blow to what Nassim Taleb calls "standardized intelligence," "epistemic arrogance," or "nerd knowledge," which is knowledge that works with phony bell curves and pretends that everything is necessary. Daoism and Zen Buddhism design a sort of "absolute existentialism" into which no "Platonified" intelligence can cut watertight compartments; and this is only possible because Daoism and Zen Buddhism achieve a coexistence of contingency and necessity. Essences are only potential, whereas *in actu* there is only existence. The mind constructs a fake reality of necessities, which makes us lose our natural flexibility of mind. However, contingency is an integral part of life and nature, not only because almost anything can happen at any moment, but also because we can never be sure that anything in our lives (in the past as well as in the present) has been determined by necessity. We can never pretend that the roles of managers, teachers, or fathers that we have been playing have been bestowed upon us with absolute necessity. And once we are aware of this contingency, we will no longer play these roles with absolute sincerity. Necessity is reserved for people who are convinced of essences and authenticities, whereas Zhuang Zhou is simply "acting happy with himself and with wishes gladly fulfilled" without having any pretensions toward the sincerity or authenticity of his role.

Those who desire necessity and discard contingency are looking for an authentic life, an authentic language, or an authentic artistic style in which everything is "real," and nothing is pretended. In short, in which everything is the way it must necessarily be. In art, they will most probably look for a maximum of realism and end up with kitsch. Though they believe they are looking for reality, from a Daoist point of view, the necessities they are looking for are only appearances. Reality is rather that all our roles and actions, as well as the reality that art is trying to depict, are social constructs: they are temporary, contingent, incongruent, or, to use Daoist vocabulary, they are subject to the "transformation of things" (*wu hua* 物化). Skepticism toward necessity and the acceptance of contingency is therefore always the most "authentic" attitude.

Life Coaching and Fake Necessities

In this chapter, I contrasted Buddhism and Daoism with the conspiratorial mindset, but it is, of course, possible to contrast these philosophies with many other manifestations of late Western modernity. In the above chapters, I evoked algorithms and their exaggerated search for necessities. In this section, I want to discuss the phenomenon of life coaching. Since life coaching sees itself as a lifestyle philosophy, it can very well be discussed and evaluated in the context of Buddhist and Daoist precepts. Just like algorithms, life coaching programs, personal development courses, as well as positive thinking books, establish necessities by excluding contingency. This goes for positive thinking programs of the 1950s, for "humanist psychology" of the 1960s, for "positive psychology" of the 1990s, as well as for the most recent alternative management strategies. It goes less for New Age-inspired methods because the latter are somehow linked to Eastern philosophies. But even the latter are arguably led by the fear of the uncertain and the belief that, in order to have the best life in terms of health, ethics, and aesthetics, life must be optimized by spelling out necessary rules that are supposed to lead to wealth, efficiency, and superiority. For New Age, it is the "true self" that needs to be discovered, which means that the contingencies of life (birth, abilities, etc.) must be overcome. The contemporary expansion of algorithms, unwarranted conspiracy theories, and the "life coaching" business are similar. Just like the conspiratorial mindset, New Age movements since the 1960s issue vigorous "wake up" calls, inviting adepts to discover their "interior force" to reach the fullness of their authentic being by becoming aware of necessities that were, so far, hidden. However, such contemporary pushes toward individualization and the finding of the true self are flagrant manifestations of a fallacy because, in the end, such approaches do not point to any kind of reality. As a matter of fact, reality is always contingent, which means that there is no "true self" to be found. Despite this, lifestyle consultants advertise a certain authenticity of human existence as necessities that they claim can be retrieved in the form of ideals, images, or experiences. Despite frequent appeals to "Eastern" sources, this most clearly contrasts with Daoism, for which there are no such essences in the form of ideals, images, or experiences: any "authentic" way of life can only emerge and be experienced within a realm of contingency. Only through a Daoist "carefree wandering" (*you* 遊), will the "self" emerge without being created and without being found or revealed in the form of an authentic being. It can even emerge without being liberated from the shackles of (contingent) evil.

Of course, life coaching programs do not simply point to ideals, images, or essences and are, in fairness, more sophisticated. They are not simply consultancy sessions in which experts set rules and guidelines. In some ways, coaching programs follow an apparently "Daoist" idea of free and easy rambling, meaning that the client must find his/her "self" on his/her own because he/she is *only* "coached" and not *taught* by a teacher or advised by a consultant. Coaching is not help but always "self-help," which means that despite its focus on necessity, life coaching has not entirely abandoned the idea of contingency. However, here it just follows the strategy of algorithms. The main trick of life coaching is even that it *pretends* to replace necessity with contingency, which is in keeping with the principles of modern capitalism. The identity-fashioning market concentrates on self-directed learning and self-fulfillment leading to the idea that "the coach functions only as a tool used by the client for her own purposes," as writes Michal Pagis (2016: 1095) who has interviewed a large number of life coaches for his research on the topic. Most of the coaches Pagis interviewed insisted on the ludic aspect of coaching. Coaching is not comparable with medical cures based on necessities. By leaving the final choice of everything to the client, coaching *seems* to work with contingencies as the coach never suggests necessary rules. In a study, a coach said: "When I coach, I coach. I have to be careful not to be the consultant that is in me. Sometimes, if I coach someone in an area that is relevant to my knowledge, like opening a business, I might consider switching hats, but I am very careful to make the distinction" (Pagis 2016: 1096).

To the client, this ludic aspect is more convincing than the straightforward insistence on necessity because the acceptance of contingency seemingly provides freedom. However, this freedom is only the "freedom of algorithms" as it is still based on the assumption that some truly necessary self does exist. Also, coach and client still believe in language. "Good and bad" express necessary values that had been hidden but could be revealed through coaching. In the end, despite its apparently ludic input, coaching believes in rules and thinks that anything in the world can be represented as definitely fixed content. However, real knowledge about the world is not knowledge about "good and bad" or about some imaginary "true self." In the end, both personal development philosophies and algorithms weave around us a veil that they want to develop into an ego. Like the Greek sophists, their techniques create illusions of determinate forms by concentrating on the individual (that is, their hard and soft skills, rhetoric, persuasion) and by neglecting the contingency that becomes obvious when looking at the whole. Eventually, this approach can prevent the client from seeing the reality of their selves. The client is supposed to discover their true self through action. A fake program of "emergence" appears when "finding yourself" is not suggested as a rule-following activity but rather as an adventure. It is fake because, in the end, this "adventure" is no different from self-discoveries made on Amazon or YouTube when we "discover" ourselves through the selected suggestions. The idea that the coaching only "brings out" what the client already has—necessarily—within themselves follows the logic of algorithms. The finding of the self is not based on adventurous rambling or carefree wandering. The algorithm suggests nothing new but shows only the client's own choices that are "necessary" but had so far been hidden. We might believe that we are "freely wandering" on Amazon or YouTube, but in reality, we are intensely looking for a ready-made self that we expect exists "somewhere" and that needs to be discovered. The algorithm pretends to make us aware of what, deep inside, we necessarily want. This procedure is sold as freedom and individuality, though in reality, such "individualism" locks the individual into necessities. It is neither an adventure nor a liberation. True freedom is contingency.

At the same time, the "true self" remains vague and cannot be found, which creates another parallel with the conspiratorial mindset. The selected options, the "likes," and the number of views can be measured whereas the self that enacted them can't. The purpose of the whole project, which is to provide some sort of "happiness," cannot be measured either. As a result, happiness must be mutated into wellness or well-being. Already in the early nineteenth century, the utilitarian philosopher Jeremy Bentham shifted the idea of happiness to the more utilitarian term "satisfaction," which has the advantage that it can be—at least vaguely—measured. One is satisfied when one receives what one expected to receive. Wellness is the happiness of meritocratic societies in which selves are submitted to algorithms and life coaching. Wellness is measurable because we receive what we expect.

Life coaches who launch appeals to "be yourself" can easily follow a utilitarian market logic based on the above-described ethics of merit. If only you make an effort, or if you listen to the right coaches, you can "become yourself." Again, as in the case of the conspiratorial mindset, the appeal to get rid of all preconceptions and limiting beliefs can sound Buddhist or Daoist in the broadest sense. Like Daoists or Buddhists, the coach urges the client to abandon the futile necessities that are rooted in their mind. However, while these Asian philosophies attempt to deliver us from anxieties and ressentiments by making us aware of the contingency of life, life coaching programs (just like algorithms and unwarranted conspiracy theories) do the contrary. For them, the world is not fortuitous but full of "bad" necessities that must be abandoned in order to reach a truth (the real self). The self is here conceived as a "good" necessity. Life coaching, even of the New Age variety that recommends an apparently anti-Capitalist "doing nothing," still remains inscribed in the ethical logic of meritocratism, which is a "necessitism." No matter in what shape they appear, all these strategies are opposed to contingency. Instead of relieving the individual of anxieties caused by necessities, the frantic search for a "necessary self" disconnected from all contingencies can only create new anxieties. Apart from that, there is much "neoliberal" input in positive thinking programs. Many a time their purpose is to make people more efficient through a regeneration of their moral forces. Many are inscribed in a utilitarian pragmatism or Benthamian individualism that makes efforts to reach the most individual kind of happiness.

As mentioned, the idea of the life coach is not new and has its predecessor in the ancient sophists who taught "excellence" (*aretê*) as a technique of self-improvement through rhetoric and persuasion. Just like today's marketing experts, the sophists delivered instructions about the most efficient presentation of the self. Against this, Daoism stands for aimless roaming, rambling, or sauntering and does not look for any necessities. Wandering without a destination is the opposite of any self-development program. For Daoism, seeing the world (the cosmos) differently means to stop thinking of the self in a conventional way: for example, it means to "forget about success and reputation, [and] personal interests" (Lundberg 2016: 213). The above-described self-development philosophies take the contrary approach. Seen from this angle, they contain an intrinsic logic. There are false necessities "out there" that are evil and which must be overcome by finding "the truth." And just as for the conspiratorial mindset, the "truth" is vague and can never be clearly spelled out.

Meritocracy sees the conflict between the ideal "self-made" self and its social embeddedness as a paradox that must be passed over by reaching for "true individualism." Social necessities are declared contingent and therefore evil. The necessary self needs to be discovered. In contrast, for Daoism, the liquidation of the clash between the individual self and social expectations is "carefree wandering." Carefree wandering has nothing to do with individualism: one always wanders within society, and "individuality" can only be found amid the contingency constituted by the environment. Adventurous wandering is always the discovery of others. Meritocracy uses individualism to eliminate the contingency produced by the environment. Obviously, meritocracy believes in self-made success: making it "on one's own" is more valued than success due to the help of others. What bothers meritocratic identity coaches most is that society is not a stable value but constantly changing, that it contains contingency. For a meritocrat, a stable identity can best be built against a stable background (which is increasingly difficult to obtain in "postmodern" societies) or by simply ignoring shifting backgrounds and concentrating on the ego. Once there is success, merit might be redistributed for reasons of charity; but the real competition is individual: the individual has to help himself, which is well expressed by the term "self-help." Not only are self-help philosophies rooted in meritocracy, but meritocracy itself is a self-help philosophy. The conspiratorial mindset, meanwhile, has found yet another solution. It consults fake experts and construes society as a static and hostile entity. These "experts" replace community, government, and family. As a result, the conspiratorial mind believes it has found its own, individual truth that only it (together with a few other conspiring individuals) can appreciate.

Is it still possible to suggest skepticism as an option in a time of Covid skepticism, climate skepticism, and even "globe skepticism"? Yes, because all these skepticisms look for necessities in the form of an essence. It has already been said in Chapter 3 that the conspiratorial mindset does not follow real skepticism. Daoism assumes that essences do not exist in the first place, which represents a much more consistent form of skepticism. Reality is created neither by authentic people nor by conspirators but emerges while we are living our lives. Obstacles exist, but even they should not be systematically spelled out in the form of rules, ideals, anti-ideals, images, essences, or conspiracies. While our lives are enacted and experienced, the world is in constant transformation. Emergence rather than creation is an important Daoist concept. It is also most essential to Chinese "creation" myths, which marks a major difference between Christian and Daoist accounts of how the world came about. As mentioned, Moeller explains that "the God of the Bible [...] created the world, but *tian* [heaven] in classical Chinese *is* the world. [...] *Tian* is *natura naturans*: "nature naturing" (Moeller 2006: 44). More than biblical myths, Chinese cosmology is prone to prevent unwarranted conspiracy theories.

Contingency in Dreams

The "authentic lifestyle seeker," just like the conspiratorial mindset, contradicts the Daoist or the Zen-Buddhist view in the most obvious fashion. Daoists and Zen-Buddhists are skeptical of necessities, while the conspiratorial mindset is skeptical of contingencies. Out of ressentiment, the latter builds a wall of alternative necessities around contingencies and thus believes himself protected from a reality in which things "just happen." Of course, as has been shown above, the conspiratorial mindset might also contest necessities, for example, the necessity of getting vaccinated, or the necessary link between lung cancer and smoking, or between HIV and AIDS (see Lewandowsky et al. 2013). But in general, for the conspiratorial mindset, necessity means "reality," and it characterizes the realm of contingency as a dream, suggesting that those who do *not* believe in the conspiracy live in a dream world. "Wake up" is a common appeal issued by the conspiratorial mindset. The problem is that it falsely believes that dreams are constituted of contingency, that in a dream anything can happen, and that—in opposition—reality is determined by necessities. The opposite is the case: it is very plausible to say that in dreams, things are more necessary than in reality. Indeed, dreams are more like what has been said in the preceding chapter about art. Dreams have an inner logic, and *from the point of view of the dream*, all actions look completely necessary. Only when looking at the dream from the outside (which is the only view that is normally permitted for dream analysis) does the dream seem confused and composed randomly "by chance." Like art, dreams are paradoxes. In dreams, things are necessary and contingent at the same time. But instead of frantically looking for necessities (as did Freud), when we dream, we rather have the feeling that in "dream actions," necessity and contingency do not matter. We might think about necessities once we are awake, but the dream develops "by chance" without meeting any resistance from reflection, which is precisely why the dream can also appear as necessary. The dream overcomes the distinction between the necessary and the contingent precisely because there is no criterion *in the dream* that could establish such a distinction; such criteria exist only outside the dream. The psychoanalyst Jean Levaillant very aptly suggests that the dream "eats everything" (1979: 15) because while we are dreaming, there is no conscious thinking that could establish differences between necessity and contingency. As a result, in the dream, contingency appears real, which is precisely the view that Zen Buddhism and Daoism suggest as a model of reality. It does not mean that we live in a dream, but, just on the contrary, the fact that "the dream becomes real" signifies that the contingent-necessary character of reality is fully recognized. All this works in parallel with the above suggestion that "life is art." Contingency is real, whereas the necessity that we artificially create while looking at life and dreams from an outside position is unreal. This was also the position of the French "Science of the Coincidence."

It is better to say that in dreams, the distinction between necessity and contingency *does* exist, but that it does not matter. This also characterizes the way of seeing we employ when looking at art, and it corresponds to the state of mind of the artist: everything is free and could very well be otherwise, but the "right" line in a drawing seems to have been produced *necessarily*, though it obviously emerged *coincidentally*. The artist thus acts in a "dreamlike" way: he draws lines as in a dream and finds the necessary placement of the line without assuming any pre-fixed rules. In a way, he *creates* the rules while he acts within a universe in which, strictly speaking, nothing is necessary. His art emerges while he draws.

Not everybody can become an artist, and not everybody might even want to become a Daoist. However, it is certain that if we adopt this "dream model" of action as an ideal for life, it will prevent us from frantically looking for conspiracies. In Daoism, there is the concept of *ziran* (自然, literally meaning "nature" in modern-day language), which is here used in the sense of "of its own" or "by itself." It suggests that we should always act naturally and spontaneously, and is thus similar to the Greek *automaton*, which, characteristically, also means "coincidence." For example, our activities should not be calculated by algorithms but rather be obtained by freely and "naturally" following the course of events that depend on contingency as much as on necessity. The main idea is that in *ziran* we do not *reflect* on contingency and necessity. *Ziran* can also be defined as "*yi ming* (以明)," which means "going along with what is most obvious," or as "*yin shi* 因是" ("going along with whatever is present/affirmed by the situation"). The concept is also similar to the more popular idea of *wuwei* (無為). *Wuwei* suggests we do not follow necessary rules; at the same time, it does not want us to be incapable of action because there would be only contingencies. *Wuwei* does not suggest that everything is random because that would mean that our actions lead nowhere. *Wuwei* actions are not goal-oriented in the classical sense (meaning that no goal has been fixed and essentialized beforehand), but eventually, the action does reach a goal. As if acting in a dream, *wuwei* overcomes both necessity and contingency. In *ziran*, one simply "follows" without following *something*. Without following necessary guidelines that are supposed to lead to some ideal or to some *Wunschtraum* of a necessary form of being. Or to something that is believed to be authentic or a "true self."

While I am acting (or while I am dreaming), I do not know what the necessity is; nor do I know what is authentic; I might only discover it gradually. While I am acting, I only follow contingencies (though without seeing them as contingencies). I discover my potential, my originality, and the necessity of my actions while living and acting amid contingencies. The originality of my actions is not inscribed in a necessary rule that has been issued beforehand, but it emerges. Within these constellations, fanaticism, the firm belief in unjustifiable conspiracy theories, and closed-mindedness become quasi-impossible. At the same time, *wuwei* is not a "contingency theory" (more on this will come in the conclusion) that preaches relativism.

The above model of action matches what has been said earlier about aesthetics. No matter whether artistic originality emerges slowly or shows itself in a sudden flash: it is not found through an active search for necessities (such as a supposed set of rules for art) but rather through a playful activity/passivity submitted to coincidences. In this sense, Daoist action is always aesthetic, too. It depends on a contemplative attitude that refrains from ethics-inspired action: it is always calm and aims to capture the broader picture of situations before acting. Like *wuwei*, art is the fusion of order with disorder: and it is this perfect fusion that makes art "real." The reality of art is not the necessary reality "out there" or "in there" (in the artist's mind) that an artist wants to copy. Nor is it the "reality" spelled out by algorithms using sophisticated calculations, technical terms, and logic. The real is rather a dreamlike reality determined by coincidences, but which will appear, in art, as though it could *not* be otherwise.

There is a human tendency to look at the world in terms of good and bad, male and female, as well as contingency and necessity. The conspiratorial mindset believes it has found "reality" by distinguishing the necessary from the contingent and holds, for example, that those who believe that the coronavirus was created by coincidence are living in a dream. For Daoism, distinctions between contingency and necessity are always issued in terms of language. Therefore, we can also say that the Daoist reality is a pre-linguistic or non-linguistic reality. It is not a dream but the reality we live in. In this reality, necessities have not been crystallized. Not only in dreams but also in our everyday reality are necessity and contingency blurred. We try to render "reality" more precise through "Cartesian terminologizations," that is, by giving names, offering definitions, and drawing bell curves. Eventually, we come to distinguish between necessity and contingency, but *in reality*, the good and the bad, the necessary and the contingent, and so on, constantly morph into one another.

Reality is impermanent, and an example of such a reality is that of Zhuang Zhou and the butterfly, in which everything is subject to continuous change and reversal. The parable shows that the correct perception of the real depends, paradoxically, on our ability to perceive reality like a dream. This means that only when we are indifferent toward the distinction between the necessary and the contingent and do not jump to conclusions about what is necessary can we grasp what is real. The conspiratorial mindset does the opposite, and by doing so, it falsifies reality. Its ambition is grounded in the desire to have a "correct" view of reality, which basically signifies a view that acknowledges what is necessary. However, such a correct view is not possible because too often, too many aspects of reality escape our control, which is why the Japanese philosopher Kuki Shūzō (1888–1941) has called contingency, under Zen-Buddhist influence as well as under the influence of French "Science of Contingency," the "reality of the real as real" or "simple reality."[1]

CONCLUSION

How to live with contingency? The Greeks elevated Fortuna to the status of a goddess and worshipped her in order to diminish arbitrariness. The Middle Ages managed to separate the contingent from the necessary by creating a solid theological framework. In these times, people could retreat, whenever facing contingency, into a quiet center of necessity guarded by God. Today, too many "necessities," many of them complex, incomprehensible, not necessary at all, or simply fake, invade our lives. In our consumer-oriented societies, more than in the Middle Ages, we are overwhelmed with so-called "necessities." These "necessities" are not as fixed and well established as they were in the past but are rather fleeting and impermanent. They are no longer rooted in a lifestyle transmitted from generation to generation following traditional, unchanging structures. In the past, the quietude of a religious center could overlap with the law-bound and purposeful environment of the almost universally rural communities, from which contingency was largely excluded. In modernity, both necessity and contingency are fluid phenomena and less clearly distinguishable.

Contingency is feared more than ever, as the loss of central authority and the multiplication of relationships between individual elements lead to disorientation and anxiety. The conspiratorial mindset "solves" the problem by creating transcendental or imaginary unities. However, it does not establish "real" necessities, nor does it manage to cope with existing contingencies. In the end, unwarranted conspiracy theories lead to even more stress and ressentiment. Similarly, merit-oriented societies treat individuals as though they could be in control of everything, when obviously, way too many things are beyond our control. In this way, meritocracies create new anxieties.

Conspiracy Skepticism

At the same time, the conspiratorial mindset does not have the serenity of Greek Pyrrhonians, who strove to live in a state of eternal suspension of judgment in order to avoid all obligations that could reach them in the form of necessities. Skeptical thought was initiated in Greece by pre-Socratic philosophers such as Xenophanes and Theophrastus; Democritus can be seen as a proto-skeptic, and Pyrrho of Elis (c. 360–270 BCE) molded skepticism into a subtle form of psychological philosophy.[1]

David Coady thinks that "conspiracy theory resembles traditional skeptical hypothesis, such as Descartes's evil demon hypothesis" (Coady 2006: 121) because it transcends the obvious, empirical world and looks for absolute truths. This fits the pattern of Cartesian temporary skepticism but not that of the Greek skeptics who looked for an eternal suspension of judgment. Proponents of the conspiratorial mindset are not skeptics because they simply reject certain elements and believe in others (for example, in hydroxychloroquine or Ivermectin at a time when no conclusive trials had proven their safety). Whereas the anti-Platonic Skeptics rejected *all* theories, the conspiratorial mindset still aspires to master the contingency-necessity problem with the help of theories. In principle, no "theorist" can be a skeptic because skepticism is traditionally evidence-based and empirical (at least since the skepticism model of Sextus Empiricus). Pyrrhonians hold that all theories are equally valid and that none should ever be embraced.

At the same time, the conspiratorial mindset locks itself into an endless loop of doubt, a doubt that will often even doubt its own evidence and conclusions. Peter Knight points to alien abduction theories which have "become an active ongoing process deferring any sense of conclusion" (Knight 2002: 11). The enigmas are not *supposed* to be solved because the conspiratorial mindset prefers to enclose itself in a coil of speculations: in a coil of theories. Can this be considered a kind of eternal suspension of judgment? No, it is not real skepticism because the conspiratorial mindset still creates alternative theories. True, as with the skeptics, the aim of these claims is not really to prove the competing theories wrong; however, the baseless theories are used as an intellectual and emotional refuge, which contradicts any skeptical principle.

Today, the Pyrrhonians are those who *doubt* unwarranted conspiracy theories. They doubt but do not necessarily offer alternative theories. It has been shown in Chapter 3 that for a conspiracy skeptic, it is typically impossible to have solid evidence or first-hand knowledge of a theory's factual falsehood, especially in knowledge societies in which much knowledge is outsourced. Lee Basham therefore calls conspiracy skeptics "agnostics": "The proper epistemic reaction to many contemporary unwarranted conspiracy theories is (at best) a *studied agnosticism*. Typically, we are not in any position to seriously

---

1 Almost all of Pyrrho's writings are lost, but Sextus Empiricus summarized the Pyrrhonian arguments about 400 years later.

credit or *discredit* these conspiratorial possibilities" (2006: 72). Conspiracy skepticism is not a systematic distrust; it is merely the expression of a conviction that the world is too complex to make any final statements. Similarly, when the ancient Skeptic engages in a suspension of judgment, he is seeking to overcome limits imposed by necessity and contingency, in an attempt to experience *reality* in its fullness, that is, in its complexity. Agamben writes: "The Skeptics viewed suspension not simply as indifference but as an experience of possibility or potentiality. What shows itself on the threshold between Being and non-Being, between sensible and intelligible, between word and thing, is not the colorless abyss of the Nothing but the luminous spiral of the possible" (1999: 257/Ital. 1993: 69).

It is not that conspiracy skeptics are convinced that all public institutions, politicians, scientists, and so on, are too reliable to the point that conspiracies are simply impossible. They merely question probabilities and speak of unlikelihood, which comes very close to the Pyrrhonian suspension of judgment. It is *unlikely* that, in such a complex world, a few players should firmly hold the strings to everything. The conspiracy skeptic does not fanatically adhere to disbelief. Doing so would mean moving closer to the model of the conspiratorial mindset. The Skeptic does not produce a better theory.

It has already been said that when faced with the conspiratorial mindset's insistence on certain "necessities," it is useless to produce better theories. What Frankfurt calls "bullshit" (and unwarranted conspiracy theories are bullshit) is almost impossible to refute, be it only because we would not have the time to do so. The "Brandolini principle," coined by Italian software engineer Alberto Brandolini, and which Bergstrom and West see as perhaps the most important principle in bullshit studies, declares that "the amount of energy needed to refute bullshit is an order of magnitude bigger than [that needed] to produce it" because "an idiot can create more bullshit than you could ever hope to refute" (Bergstrom and West 2021: 11). The conclusion is that bullshit can best be rejected not by refuting it but by suspending one's judgment. Together with irony, the suspension of judgment remains the most efficient strategy to cope with unfounded conspiracies.

At the same time, contingency should not be seen as an epistemic and ethical "insignificance" that can be opposed to the epistemically and morally more "heavy" necessity. Contingency can be very significant, even ethically, as Gould correctly notes: "The literati embrace contingency because no other theme so affirms the moral weight, and the practical importance, of each human life" (Gould 2002: 1342). Ethically speaking, contingency can be more meaningful than necessity.

In the last chapter, I asked if it still makes sense, in a time of vaccination skepticism, climate skepticism, and even "globe skepticism," to suggest skepticism as a solution. It does, but skepticism must be well defined. Skepticism, when practiced properly, is neither based on ressentiment nor does it instill ressentiment; instead, it tends to lead to restrained behavior and tolerance. Both the ancient skeptic and the conspiratorial mindset choose to quit the arena of "reasonable" Platonic discussions; but the skeptic has no ressentiment in doing so. The skeptic tries to reach happiness (*ataraxia*) through a suspension of judgment, in which case any resentment needs to be likewise suspended. Pyrrho saw Plato's certitudes as mere appearances: they *can* be accepted, but only as appearances. None of them is truer or more real than the other. There is no ressentiment toward falsehood here.

The conspiratorial mindset suspends judgment too, as it usually does not provide a conclusive theory capable of proving that all other theories are false. Its "theory" is one of "evil conspirators" lurking behind everything. The identity of these conspirators is mystified and never spelled out. This mindset works with "alternative" theories or "alternative" facts, which means that it questions existing theories, not because it initially discovered flaws in the theories, but because it resents them. Instead of creating a pertinent theory that replaces the existing one, it is left with an alternative world.

When speaking of alternative facts, we suspend our judgment and accept two truths, which come strangely close to the Greek *epochè*. The problem is that for the conspiratorial mindset, the motivation for this suspension is too often ressentiment, whereas the Greek *epochè* aims to overcome all ressentiment in order to reach *ataraxia*. In other words, the conspiratorial mindset still regrets that its alternative truth is *only* an alternative: it would like for it to be an absolute truth but cannot provide sufficient arguments. This is not the skepticism that Pyrrho or Sextus Empiricus had in mind.

At the root of the conspiratorial mindset are two things: ressentiment and a desire to be independent of all official theories, ideologies, systems, and influences. Like the ancient Skeptics, the conspiratorial mindset maintains the dream of a self-reliant and self-determined individuality; but unlike the Skeptics, the former are convinced that evil necessities prevent them from realizing this dream. As mentioned, Americans are—after the Middle East[2]— the champions of unwarranted conspiracy theories because American culture maintains a myth of absolute freedom, a freedom so much idealized that it can never be materialized. The conspiratorial mindset resents evil powers (government, socialism, etc.) that might curb this freedom. This skeptical investigation of "conventional" theories does not lead to the psychological

---

2 According to Pipes, in the Middle East, conspiracy theories "provide a key to the political rule" (Pipes 1996: 2).

equilibrium sought after by Pyrrhonians, but rather to biases and preconceptions that make such an equilibrium impossible. Instead of peace of mind, the conspiratorial mindset obtains panic, which reinforces his conspiracist thinking.

The astrophysicist Carl Sagan, in a text supposed to prevent people from falling victim to pseudoscience and mystifications, once gave the following advice: "Try not to get overly attached to a hypothesis just because it's yours. It's only a way station in the pursuit of knowledge. Ask yourself why you like the idea. Compare it fairly with the alternatives. See if you can find reasons for rejecting it" (2007: 7). Nicholas Taleb gives similar advice to stock exchange traders whose job is to deal with contingency: bad traders "get married to their positions" (2001: 92), which eventually makes them fail. A perpetual openness to new theories, an attitude that Taleb derives from Karl Popper's philosophy of open systems and liberal democracy, is essential for good trading. Max Scheler, already in 1905, said the same: avoid absolute necessities such as nationalist, religious, or personal pride. He believed that this could prevent ressentiment thinking and conspiratorial ideation. This is the skepticism that comes close to the Greek one.

Contingency Theories

At the same time, we should not venture toward the other extreme, which Skip Willman has dubbed "contingency theory," and which he frames as the contrary of the unwarranted conspiracy theory (2002: 36). In no case should necessity simply be replaced with contingency. When we state that contingency can exist and that not all evil must have necessary causes, we are not replacing necessity with contingency. It has been shown in Chapter 3 that scientific accounts attributing all events to contingency are unsatisfactory. Events must become intelligible, and contingency must always be elucidated in contexts that provide some amount of necessity. "Contingency theories" foreground the complexity of systems and state that connections are too loose to make any statements at all. They end up as the kind of relativism that Alan Bloom criticized (see Chapter 5); when everything is contingent, everything is possible, and fatalism is the result. According to Willman, in the modern world, the "contingency theorist" falls victim to multinational capitalism because he can ever question economies where power is in the hands of a few.

For yet another reason, the unwarranted conspiracy theory should not be contrasted with the contingency theory. The "necessities" that unwarranted conspiracy theories quote are typically blurred and enigmatic. In its desperate attempt to cope with contingency, the conspiratorial mindset creates an odd mixture of fatalism and sublimated combative attitudes, all directed against obscure necessities. In a way, the protagonist of the conspiratorial mindset *is himself* a contingency theorist because his necessities are fake. Therefore, the contingency theory is not the converse of the unwarranted conspiracy theory.

How can the happenings of the world be explained without falling into either contingency fatalism or the fuzzy determinism of indefensible conspiracy theories? The resulting position will be founded on a paradox, though eventually, the model is no less paradoxical than the conspiracism model itself, which is why it can be seen as the unwarranted conspiracy theory's direct converse. Rorty, in his book on irony, attempts to sketch a skeptical attitude based on a contingency mindset. He is fascinated by a sentence from the liberal Austrian economist Joseph Schumpeter (1883–1950): "To realize the relative validity of one's convictions and yet stand for them unflinchingly, is what distinguishes a civilized man from a barbarian" (1989: 46).[3] The statement describes a paradox because it suggests being relativistic yet also standing for one's opinions unflinchingly. For Schumpeter, this moral attitude is a matter of "civilization," which points, in all its vagueness, to style, lifestyle, or some other form of cultural conditioning. Schumpeter's civilized person is fully aware of the contradiction that this maxim expresses. They do not eliminate the relativism in order to act single-mindedly. It would be wrong to say that Schumpeter's civilized person is brainwashed by civilization; she is merely culturally conditioned and aware of this conditioning. But she is not a "contingency theorist." Rorty calls this attitude a commitment "combined with a sense of the contingency of their own commitment" (61) and describes it as emblematic of a shift from epistemology to politics (68). I would interpret it rather as a shift from epistemology to aesthetics. This skepticism reaches for an openness toward a multitude of possibilities. Like Scheler, Rorty insists that we should "try to get to the point where we no longer worship anything, where we treat nothing as a quasi-divinity" (22). Rorty sees this line of thought confirmed by Nietzsche and Freud. Our language, conscience, and community are products of chance and have no absolute value. Yet we might still follow this civilization "unflinchingly."

This attitude, which reflects a great deal of Pyrrhonian skepticism, could also be called "necessity idiocy" because it does not create a relativist position based on "contingency theories" but is simply blind—or pretends to be blind—to necessities. Being blind to necessity does not mean that one sees everything in terms of contingency. I derive the term "necessity idiocy" or "necessity fool" from Hans-Georg Moeller's writings on the "moral fool" in ethics. Moeller is inspired by Eastern philosophies, especially Daoism, a

---

3 Schumpeter's sentence was quoted by Isaiah Berlin and has been criticized by Sandel.

philosophy that refrains from ethical theories or often—similar to Pyrrhonian skepticism—from all theories (Moeller 2009: 10).

As Schumpeter's example shows, "necessities" can be followed, but they must not be followed as quasi-divinities. It simply makes sense to follow them within a certain civilizational context. Necessity idiocy is nothing other than a realistic attitude in the Stoic sense. The Stoic is exclusively concerned with the "is" of a given situation, and not with the "could be"; whether what happens is necessary or coincidental. Whatever happens, happens. Complaining about contingencies or necessities creates illusions, vain hopes, and resentment. It leads to theories about what could be or should be. The Stoic accepts the world as it is, which is not naïve apathy but realism. Marcus Aurelius, the Roman emperor and Stoic, is effective in his responses to challenges precisely because he is a realist. He accepts the necessary reality, but he is not impressed by it. Very often, necessities turn out to be less necessary than they appear, as says Seneca in *On Anger*: "[Some things] can be terrifying and riotous and deadly. Greatness, whose strength and stability is goodness, they will not have. To be sure, in their speech and their strivings and all their trappings they will produce a credible impression of greatness. They will make a statement that you might reckon belongs to a great spirit" (2014: 33). Seneca speaks of Caligula.

In Chapter 11, it was shown that this Stoic attitude makes unwarranted conspiracy theories quasi-impossible. Moeller does not discuss conspiracy theories but believes that as today, ethical teachings are no longer centralized by the church but liberally distributed by mass media (170), a certain idiocy, that is, a willful non-understanding of ethics, is the most appropriate approach to be taken by enlightened modern humans. A "moral fool" is simply blind with respect to moral judgments, though he still follows the law. Much morality is sparked by (sublimated) anger and resentment, and from a Zen-Buddhist or Daoist perspective, a morality of anger is inacceptable (61). The Daoist criticism of ethics emerges as an alternative (64). Just like Schumpeter's "civilized man," the "necessity fool" refuses to recognize necessary principles, all without falling into the relativist position of contingency theories. He does not base his opinion on any theory. According to Moeller, such an "idiocy" is the most typical Daoist position:

> [The Daoist sage] does not know how he would know anything in the first place. The Daoist sage simply does not operate in a mode of knowing and also not [in a mode] of "critical" knowing in a relativist or skeptical form. Rather than a skeptic or a relativist, the sage is simply someone who has not yet been exposed to intellectual knowledge; he is an ultimate simpleton, a perfect idiot. (2006: 118)

The phlegm and the indifference that we find expressed in this position are precisely what the conspiratorial mindset is lacking most. The "amorality" that results from a Daoist ethical stance that sees aesthetics (contingency) and tries to ignore ethics (necessity) is also reflected in another term: Pierluigi Barrotta's idea of an "ameritocratic" society. For Barrotta, this is a truly liberal society (Barrotta 1999: 14).

How do we most efficiently avoid unwarranted conspiracy thinking? The alternatives that have been presented in this book highlight the notions of play and game as essential aspects of any efficient philosophy of contingency. Play faces contingency "head on"; it cannot afford any kind of determinism, but it cannot base itself on "contingency theories" either. Play does not avoid the coincidence by transforming it into necessity, but it does not fall into deterministic fatalism either. Fatalism would mean the end of play. In play, contingency is simply seen for what it is: an impossibility to predict the future. The "contingency-only" option that has been presented in Chapters 8 and 9, and which became relatively popular in the early twentieth century, is not a "contingency theory" in Willman's sense. First, French philosophy of contingency saw reality as contingent; later, existentialism suggested that we are thrown into a nonsensical situation with which we can only cope if we acknowledge the contingency that we are exposed to. Quantum mechanics developed similar views in science. This is not fatalism but rather an attempt to live without fake necessities and fake transcendentalities. Life is an undetermined game, and even God is a gambler. If we accept life as facticity, we will be neither surprised by contingencies nor resent them. Of course, not all necessities *are* contingencies, but they can be interpreted as contingencies. Sartre explained this with regard to the ill athlete, who should see his illness not as a necessity destroying his athletic career but rather as a coincidence enabling him to develop other activities. This book also suggested irony, or more precisely, Nietzsche's tragic irony. The ironic belief that much of our fate is due to coincidences avoids the poisoning of the mind through ressentiment. Fate is not determined, not even by our worst enemies.

Contingency and Life

Contingency is not a liquid mass but rather a solid chain of events embedded in a realm that has rules and necessities. By adopting this view, coincidence can be handled and used in activities such as gambling or art. All of life can be seen as a game too. It is a game in which one always plays against one predominant necessity: death. But death is not an *immediate* necessity because it can be postponed; and how much it can be postponed depends, to a considerable extent, on the correct handling of contingencies. While one plays against death, one must assume contingencies. The match against death cannot be won, but what matters is the play. Seeing death looming at the end of the game helps one accept contingencies in a more playful fashion. They are then not fought off but integrated, in an existentialist manner, into the game. Accepting loss as the inevitable outcome of a game helps one cope with contingencies. Then coincidences will not plunge us into desperation by initiating a frantic search for "necessary" alternatives. Good gamblers never do this. Contingency cannot be overcome, but it can be accepted, and sometimes even seen as a chance. As contingency is both a condemnation and a chance, it can never be an evil. It instills skepticism, restraint, and tolerance, which are also the three major virtues of a good gambler. A gambler is not fatalistic; he does not simply give up but rather allows his will to flow along emerging contingencies. There is no such thing as an "evil game" just as there is no "perfect game." The reality of the game is not *created* in the name of evil or perfection, but each game emerges individually as an entity. We cannot escape Fortuna's decision, but we can learn strategies to withstand its consequences and accept them without falling into a conspiratorial mindset. Fortuna is not evil or manipulated by evil powers. Sandel finishes his book on meritocracy with a philosophical observation that approaches Rorty's ironism: "A lively sense of the contingency of our lot can inspire a certain humility: 'There, but for the grace of God, or the accident of birth, or the mystery of fate, go I.' Such humility is the beginning of the way back from the harsh ethic of success that drives us apart. It points beyond the tyranny of merit toward a less rancorous, more generous public life" (Sandel: 228). Teaching humility toward necessities has also been on the program of many religions. We have no divine insights (we are no gods) and must skeptically evaluate our beliefs about what is necessary in light of possible contingencies. Finally, science, too, teaches, or at least should teach, a similar open-minded skepticism.

BIBLIOGRAPHY

Aaronovitch, David. 2011. *Voodoo Histories: The Role of the Conspiracy Theory in Shaping Modern History*. New York: Riverhead Books.
Abe, Masao. 1985. *Zen and Western Thought*. Houndsmill: MacMillan.
———. 1995. *Buddhism and Interfaith Dialogue*. Honolulu: Hawai'i University Press.
Adamson, Peter. 2013. "From the Necessary Existent to God" in P. Adamson (ed.), *Interpreting Avicenna: Critical Essays*. Cambridge: Cambridge University Press, 170–89.
Agamben, Giorgio and Gilles Deleuze. 1993. *Bartleby: La formula della creazione*. Macerata: Quodlibet.
———. 1999. "Bartleby, or on Contingency" in Daniel Heller-Roazen (ed.), *Potentialities: Collected Essays in Philosophy*. Stanford: Stanford University Press, 243–71.
———. 1999b. "The Passion of Facticity" in *Potentialities: Collected Essays in Philosophy*. Stanford: Stanford University Press, 185–204.
———. 2005. "La passione della fatticità" in *La Potenza del pensiero: Saggi e conferenze*. Milano: Neri Pozza, 289–319.
Ahmed, Leila. 2011. *A Quiet Revolution: The Veil's Resurgence, from the Middle East to America*. New Haven and London: Yale University Press.
Alain [Emile Chartier]. 1920. *Propos* (Vol. 1). Paris: Nouvelle Revue Française.
Al-Ghazālī, Abu Hamid. 2011. *Faith in Divine Unity and Trust in Divine Providence* (trans. David Burrell). Louisville, KY: Fons Vitae.
Aquinas, Thomas. 1911. *Summa Theologiae* (Vol. I). London: Burns Oates & Washbourne.
Argentino, Marc-André. 2023. "Qvangelicalism: QAnon as a Hyper-Real Religion" in F. Piraino, M. Pasi, and E. Asprem (eds.), *Religious Dimensions of Conspiracy Theories: Comparing and Connecting Old and New Trends*. New York: Routledge, 257–79.
Aristotle. 1933. *Metaphysics Books I–IX* (trans. H. Tredennick) (Loeb). Cambridge, MA: Harvard University Press.
———. 1955. *On Interpretation* in *The Organon, The Categories, On Interpretation* (trans. H. Tredennick) (Loeb). London: Heinemann.
———. 1963. *The Physics* (trans. P. H. Wicksteed and F. H. Cornford) (Loeb). London: Heinemann.
———. 1985. "Of the Heavens" in J. Barnes (ed.), *The Complete Works of Aristotle*. Princeton: Princeton University Press.
Aron, Raymond. 1984. "Le Siècle de la contingence dans le Vingtième siècle" in *Revue d'histoire* 1, 98–110.
Asad, Talal. 2003. *Formations of the Secular: Christianity, Islam, Modernity*. Stanford: Stanford University Press.
Asprem, Egil, F. Piraino, and M. Pasi (eds.) 2022. *Religious Dimensions of Conspiracy Theories: Comparing and Connecting Old and New Trends*. New York: Routledge.

Augustine of Hippo. 2009 [426]. *The City of God* [*De Civitate Dei*]. Peabody, MA: Hendrickson.
Badran, Margot. 2009. *Feminism in Islam: Secular and Religious Convergences*. Oxford: Oneworld.
Baeyer-Katte, Wanda von. 1965. "Die historischen Hexenprozesse: Der verbürokratisierte Massenwahn" in W. Bitter (ed.), *Massenwahn in Geschichte und Gegenwart. Ein Tagungsbericht*. Stuttgart: Klett, 220–31.
Barkun, Michael. 2018. "Foreword" in A. Dyrendal, D. Robertson, and E. Asprem (eds.), *Handbook of Conspiracy Theory and Contemporary Religion*. Leiden: Brill, ix–x.
Barrotta, Pierluigi. 1999. *I demeriti del merito: Una critica liberale alla meritocrazia*. Soveria Manelli: Rubinetto.
Barruel, Augustin de. 1799. *Memoirs Illustrating the History of Jacobinism*. Part I Vol I *The Antichristian Conspiracy*. New York: Hudson and Goodwin.
Basham, Lee and M. R. X. Dentith. 2016. "Social Sciences Conspiracy Theory Panic: Now They Want to Cure Everyone" in *Social Epistemology Review and Reply Collective* 5: 10, 12–19.
———. 2006. "Living with the Conspiracy" in D. Coady (ed.), *Conspiracy Theories. The Philosophical Debate*. Farnham: Ashgate, 61–76.
———. 2018. "Joining the Conspiracy" in *Argumenta* 3: 2, 271–90.
Baudelaire, Charles. 2006. "The Painter of Modern Life" in *Selected Writings on Art and Literature*. London: Penguin, 390–435.
Baudrillard, Jean. 1983. *Les Stratégies fatales*. Paris: Grasset.
———. 2005. *The Conspiracy of Art: Manifestos, Interviews, Essays*. Cambridge, MA: MIT Press.
Beck, Ulrich. 1986. *Risikogesellschaft: Auf dem Weg in eine andere Moderne*. Frankfurt: Suhrkamp.
———. 1992. *Risk Society: Towards a New Modernity*. Thousand Oaks, CA: Sage.
Bergson, Henri. 1991 [1907]. *L'Evolution créatrice* Paris: Alcan. Engl.: *Creative Evolution* (trans. by A. Mitchell). New York: The Modern Library, 1944.
Bergstrom, Carl and Jevin D. West. 2021. *Calling Bullshit: The Art of Skepticism in a Data-Driven World*. New York: Random House.
Bieberstein, Johannes Rogalla von. 1976. *Die These von der Verschwörung, 1776–1945. Philosophen, Freimaurer, Juden, Liberale und Sozialisten als Verschwörer gegen die Sozialordnung*. Bern: Peter Lang.
Blanqui, Auguste. 1872. *Eternité par les astres*. Paris: Germer Baillière.
Bloom, Allan. 1987. *The Closing of the American Mind*. New York: Simon and Schuster.
Blumenberg, Hans. 1950. *Die ontologische Distanz. Eine Untersuchung über die Krisis der Phänomenologie Husserls*. Kiel University, Unpublished habilitation.
———. 1985. *The Legitimacy of the Modern Age*. Cambridge, MA: MIT Press.
———. 1987. "An Anthropological Approach to the Contemporary Significance of Rhetoric" in K. Baynes, J. Bohman, and Th. McCarthy (eds.), *After Philosophy? End or Transformation*. Cambridge: MIT Press, 429–58.
———. 1997. *Die Vollzähligkeit der Sterne*. Frankfurt: Suhrkamp.
Boarelli, Mauro. 2019. *Contro l'ideologia del merito*. Bari: Laterza.
Boethius. 1785 [524]. *Consolation of Philosophy*. London: Dilly.
Boll, Marcel. 1966. *Les Certitudes du hasard*. Paris: Presses universitaires de France.
Borel, Emile. 1938a. *Le Hasard*. Paris: Alcan.
———. 1938b. *Le Jeu, la chance et les théories scientifiques modernes*. Paris: Gallimard.

Borges, Jorge Luis. 1981. "The Mirror of Enigmas" in *Labyrinths*. Harmondsworth: Penguin, 244–47.
Borst, Arno. 1965. "Mittelalterliche Sekten und Massenwahn" in W. Bitter (ed.), *Massenwahn in Geschichte und Gegenwart. Ein Tagungsbericht*. Stuttgart: Klett, 173–78.
Bortolotti, Lisa and Anna Ichino 2020. "Conspiracy Theories May Seem Irrational – But They Fulfill a Basic Human Need" in *The Conversation* Dec. 9.
Bost, P. R., S. G. Prunier, and A. J. Piper. 2010. "Relations of Familiarity with Reasoning Strategies in Conspiracy Beliefs" in *Psychological Reports* 107, 593–602.
Botz-Bornstein, Thorsten. 2010. "What does it Mean to be Cool?" in *Philosophy Now* September.
———. 2015. "Kitsch and Bullshit" in *Philosophy and Literature* 39: 2, 305–21.
———. 2015b. *Transcultural Architecture: Limits and Opportunities of Critical Regionalism*. New York: Ashgate/Routledge.
———. 2016. "The Aesthetic Experiences of Kitsch and Bullshit" in *Aesthetics and Literature* 26, 1–22.
———. 2019. *The New Aesthetics of Deculturation: Neoliberalism, Fundamentalism and Kitsch*. London: Bloomsbury.
———. 2019b. *The Political Aesthetics of ISIS and Italian Futurism*. Lanham: Lexington.
———. 2020. *Micro and Macro-Philosophy. Organicism in Biology, Philosophy, and Politics*. Leiden: Brill.
———. 2021. *The Philosophy of Lines: From Art Nouveau to Cyberspace*. New York: Palgrave.
Boutroux, Emile. 1908 [1874]. *De la Contingence des lois de la nature*. Paris: Alcan.
———. 1916. *The Contingency of the Laws of Nature* (trans. Fred Rothwell). London and Chicago: Open Court.
Bouveresse, Jacques. 1993. *L'Homme probable: Robert Musil, le hasard, la moyenne et l'escargot de l'histoire*. Paris: Éditions de l'Éclat.
Brachfeld, Oliver. 1965. "Zur Psychopathologie der Weltverschwörungen" in W. Bitter (ed.), *Massenwahn in Geschichte und Gegenwart. Ein Tagungsbericht*. Stuttgart: Klett, 111–17.
Bréhier, Émile. 1928. *Histoire de la philosophie. Tome II: La philosophie moderne*. Paris: Alcan.
Breton, André. 1924. *Manifeste du surréalisme*. Paris: Editions du Sagittaire.
Brotherton, Rob. 2015. *Suspicious Minds: Why We Believe Conspiracy Theories*. London: Bloomsbury.
Buenting, Joel and Jason Taylor. 2010. "Conspiracy Theories and Fortuitous Data" in *Philosophy of the Social Sciences* 40: 4, 567–78.
Burns, Dylan. 2020. *Did God Care? Providence, Dualism, and Will in Later Greek and Early Christian Philosophy*. Leiden: Brill.
Büssow, Johann. 2016. "Mohammed 'Abduh: The Theology of Unity" B. Bentlage et al. (eds.), *Religious Dynamic under the Impact of Imperialism and Colonialism*. Leiden: Brill, 141–59.
Byford, Jovan. 2011. *Conspiracy Theories: A Critical Introduction*. New York: Palgrave Macmillan.
Canguilhem, Georges. 1947. "Note sur la situation faite en France à la philosophie biologique" in *Revue de Métaphysique et de Morale* 3–4, 322–32.
Cardon, Dominique. 2015. *A Quoi Rêvent les Algorithmes? Nos Vies à l'heure des big data*. Paris: Seuil.
Carpentier, Laurent. 2021. "L'Algorithme, nouvelle machine à tubes" in *Le Monde* 15 Feb.
Cassam, Quassim. 2019. *Conspiracy Theories*. Oxford: Polity Press.

Cichocka, Aleksandra, M. Marchlewska, and A. Golec de Zavala. 2016. "Does Self-Love or Self-Hate Predict Conspiracy Beliefs? Narcissism, Self-Esteem, and the Endorsement of Conspiracy Theories" in *Social Psychological & Personality Science* 7, 157–66.

Cilliers, Johan. 2010. "The Unveiling of Life: Liturgy and the Lure of Kitsch" in *HTS Theological Studies* 66: 2, npn.

Clarke, Steve. 2002. "Conspiracy Theories and Conspiracy Theorizing" in *Philosophy of the Social Sciences* 32: 2, 131–50.

Coady, David. 2006. "An Introduction to the Philosophical Debate about Conspiracy Theories" in D. Coady (ed.), *Conspiracy Theories. The Philosophical Debate*. Farnham: Ashgate, 1–12.

———. 2007. "Are Conspiracy Theorists Irrational?" in *Episteme* 4: 2, 193–204.

———. 2012. *What to Believe Now: Applying Epistemology to Contemporary Issues*. Hoboken: Wiley Blackwell.

———. 2017. "Cass Sunstein and Adrian Vermeule on Conspiracy Theories" in *Argumenta* 6, 291–302.

———. 2023. "Conspiracy Theory as Heresy" in *Educational Philosophy and Theory*, 55: 7, 756–59.

Comte, Auguste. 1851–54. *Système de politique positive, ou traité de sociologie instituant la religion de l'Humanité* (4 vols.). Paris: Carilian-Goeury. Engl.: *System of Positive Polity*. London: Longmans, 1875–1877.

Conche, Marcel. 2002. "La Métaphysique du hasard" in *Revue de philosophie et de sciences humaines* 9, 1–11.

Cubitt, Geoffrey. 1993. *The Jesuit Myth: Conspiracy Theory and Politics in Nineteenth Century France*. Oxford: Clarendon Press.

Dalferth, Ingolf and Philipp Stoellger. 2000. "Introduction" Dalferth and Stoellger (eds.), *Vernunft, Kontingenz und Gott: Konstellationen eines offenen Problems*. Tübingen: Mohr-Siebeck.

Danesi, Marcel. 2023. *Politics, Lies and Conspiracy Theories: A Cognitive Linguistic Perspective*. New York: Routledge.

Darwin, Charles. 1859. *On the Origin of Species by Means of Natural Selection, or Preservation of Favored Races in the Struggle for Life*. London: Murray.

Dentith, M. R. X. 2014. *The Philosophy of Conspiracy Theories*. New York: Palgrave.

———. 2018. "Conspiracy Theories and Philosophy: Bringing the Epistemology of a Freighted Term into the Social Sciences" in J. Uscinski (ed.), *Conspiracy Theories and the People Who Believe Them*. Oxford: Oxford University Press, 94–108.

———. 2019. "Conspiracy Theories on the Basis of the Evidence" in *Synthese* 196, 2243–61.

———. (ed.) 2024. *The Philosophy of Conspiracy Theories: Concepts, Methods and Theory*. New York: Routledge.

Derrida, Jacques. 1987–98. *Psyché: Inventions de l'autre. Nouvelle édition augmentée*. Paris: Galilée.

———. 2007. "My Chances / Mes chances: A Rendezvous with Some Epicurean Stereophonies" in *Psyche: Inventions of the Other* (Vol. I). Stanford: Stanford University Press, 344–76.

Di Cesare, Donatella. 2021. *Il complotto al potere*. Turin: Einaudi.

Dōgen. 1972. "*Shōbōgenzō Zenki*," "Total Dynamic Working," and "*Shōji*" "Birth and Death (trans N. Wadell and Masao Abe) in *The Eastern Buddhist New Series* 5: 1, 70–80.

Doren, Alfred. 1924. "Fortuna im Mittelalter und in der Renaissance" in F. Saxl (ed.), *Vorträge der Bibliothek Warburg 1922/1923* (Part II). Leipzig; Berlin: Teubner, 71–144.

Douglas, Karen and Robbie M. Sutton. 2018. "Why Conspiracy Theories Matter: A Social Psychological Analysis" in *European Review of Social Psychology* 29: 1, 256–98.

Driesch, Hans. 1908. *The Science and Philosophy of the Organism*. London: Adam and Charles Black.

———. 1908b. "Bergson, der Biologische Philosoph" in *Zeitschrift für den Ausbau der Entwicklungslehre* 2, 48–55.

Duetz, J. C. M. and M. R. X. Dentith. 2022. "Reconciling Conceptual Confusions in the *Le Monde* Debate on Conspiracy Theories" in *Social Epistemology Review and Reply Collective* 11: 10, 40–50.

Engels, Friedrich. 1952 [1883]. *Dialektik der Natur*. Berlin: Diet.

———. 2004 [1884]. *The Origin of the Family, Private Property and the State*. Chippendale, Australia: Resistance Books.

———. 2010. "Dialectics of Nature" in *Collected Works of Marx and Engels* (Vol. 25). London: Lawrence & Wishart, 313–589.

Forgas, Joseph P. and Roy F. Baumeister. 2019. "*Homo Credulus*: On the Social Psychology of Gullibility" in J. Forgas and R. Baumeister (eds.), *The Social Psychology of Gullibility: Fake News, Conspiracy Theories, and Irrational Beliefs*. New York: Routledge, 1–17.

Foucault, Michel. 1977. "La Fonction politique de l'intellectuel. Entretien avec Michel Foucault" in *Dits Ecrits* 3: 192, 140–60.

Fourier, Charles. 1844 [1822]. *Théorie de l'unité universelle* (4 Vol.). Paris: Presses du Réel.

Frankfurt. Harry G. 2005. *On Bullshit*. Princeton: Princeton University Press.

Freud, Sigmund. 1904. *Zur Psychopathologie des Alltagslebens Über Vergessen, Versprechen, Vergreifen, Aberglaube und Irrtum*. Berlin: Karger.

———. 1945 [1919]. "Das Unheimliche" in *Gesammelte Werke* XII. London: Imago, 227–68.

———. 1963 [1910]. *Leonardo da Vinci, A Memory of his Childhood*. Harmondsworth: Penguin.

Friedman, Milton. 1951. "Neo-Liberalism and its Prospects" in R. Leeson and C. G. Palm (eds.), *The Collected Works of Milton Friedman*. Stanford: Hoover Institution on War, Revolution, and Peace, 89–93.

Goertzel, Ted. 1994. "Belief in Conspiracy Theories" in *Political Psychology* 15: 4, 731–42.

Goldschmidt, Victor. 1982. *Temps physique et temps tragique chez Aristote*. Paris: Vrin.

Goldstein, Kurt. 1995. [1934]. *The Organism: A Holistic Approach to Biology Derived from Pathological Data in Man*. New York: Zone Books.

Gombrich, Ernst H. 1979. *The Sense of Order: A Study in the Psychology of Decorative Art*. London: Phaidon.

Gould, Stephen Jay. 2002. *The Structure of Evolutionary Theory*. Cambridge, MA: Harvard University Press.

Graeber, David. 2018. *Bullshit Jobs: A Theory*. Harmondsworth: Penguin.

Graevenitz, Gerhart von and Odo Marquard. 1998. "Vorwort" to O. Marquard, E. Marquard, M. Christen, and G. von Graevenitz (eds.), *Kontingenz* (Vol. 17 of *Poetik und Hermeneutik*). Paderborn: Wilhelm Fink.

Gray, Matthew. 2010. *Conspiracy Theories in the Arab World: Sources and Politics*. New York: Routledge.

Griffin, Roger. 1992. *The Nature of Fascism*. New York: Routledge.

Guyau, Jean-Marie. 1887. *L'Irreligion de l'avenir: Etude sociologique*. Paris: Alcan.

Hacking, Ian. 1990. *The Taming of Chance*. Cambridge: Cambridge University Press.
Hagen, Kurtis. 2022. *Conspiracy Theories and the Failure of Intellectual Critique*. Ann Arbor: University of Michigan Press.
Harris, Keith. 2018. "What's Epistemically Wrong with Conspiracy Theorizing?" in *Royal Institute of Philosophy Supplement* 84, 235–57.
Hawking, Stephen. 1999. "Does God Play Dice?" on Hawking's Website: http://www.hawking.org.uk/does-god-play-dice.html. Last accessed 3 Sept. 2018.
Hayek, Friedrich. 2003 [1943]. *The Road to Serfdom* [condensed version]. London: Institute of Economic Affairs.
Hegel, Georg Wilhelm Friedrich. 1955 [1837]. *Vorlesungen über die Philosophie der Weltgeschichte*, Vol. I: *Die Vernunft in der Geschichte* (ed. J. Hoffmeister). Hamburg: Meiner.
———. 1969. *Science of Logic* (trans. A.V. Miller). Atlantic Highlands: Humanities Press.
———. 1971. "Introduction to the History of Philosophy" in Q. Lauer (ed.), *Hegel's Idea of Philosophy*. New York: Fordham University Press, 67–136.
———. 1986 [1837]. *Vorlesungen über die Geschichte der Philosophie* [VGP]. Frankfurt: Suhrkamp.
———. 1986b. *Wissenschaft der Logik II* (Werke 6). Frankfurt: Suhrkamp.
———. 2010. *The Science of Logic*. Cambridge: Cambridge University Press.
Heidegger, Martin. 1931. "Vorlesung über Aristoteles Metaphysik" in *Gesamtausgabe* Abt. 2 Bd. 33. Frankfurt: Klostermann.
———. 1972 [1914]. "Die Lehre vom Urteil im Psychologismus" in *Frühe Schriften*. Frankfurt: Steiner.
———. 1980. *Being and Time* (trans. J. Macquarrie and E. Robinson). Oxford: Blackwell.
———. 1983 [1929/30]. *Die Grundbegriffe der Metaphysik* (GA 29/30). Frankfurt: Vittorio Klostermann.
———. 1986. *Sein und Zeit*. Tübingen: Niemeyer.
Heine, Steven. 1985. *Existential and Ontological Dimensions of Time in Heidegger and Dogen*. Albany: State University of New York Press.
Henrich, Dieter. 1971. *Hegel im Kontext*. Frankfurt: Suhrkamp.
Hofstadter, Richard. 2012 [1964]. *The Paranoid Style in American Politics*. New York: Knopf-Doubleday.
Horkheimer, Max. 1934. "Zu Bergsons Metaphysik der Zeit" in *Zeitschrift für Sozialforschung* 3: 3, 321–42.
Inayatullah, Sohail and Gail Boxwell. 2003. "Introduction: The Other Futurist" in S. Ziauddin (ed.), *Islam, Postmodernism and Other Futures: A Ziauddin Sardar Reader*. London: Pluto Press, 1–25.
Jameson, Frederic. 1988. "Cognitive Mapping" in C. Nelson and L. Grossberg (eds.), *Marxism and Interpretation of Culture*. London: Macmillan, 347–57.
Joas, Hans and Wolfgang Knöbl. 2013. *War in Social Thought: Hobbes to the Present*. Princeton: Princeton University Press.
Jullien, François. 2017. *Dé-coïncidence. D'où viennent l'art et l'existence*. Paris: Grasset.
Kail, Michel, 1993. "Sartre et Bergson" in *Études sartriennes* 5, 167–78.
Kant, Immanuel. 1974 [1781]. *Kritik der reinen Vernunft 1*. Werkausgabe III. Frankfurt: Suhrkamp.
———. 1998 [1793]. *Religion within the Bounds of Bare Reason* (trans. A. W. Wood and G. di Giovanni). Cambridge: Cambridge University Press.
Keeley, Brian. 2006. "Of Conspiracy Theories" in D. Coady (ed.), *Conspiracy Theories. The Philosophical Debate*. Farnham: Ashgate, 45–60.

Keyes, Ralph. 2004. *The Post-Truth Era: Dishonesty and Deception in Contemporary Life*. New York: St. Martin's Press.
Knight, Peter. 2000. *Conspiracy Culture: From the Kennedy Assassination to The X-Files*. London: Routledge.
———. 2002. "Introduction" to P. Knight (ed.), *Conspiracy Nation: The Politics of Paranoia in Postwar America*. New York: New York University Press, 1–20.
Koselleck, Reinhart. 1983. *Vergangene Zukunft. Zur Semantik geschichtlicher Zeiten*. Frankfurt: Suhrkamp.
Koyré, Alexandre. 1962. *Du Monde clos à l'univers infini*. Paris: Presses Universitaires de Paris.
———. 1968. *Newtonian Studies*. Chicago: University of Chicago Press.
Krauss, Veiko. 2014. *Gene, Zufall, Selektion: Populäre Vorstellungen zur Evolution und der Stand des Wissens*. Springer Spektrum. Berlin: Springer.
Kristol, Irving. 1970. "'When Virtue Loses All Her Loveliness'—Some Reflections on Capitalism and 'The Free Society'" in *The Public Interest* Fall, 1–9.
Kuki, Shūzō. 1981. 偶然性の問題 (*Gūzensei no mondai*; *The Problem of Contingency*) in *Zenshū* 2. Tokyo: Iwanami Shoten.
Kundera, Milan. 1999. *The Unbearable Lightness of Being*. New York: Harper & Collins.
Laplace, Pierre Simon. 1902. *A Philosophical Essay on Probabilities*. New York: Wiley.
———. 1984 [1796]. *Exposition du système du monde*. Paris: Fayard.
———. 2009 [1814]. *Essai philosophique sur les probabilités*. Cambridge: Cambridge University Press.
Lasch, Christopher. 1979. *The Culture of Narcissism: American Life in an Age of Diminishing Expectations*. New York, London: Norton.
Laskar, Jacques. 1989. "A Numerical Experiment on the Chaotic Behavior of the Solar System" in *Nature* 338, 237–38.
Le Dantec, Félix. 1907. "Le Hasard et la question d'échelle" in *La Revue du Mois*, 273–88.
Leibniz, Gottfried Wilhelm. 2005 [1710]. *Theodicy: Essays on the Goodness of God, the Freedom of Man and the Origin of Evil*. Chapel Hill, NC: Project Gutenberg.
Leucippius. 1999. "Fragments" in C. C. W. Taylor (ed.), *The Atomists: Leucippus and Democritus. Fragments. A Text and Translation with Commentary*. Toronto: University of Toronto Press, 2–52.
Leung, Tommy. 2014. "Good Parasite, Bad Parasite: Nature has a Job for Everyone" in *The Conversation* March 14.
Levaillant, Jean. 1979. "Avant Rêve" in Paul Valéry, *Questions du rêve (Cahiers Paul Valéry III)*. Paris: Gallimard, 13–19.
Levin, Nora. 1973. *The Holocaust: The Destruction of European Jewry 1933–1945*. New York: Schocken.
Levy, Neil. 2007. "Radically Socialized Knowledge and Conspiracy Theories" in *Episteme: A Journal of Social Epistemology* 4: 2, 181–92.
Lewandowsky, Stefan, J. Cook, K. Oberauer, and M. Marriott. 2013b. "Recursive Fury: Conspiracist Ideation in the Blogosphere in Response to Research on Conspiracist Ideation" in *Frontiers in Psychology* 4: 73, 1–15.
Lewandowsky, Stefan, Gilles Gignac, and Klaus Oberauer. 2013. "The Role of Conspiracist Ideation and Worldviews in Predicting Rejection of Science" in *PLOS ONE* 10: 8 (e75637).
Lichtenberg, Georg Christoph. 1992 [1776–1779]. "Sudelbuch F" in *Schriften und Briefe* Bd. 1. Frankfurt: Insel.

Lichtheim, George. 1961. *Marxism: An Historical and Critical Study*. London: Routledge.
Lipovetsky, Gilles. 1983. *L'Ere du vide: Essais sur l'individualisme contemporain*. Paris: Gallimard.
Locke, John. 1999 [1690]. *An Essay Concerning Human Understanding*. Oxford: Oxford University Press.
Longinus. 2006. *On the Sublime*. Chapel Hill, NC: Project Gutenberg.
Lucretius. 2018. *On the Nature of Things* (Vol. V 2). Minneapolis: Franklin Classics Trade Press.
Lundberg, Brian. 2016. "A Meditation on Friendship" in R. Ames (ed.), *Wandering at Ease in the Zhuangzi*. New York: SUNY Press, 211–18.
Machan, Tibor R. 1977. "Kuhn, Paradigm Choice and the Arbitrariness of Aesthetic Criteria in Science" in *Theory and Decision* 8: 4, 361–62.
Mandel, Ernest. 1989. "How to Make No Sense of Marx" in R. Ware and K. Nielsen (eds.), *Analyzing Marxism. New Essays on Analytical Marxism*, supplementary volume of *The Canadian Journal of Philosophy* 15, 105–32.
Mandik, Pete. 2007. "Shit Happens" in *Episteme* 4: 2, 205–18.
Marcuse, Herbert. 1964. *One-Dimensional Man: Studies in the Ideology of Advanced Industrial Society*. Boston: Beacon.
Marquard, Odo, E. Marquard, M. Christen, and G. v. Graevenitz (eds.). 1998. *Kontingenz* (Vol. 17 of *Poetik und Hermeneutik*). Paderborn: Wilhelm Fink.
Marsden, George M. 2006. *Fundamentalism and American Culture*. Cary, NC: Oxford University Press
Marx, Karl and Friedrich Engels. 1968 [1841]. "Differenz der demokritischen und epikureischen Naturphilosophie" in *Marx-Engels-Werke (MEW), Ergänzungsband 1*. Berlin: Diez.
———. 2012. *The Communist Manifesto: A Modern Edition*. London: Verso.
Massie, Pascal. 2011. *Contingency, Time, and Possibility. An Essay on Aristotle and Duns Scotus*. Lanham: Lexington.
Mauthner, Fritz. 2012 [1910]. *Wörterbuch der Philosophie*. Altenmünster: Jazzybee Verlag.
Mazarr, Michael. 2007. *Unmodern Men in the Modern World: Radical Islam, Terrorism, and the War on Modernity*. Cambridge, MA: Cambridge University Press.
McIntyre, Lee. 2018. *Post-Truth*. Cambridge, MA: MIT Press.
Meillassoux, Quentin. 2008. *After Finitude: An Essay on the Necessity of Contingency*. London: Bloomsbury.
Merleau-Ponty, Maurice. 1945. *Phénoménologie de la perception*. Paris: Gallimard.
Mikušková, Eva Ballová and Vladimíra Čavojová. 2020. "The Effect of Analytic Cognitive Style on Credulity" in *Frontiers of Psychology* Oct. 15. https://doi.org/10.3389/fpsyg.2020.584424
Minic, Dimitri. 2022. "Les élites politico-militaires russes croient que le monde leur est hostile et que les Etats-Unis sont omniscients" in *Le Monde* 4/4/2022.
Mintz, Frank. 1985. *The Liberty Lobby and the American Right: Race, Conspiracy, and Culture*. Westport: Greenwood.
Mises, Ludwig von. 1962 [1944]. *Bureaucracy*. New Haven: Yale University Press.
Moallem, Minoo. 2005. *Between Warrior Brother and Veiled Sister: Islamic Fundamentalism and the Politics of Patriarchy in Iran*. Berkeley and Los Angeles: University of California Press.
Moeller, Hans-Georg. 1999. "Zhuangzi's 'Dream of the Butterfly': A Daoist Interpretation" in *Philosophy East and West*. 49: 4, 439–50.
———. 2006. *The Philosophy of the Daodejing*. New York: Columbia University Press.

———. 2009. *The Moral Fool: A Case for Amorality.* New York: Columbia University Press.
Monod, Jacques. 1970. *Le Hasard et la Nécessité. Essai sur la philosophie naturelle de la biologie moderne.* Paris: Seuil.
———. 1971. *Chance and Necessity. An Essay on the Natural Philosophy of Modern Biology.* New York: Alfred A. Knopf.
More, Mabogo Percy. 2021. *Sartre on Contingency: Antiblack Racism and Embodiment.* Lanham: Rowman & Littlefield.
Nagarjuna. 2015. *The Philosophy of the Middle Way* [Mulamadhyamakakarika] (trans. and comment by D. Kalupahana). New York: SUNY Press.
Napolitano, M. Giulia. 2021. "Conspiracy Theories and Evidential Self-Insulation" in S. Bernecker, A. Flowerree, and T. Grundmann (eds.), *The Epistemology of Fake News.* Oxford: Oxford University Press, 82–105.
Napolitano, M. Giulia and Kevin Reuter. 2021. "What is a Conspiracy Theory?" in *Erkenntnis* 88, 2035–62.
Nicholson, Daniel J. 2014. "The Return of the Organism as a Fundamental Explanatory Concept" in *Biology Philosophy Compass* 9/5, 347–59.
Nietzsche, Friedrich. 1969. *Thus Spoke Zarathustra* (trans. R. J. Hollingdale). London: Penguin.
———. 1970. *Nachgelassene Fragmente 1887–1888* in *Werke* (Kritische Gesamtausgabe ed. by Giorgio Colli and Montinari) Vol. 8: 2. Berlin-New York: Walter de Gruyter.
———. 1988. *Unzeitgemäße Betrachtungen I-IV; Die Geburt der Tragödie; Nachgelassene Schriften 1870–1873* in *Werke*, KA Vol. 8: 2. Berlin-New York: Walter de Gruyter.
———. 1997 [1889]. *Twilight of the Idols or how to Philosophize with the Hammer* (trans. R. Polt). Indianapolis: Hackett.
———. 1997b. *Untimely Meditations* (trans. R. J. Hollingdale). Cambridge, MA: Cambridge University Press.
———. 2006. *On the Genealogy of Morality.* Cambridge, MA: Cambridge University Press.
Nisbett, Richard E. and Lee Ross. 1980. *Human Inference: Strategies and Shortcomings of Social Judgment.* Englewood-Cliffs, NJ: Prentice-Hall.
Odenwald, Stan. 1998. *The Astronomy Café.* New York: W.H. Freeman.
Orr, Martin and Ginna Husting. 2018. "Media Marginalization of Racial Minorities: 'Conspiracy Theorists' in U.S. Ghettos and on the 'Arab Street'" in J. Uscinski (ed.), *Conspiracy Theories and the People Who Believe Them.* Oxford: Oxford University Press, 82–93.
Pagán, Victoria Emma. 2004. *Conspiracy Narratives in Roman History.* Austin: University of Texas Press.
Pagis, Michal. 2016. "Fashioning Futures: Life Coaching and the Self-Made Identity Paradox" in *Sociological Forum* 31: 4, 1083–110.
Pamuk, Orhan. 2020. "What the Great Pandemic Novels Teach Us" in *The New York Times*, April 23 https://www.nytimes.com/2020/04/23/opinion/sunday/coronavirus-orhan-pamuk.html
Pigden, Charles. 2006. "Popper Revisited or What's Wrong with Conspiracy Theories?" in D. Coady (ed.), *Conspiracy Theories. The Philosophical Debate.* Farnham: Ashgate, 17–44.
———. 2007. "Conspiracy Theories and the Conventional Wisdom" in *Episteme: A Journal of Social Epistemology* 4: 2, 219–32.
Pipes, Daniel. 1996. *The Hidden Hand: Middle East Fears of Conspiracy.* London: St. Martin's Press.

———. 1997. *Conspiracy: How the Paranoid Style Flourishes and Where It Comes From*. New York: Free Press.
Plato. 1925. "Laws" in *Plato in Twelve Volumes*, Vol. X and XI. Trans. H. N. Fowler (Loeb Classical Library). Cambridge, MA: Harvard University Press; London: William Heinemann.
———. 1992. *Republic* (trans. G. M. A. Grube). Indianapolis: Hackett.
Poincaré, Henri. 1903. *La Valeur de la science*. Paris: Flammarion.
———. 1905. *Science and Hypothesis*. London and Newcastle: Walter Scott.
———. 1908. *Science et méthode*. Paris: Flammarion.
Polybius. 1979. *The Rise of The Roman Empire*. Harmondsworth: Penguin.
Popper, Karl. 1969. *The Open Society and Its Enemies*. New York: Routledge and Kegan Paul.
———. 1972. *Objective Knowledge, an Evolutionary Approach*. Oxford: Oxford University Press.
Raab, M. H., S. A. Ortlieb, N. Auer, K. Guthmann, and C. C. Carbon. 2013. "Thirty Shades of Truth: Conspiracy Theories as Stories of Individuation, not of Pathological Delusion" in *Frontiers Psychology* 9: 406.
Räikkä, Juha. 2009. "The Ethics of Conspiracy Theorizing" in *Journal Value Inquiry* 43, 457–68.
Räikkä, Juha and Lee Basham. 2019. "Conspiracy Theory Phobia" in J. Uscinski (ed.), *Conspiracy Theories and the People Who Believe Them*, New York: Oxford University Press, 178–86.
Ravaisson, Félix. 1868. *La Philosophie en France au XIXe siècle*. Paris: Hachette.
Rawls, John. 1971. *A Theory of Justice*. Cambridge, MA: Belknap Press.
Richmond, Sarah. 2007. "Sartre and Bergson: A Disagreement about Nothingness" in *International Journal of Philosophical Studies* 15: 1, 77–95,
Rieger, Stefan. 1997. *Speichern, Merken: die künstlichen Intelligenzen des Barock*. München: Fink.
Robertson, D. G. 2024. *Religion and Conspiracy Theories: An Introduction*. New York: Routledge.
Rorty, Richard. 1989. *Contingency, Irony, and Solidarity*. Cambridge: Cambridge University Press.
Rupke, Nicolaas. 2006. "Christianity and the Sciences" in Sheridan Gilley and Brian Stanley (eds.), *The Cambridge History of Christianity: Volume 8, World Christianities c.1815–c.1914*. Cambridge: Cambridge University Press, 164–80.
Ruyer, Raymond. 1946. *Éléments de psychobiologie*. Paris: Presses Universitaires de France.
Sagan, Carl. 2007 [1995]. "The Fine Art of Baloney Detection" in B. Farha (ed.), *Paranormal Claims: A Critical Analysis*. Lanham: University Press of America, 1–12.
Sandel, Michael. 2020. *The Tyranny of Merit: What's Become of the Common Good*. Harmondsworth: Penguin.
Sardar, Ziauddin. 2003. *Islam, Postmodernism and Other Futures: A Ziauddin Sardar Reader*. London: Pluto Press.
Sartre, Jean-Paul. 1966. *La Transcendence de l'ego. Esquisse d'une description phénoménologique*. Paris: Vrin.
———. 1969. *Nausea*. New York: New Directions.
———. 1972 [1938]. *La Nausée*. Paris: Gallimard.
———. 1983. *Cahiers pour une morale*. Paris: Gallimard.
———. 1992. *Notebooks for an Ethics*. Chicago: University of Chicago Press.

Sauter, Michael J. 2019. *The Spatial Reformation: Euclid Between Man, Cosmos, and God.* Philadelphia: University of Pennsylvania Press.
Scheler, Max. 2007 [1915]. *Ressentiment.* Milwaukee: Marquette University Press.
Schluchter, Wolfgang. 2009. *Die Entzauberung der Welt. Sechs Studien zu Max Weber.* Tübingen: Mohr-Siebeck.
Schopenhauer, Arthur. 1998 [1859]. *Die Welt als Wille und Vorstellung.* München: dtv.
———. 2010 [1859]. *The World as Will and Representation* Vol. 1 (trans. J. Norman, A. Welchman, and C. Janaway). Cambridge, MA: Cambridge University Press.
Schwab, Klaus and Thierry Malleret. 2020. *COVID-19: The Great Reset.* Geneva World Economic Forum: Forum Publishing.
Seneca, Lucius Annaeus, 2014. *Delphi Complete Works of Seneca the Younger* (trans. F. J. Miller). Hastings: Delphi Classics.
Shields, Matthew. 2022. "Rethinking Conspiracy Theories" in *Synthese* 200: 331, 1–29.
Somers-Hall, Henry. 2017. "Bergson and the Development of Sartre's Thought" in *Research in Phenomenology* 47: 1, 85–107.
Stcherbatsky, Theodor. 1936. *Madhyanta-Vibhanga Discourse on Discrimination between Middle and Extremes ascribed to Bodhisattva Maiteyka and Commented by Vasubandhu and Sthiramati* (trans. and comments by Th. Stcherbatsky). Leningrad and Moscow: Academy of Sciences of USSR Press.
Steinvorth, Ulrich. 2016. *Pride and Authenticity.* New York: Palgrave.
Stevenson, Angus (ed.). 2007. "Contingency" in *Shorter Oxford English Dictionary* 6th Edition. Oxford: Oxford University Press.
Stokes, Patrick. 2016. "Between Generalism and Particularism about Conspiracy Theory: A Response to Basham and Dentith" in *Social Epistemology Review and Reply Collective* 5: 10, 34–39.
Sunstein, C. R. and A. Vermeule. 2009, "Conspiracy Theories: Causes and Cures" in *Journal of Political Philosophy* 17, 202–27.
Swami, Viren, M. Voracek, S. Stieger, Ulrich S. Tran, and A. Furnham. 2014. "Analytic Thinking Reduces Belief in Conspiracy Theories" in *Cognition* 133, 572–85.
Taleb, Nassim N. 2001. *Fooled by Randomness: The Hidden Role of Chance in the Markets and in Life.* New York: Norton.
———. 2007. *The Black Swan: The Impact of the Highly Improbably.* New York: Random House.
Tibi, Bassam. 1998. *The Challenge of Fundamentalism: Political Islam and the New World Order.* Berkeley: University of California Press.
Tsapos, Melina. 2023. "Who is a Conspiracy Theorist?" in *Social Epistemology* 37: 4, 454–63.
Valéry, Paul. 1942–43. *Cahiers XXVI.* Paris: Gallimard.
Vattimo, Gianni. 1999. *Belief* [trans. of *Credere di Credere*]. Stanford: Stanford University Press.
Virilio, Paul. 2005. *The Accident of Art.* New York: Semiotext(e).
Watson, Burton (trans.). 2013 [1968]. *The Complete Works of Zhuangzi.* New York: Columbia University Press.
Weber, Max. 2013 [1919–20]. *Wirtschaft und Gesellschaft* (Gesamtausgabe I/23). Tübingen: Mohr-Siebeck.
Wicks, Robert. 2005. "The Idealization of Contingency in Traditional Japanese Aesthetics" in *The Journal of Aesthetic Education* 39: 3, 88–101.

Wilentz, Sean. 2012. "Foreword" in Richard Hofstadter, *The Paranoid Style in American Politics*. New York: Knopf-Doubleday, i–xxx.

Willman, Skip. 2002. "Spinning Paranoia: The Antinomy of Conspiracy and Contingency in Postmodern Culture" in P. Knight (ed.), *Conspiracy Nation: The Politics of Paranoia in Postwar America*. New York: New York University Press, 21–39.

Wood, Michael J., Karen M. Douglas, and Robbie M. Sutton. 2012. "Dead and Alive: Beliefs in Contradictory Conspiracy Theories" in *Social Psychological and Personality Science* 3: 6, 767–73.

Young, Michael. 1958. *The Rise of the Meritocracy*. Harmondsworth: Penguin Books.

INDEX

Note: Page numbers followed by 'n' indicates note number(s).

5G 22, 85

Abduh, Mohammad 135
Abe, Masao 196
accident 6, 49, 51–56, 59, 62, 65, 76, 79, 90n2, 124, 130, 138, 144, 151, 164–65
actuality 50–51, 90–91, 150, 156, 172–73
Adam and Eve 4–5, 144
aesthetics 5, 10, 15–16, 24–25, 28–31, 74, 78, 173, 177–78, 180, 183, 189, 214
African Americans 29
Agamben, Giorgio 111, 156–57, 158n9, 209
AIDS 2, 57, 67, 75, 202
Alain [Emile Chartier] 162, 188
algorithms 1, 29, 46, 118, 181–88, 199
alternative history 88–89
alternative science 5–6, 34–35, 38–46, 71, 86, 88, 99, 119, 136, 146, 208–10
Amazon 200
animism 68–69
Antiquity 4, 7, 102–6
antisemitism 44
apocalyptic 3
Aquinas, Thomas 156
arete 201
Aristotle 9, 49–50, 87, 103, 106, 146, 155, 177, 189
Aron, Raymond 152
Arp, Hans 167–68
art 9, 27, 172–78
Arte Combinatoria 186–88
Asad, Talal 138
ataraxia 210
atomism 104
Augustine 107, 110–11, 157
Aurelius, Marcus 213
automaton 49n1, 117, 204

Bahnsen, Julius 125
Barrotta, Pierluigi 131, 181

Basham, Lee 20–21, 25, 208
Baudelaire, Charles 137
Baudrillard, Jean 38, 89, 140
Beck, Ulrich 58–62, 138–39, 141–42
Being 156–57
belief 24–25, 26n13, 33, 40n8
Bentham, Jeremy 201
Bergson, Henri 75, 161, 165, 168
Bernoulli brothers 138
Bertalanffy, Ludwig von 150, 165
Bible 4–5, 135, 144, 202
Big Bang 123
Binet, Alfred 138
biology 122, 149–50, 153, 165–69, 176
bitcoin 128
Black Death 108, 120
Black Swan 57–58
Blanqui, Louis Auguste 118
Bloom, Alan 96–97, 211
Blumenberg, Hans 4, 47, 71–72, 113, 158–59
Bodin, Jean 108
Boethius 111
Boll, Marcel 54, 72, 87
Borel, Emile 161–62, 166
Borges, Jorge Luis 146–47
bourgeois morality 84–85
Boutroux, Emile 91, 162, 166, 168–69, 187
Bouveresse, Jacques 125, 154
Brandolini principle 209
Bréhier, Emile 164
Breton, André 167
Brexit 38
Brotherton, Rob 30, 42, 102, 182
Buddhism (Mahayana) 3, 191–96
bullshit 94–95, 141–42, 186, 209
Bush, George 26

Caligula 213
Canguilhem, Georges 7, 73, 165–66, 174
Cantor, Moritz 138

capitalism (multinational) 8, 128, 141, 151, 180–81
Cardon, Dominique 188
Cassam, Qassim 6, 18, 20, 23, 27, 29, 35, 38–40, 47
Catholicism 45
causality 59, 72, 91n4, 139, 140, 148
chaos 72, 74, 87, 105, 145, 149
chaos theory 89, 113, 122, 142, 155, 176
chemtrails 12
Chernobyl 59
China 83, 85, 193, 202
cholera 57, 120
Christians 99, 104, 108–9, 111, 135
CIA 125
Clarke, Steve 25
clinamen 105
Coady, David 12, 21–22, 28, 96, 208
coincidence (epistemic) 66, 71, 209
coincidence (ontological) 65–66, 70–72, 76, 120, 124, 148, 152, 159–60, 172
Cold War 26
complexity 30, 43, 70, 111, 143, 162, 209, 211
Comte, Auguste 118, 163, 187
Conche, Marcel 167
confirmation bias 47n12, 54, 55, 182
contingency (definition) 49–50
contingency phobia 1, 29
contingency skepticism 65–68
contingentia 110, 112, 192
coolness 189
Copernicus 113
cosmology 4, 102–3, 110, 113, 117–18, 122, 144, 193
Cournot, Antoine Augustin 163
COVID–19, 1, 2, 19n4, 29, 55–57, 62–63, 83–84, 94, 124, 142, 202
creationism 43, 122, 135, 185
Crusades 108
cryptology 147
CryptoPunk 141
cui bono 67

da Vinci, Leonardo 123
Dadaism 23, 167, 175–76
Dalton, John 155
Danesi, Marcel 20
Daoism 3, 9, 195–205, 212–14
Darwin, Charles 7, 44, 69, 76, 121–22
Dasein 79, 155
De Barruel, Augustin 115–16
death 51–52, 193, 214–15

Deism 136, 148–49
Deleuze, Gilles 152
democracy 44–45, 71, 126, 178, 208
Democritus 104–5, 117, 167
Dentith, M. R. X. 20–21, 24, 26n11, 32n15
depression 37, 40, 51
Derrida, Jacques 6, 78, 88
Descartes, René 7, 107, 121, 187, 208
determinism 87, 89, 92, 95, 118, 121–22, 146–48, 163, 169, 187
Di Cesare, Donatella 4, 27, 43–45
dialectics 18
Diana (Princess) 65
Dionysos 98–99
DNA 123, 140–41
documentaries (conspiracy) 70
Dōgen 193–94
Dominant Institution Conspiracy Theories (DITs) 17
dreams 202–5
Driesch, Hans 150, 165
Duchamps, Marcel 167
Durkheim, Emile 138
dystopia 6, 36–37, 39–40, 150

economics 57, 119, 126–28, 181
Einstein, Albert 149–50, 154
Elders of Zion 2
emergence 122, 200, 204
endechomenon 49, 49n1, 50, 102, 107
Engels, Friedrich 8, 92, 147–48, 161
Enlightenment 6, 34, 37–38, 41–42, 45, 97, 99, 114
Enron 11
entelechy 150
Epicurus 104–5, 117, 171
epistemology 5, 12, 18, 28
epochè 210
ethics 178, 180, 188–89
evangelical Christians 4, 36n5
evolution 6, 55, 67, 69, 75, 122–23, 135–36, 146, 149, 164, 166, 168
excellence 41, 106, 127, 201
existence 3, 29, 86, 89, 91, 103, 139, 154–59, 165–66, 169, 178, 185, 192–94, 196–98

facticity 3, 10, 53, 69, 80, 91, 112, 135, 156–59, 176, 190, 214
fake news 44, 84, 116
fatalism 9–10, 95, 147, 169, 185, 194, 211–12, 214

INDEX

FEMA concentration camps 124
flat-earthers 24, 38, 67, 82, 145
folk culture 23
fortuity 2, 49, 51, 51n2, 66n1, 69, 82, 88, 154, 169, 175, 192
Fortuna 7, 110, 207
Foucault, Michel 151–52
Fourier, Charles 118
Frankfurt, Harry 94–95
Frauenstädt, Julius 125
Freemasons 34, 42, 114–15
French Revolution 42, 115–16, 120
Freud, Sigmund 73, 76–80, 87–88, 123–24
Friedman, Milton 129–30
fundamentalism 6, 30, 34–36, 136, 145
Futurism 126

Galileo 113, 138
gambling 69, 134, 154–55, 174, 176, 183, 188–90, 214–15
games 10, 96, 174, 188
Gates, Bill 1, 22, 67
genetics 139
German Revolution 115, 125
Gesellschaft-Gemeinschaft 143
globalization 114, 142
Gnosticism 41n11
Goldschmidt, Victor 177
Goldstein, Kurt 73, 165
Gombrich, Ernst 6, 72–73, 75
Gould, Stephen Jay 61, 72, 76, 122, 140–41, 167–68, 176, 209
Graeber, David 38n6, 46, 141
Gray, Mathew 4, 9, 40, 143
Greater Uncertainty Principle 154, 176
Greek culture 102, 112
Griffin, Roger 36

Hacking, Ian 138, 140
Haeckel, Ernst 150
Hagen, Kurtis 11–12, 16, 20–21, 24–25, 33
half-belief 28, 29
Hamann, Johan Georg 164
Harris, Keith 12, 21, 23, 145
Hartmann, Eduard von 165
hasard 66, 72, 89, 161–62
Hawking, Stephen 154–55, 176
Hayek, Friedrich 129–30, 181
Hegel, Georg Wilhelm Friedrich 87, 90–93, 147, 161, 175

Heidegger, Martin 6, 53, 68–69, 78–80, 98, 135, 156–59, 164
Heine, Steven 193
Heisenberg, Werner 154
Henrich, Dieter 90–91
Herder, Johann Gottfried von 164
Hinduism 192
history 44, 151
Hitler, Adolf 2
Hofstadter, Richard 24, 39–40, 112, 181
holism 150
homeopathy 43
Humboldt, Wilhelm 164
Hume, David 59
Hussein, Saddam 40
hydroxychloroquine 37

idealism 34
Illuminati 115
individualism 43, 142, 200
indulgence 9, 93–94
influenza 57–58
Inquisition 21
irony 10, 95–97, 99, 197, 212, 214–15
irrationality 13, 18, 21, 21n6, 23, 84, 110, 118
ISIS 22, 24
Islam 35–36, 111, 135
Ivermectin 208

Jacobins 115
Jameson, Frederic 37
Japanese art 194–95
Jesus 108
Jews 34, 42, 86, 108–10, 114–15
Jones, Alex 22
Jullien, François 74, 95, 106

Kant, Immanuel 41n11, 50, 136, 168, 189
karma 192
kata symbebekos 49, 88, 103, 117, 172
Keeley, Brian 7, 14–15, 31, 35, 93, 118, 143, 185
KGB 2, 125
Khomeini, Ayatollah 35
kitsch 9, 32, 93–100, 176–77, 186, 197
Knight, Peter 208
koan 196
Koselleck, Reinhart 74
Koyré, Alexandre 113
Kuhn, T. S. 16, 164
Kuki, Shūzō 205

Lachelier, Jules 163
Lagneau, Jules 163
Lamarck, Jean-Baptiste 150
language 98, 164, 195–96, 199, 205
Laplace, Pierre Simon 89, 117–18, 121, 138, 154–55, 171–72
Lasch, Christopher 44, 131
Le Dantec, Felix 150–51
Le Monde 17
Leibniz, Gottfried Wilhelm 29, 50, 111, 186–87
leprosy 120
Leucippus 105
liberalism 8, 126–31
Lichtenberg, Georg Christoph 154, 177
life coaching 198
lifestyle 33–34, 46, 143, 198, 202, 207
Locke, John 116
Longinus 174
Lucretius 104–5
Lyotard, Jean-François 152

Mainländer, Philipp 125
Marcuse, Ludwig 130
Marx, Karl 105, 125, 137, 147
Masson, André 168
materialism 92, 147, 176
mathematics 9, 54, 75, 87, 114, 119, 138, 162–163, 167, 171, 176, 181–87, 193
Mauthner, Fritz 87
McCarthy 26
Meillassoux, Quentin 96, 123, 142
meritocracy 7–8, 29, 127–36, 180–81, 201
Merleau-Ponty, Maurice 166
methodology 11
micro-macro 4, 10, 145, 149–50
Middle Ages 4, 7, 106–13
Middle East 4, 24, 210
mindset 5, 17–18, 33–34
Mises, Ludwig von 44, 138
modernity 6, 34–35, 37–38, 61, 126
Moeller, Hans-Georg 202, 212–13
Monod, Jacques 69, 140, 154, 168
monotheism 146
Musil, Robert 186
mutation 122
mystery cults 102

Nagarjuna 193
Napolitano, Giulia 21, 25
narcissism 9, 46, 48, 90, 93–99, 183, 190
nature 104–5, 140–41

negative theology 71
Neo-Darwinism 150n3
neoliberalism 129–31, 181
neo-Nazis 29
Neoplatonism 156
Nero 102
New Age 70, 198
Newton, Isaac 114, 118, 164
NGO 38, 67
Nietzsche, Friedrich 3, 10, 18, 81, 85–100, 183–84, 193
nihilism 36–37, 94–96, 99
Non-Dominant Institution Conspiracy Theories (non-DITS) 17, 34
NSA surveillance program 11

Ockham, William of 111
Oedipus 94, 99
ontological contingency 152
organic 5–7, 10, 70, 97, 112, 145, 149–53

Pamuk, Orhan 55
paranoia 13, 24
paranormal 40n8, 136
parasites 153
particularism *vs.* generalism 5, 13, 16
Pascal 138
Peirce, Charles Sanders 125
pharmakon 13, 23
philosophes 115
philosophy 18, 20–21
phronesis 119, 185, 188
Pigden, Charles 12, 20–22, 47
Pipes, Daniel 2, 4, 6, 24, 30, 34, 38, 42, 70, 102, 108, 118
pistis (trust) 171
Plato 103; Laws 104, 121; *Republic* 171–72
play 10, 96, 133, 214
Poincaré, Henri 140, 162–64, 196
poison 60–61
Political Correctness 98
Polybius 101
Popper, Karl. 4, 6–8, 72–73, 75, 124, 132
populism 71, 85, 129
positive psychology 198
possibility 50–51, 90, 156, 172, 192, 209
post-industrial society 38, 61–62, 128
post-truth 3, 29–30
Pre-Socratics 102, 208
probability 51–52, 72, 87, 122, 138–39, 166
propaganda 29, 176–77
providence 101, 111, 121

pseudoscience 6, 42, 43, 46, 47, 70, 86, 112, 132, 135, 145, 211
psychology 28, 78, 140, 198
puritanism 8, 132
Putin, Vladimir 2, 22
Pyrrho 207–10

QAnon 3, 41, 99, 132
quantum physics 155, 160, 176
Qur'an 135

racism 44, 85
Raëlians 136
Räikkä, Juha 18, 20
rationalization 112, 118, 161, 185
Ravaisson, Félix 164
Rawls, John 133
Reinke, Johannes 150, 165
relativism 20, 47, 96–98, 195, 204, 211–212
religion 128, 131–35; natural 136
Renaissance 35n4, 111, 161, 163
Renouvier, Charles 163
ressentiment 10, 81–84
Reuters, Kevin 21, 23
risk 58–60
Roman culture 102
Romanticism 162
Rorty, Richard 79, 95, 97–98, 151, 167, 171, 192, 197, 212
Russia 2, 22
Ruyer, Raymond 166

Sacks, Oliver 140
Sagan, Carl 211
Salafism 35–36
Sandel, Michael 38–39, 61, 128, 132–34, 141, 180, 215
Sandy Hook 12
Sartre, Jean-Paul 3, 157–58, 161, 168, 178–80
Satan 7, 107, 113, 145
scapegoat 42, 60, 81, 114
Scheler, Max 7, 81, 84–86, 211
Schelling, Friedrich Wilhelm Joseph von 165
Scholasticism 4, 49–50
Schopenhauer, Arthur 165, 172–73
Schumpeter, Joseph 212
Schwab, Klaus 55
science 4–5, 86–89, 135–36, 143–46
secularization 123
Seneca 82, 90, 213

Sextus Empiricus 208
Shields, Matthew 15
Simmel, Georg 126
skepticism 6, 10, 43, 52, 65, 72, 76, 97, 164, 186, 196–97, 202, 207–11
Skinner, Quentin 164
slave morality 84, 99
social media 8, 142, 186
Socrates 18, 99
sophists 186, 199–201
Soros, George 66–67
Spanish flu 57
statistics 138–43, 161, 182, 189
Stoics 82, 95, 102, 105–6, 194, 213
Stokes, Patrick 18
style (of thinking) 5, 16, 23–25, 94
sunyata 192
superstitions 18, 33, 43, 108, 109, 114, 116
Surrealism 167, 175–76

Taine, Hyppolite 163
Taleb, Nassim 39, 48, 52, 55, 66n1, 118–19, 133n5, 162–63, 190, 197
taste 17, 24, 33, 171
terrorism 116, 127
theory 119–20
tian (Chinese) 104, 202
Tibi, Bassam 35–36
time 194
tragedy 94–98, 177
Trump, Donald 41
Tsapos, Melina 20
tyche 7, 49n1, 117

Uexküll, Jakob Johann von 150, 165
UFOs 82–83
Ukraine 2
uncanny 6, 39, 60, 76–80, 174
urbanism 143
utilitarianism 201
utopia 36–37, 60

vaccinations 62, 67, 138
Valéry, Paul 175
Vattimo, Gianni 28
violence 2, 126
Virilio, Paul 53, 144, 151, 164–65
von Hartmann, Eduard 125

Wall Street 141
Weber, Max 128, 130
Weiss, Paul Alfred Weiss 150

Willman, Skip 88, 151, 211
witches 107, 109–10
Wittgenstein, Ludwig 98, 164, 196
wokeness 41, 127
Wolfowitz, Paul 40
World War II 58
Wundt, Wilhelm 140
wuwei 204–5

Young, Michael 131
YouTube 26, 182, 188, 200

Zen Buddhism 3, 193–94, 197–202
Zhuangzi 196–97, 205
ziran 204
Zufall 90n2
Zufälligkeit 90n2, 158n9, 173

www.ingramcontent.com/pod-product-compliance
Lightning Source LLC
Jackson TN
JSHW020259260325
81395JS00001B/1